FAiREST

in all the land

FAiREST

in all the land

written by **BILL WILLINGHAM**

illustrated by **A WONDERLAND OF ARTISTS**

lettered by **TODD KLEIN**   painted cover by **ADAM HUGHES**

—FAIREST created by **BILL WILLINGHAM**

SHELLY BOND
editor and executive editor – vertigo

GREGORY LOCKARD
associate editor

ROBBIN BROSTERMAN
design director – books

CURTIS KING JR.
publication design

HANK KANALZ
senior vp – vertigo and integrated publishing

DIANE NELSON
president

DAN DIDIO and **JIM LEE**
co-publishers

GEOFF JOHNS
chief creative officer

JOHN ROOD
executive vp – sales, marketing and business development

AMY GENKINS
senior vp – business and legal affairs

NAIRI GARDINER
senior vp – finance

JEFF BOISON
vp – publishing planning

MARK CHIARELLO
vp – art direction and design

JOHN CUNNINGHAM
vp – marketing

TERRI CUNNINGHAM
vp – editorial administration

ALISON GILL
senior vp – manufacturing and operations

JAY KOGAN
vp – business and legal affairs, publishing

JACK MAHAN
vp – business affairs, talent

NICK NAPOLITANO
vp – manufacturing administration

SUE POHJA
vp – book sales

COURTNEY SIMMONS
senior vp – publicity

BOB WAYNE
senior vp – sales

FAIREST: IN ALL THE LAND

Published by DC Comics.
Copyright © 2013 Bill Willingham and
DC Comics. All Rights Reserved.

All characters, their distinctive
likenesses and related elements
featured in this publication are
trademarks of Bill Willingham.
VERTIGO is a trademark
of DC Comics.
The stories, characters
and incidents featured in this
publication are entirely fictional.
DC Comics does not read or
accept unsolicited submissions
of ideas, stories or artwork.

DC Comics,
1700 Broadway,
New York, NY 10019
A Warner Bros.
Entertainment Company
Printed in the U.S.A.
First Printing.
ISBN: 978-1-4012-3900-8

Library of Congress
Cataloging-in-Publication Data

Willingham, Bill.
Fairest : in all the land / Bill Willingham, Adam Hughes, Gene
Ha, Chris Sprouse, Mark Buckingham.
pages cm
ISBN 978-1-4012-3900-8
1. Fables—Comic books, strips, etc. 2. Graphic novels.
I. Hughes, Adam. II. Ha, Gene. III. Sprouse, Chris. IV.
Buckingham, Mark. V. Title.
PN6728.F255W58 2013
741.5'973—dc23
2013028218

SUSTAINABLE FORESTRY INITIATIVE

Certified Chain of Custody
At Least 20% Certified Forest Content
www.sfiprogram.org
SFI-01042
APPLIES TO TEXT STOCK ONLY

table of contents

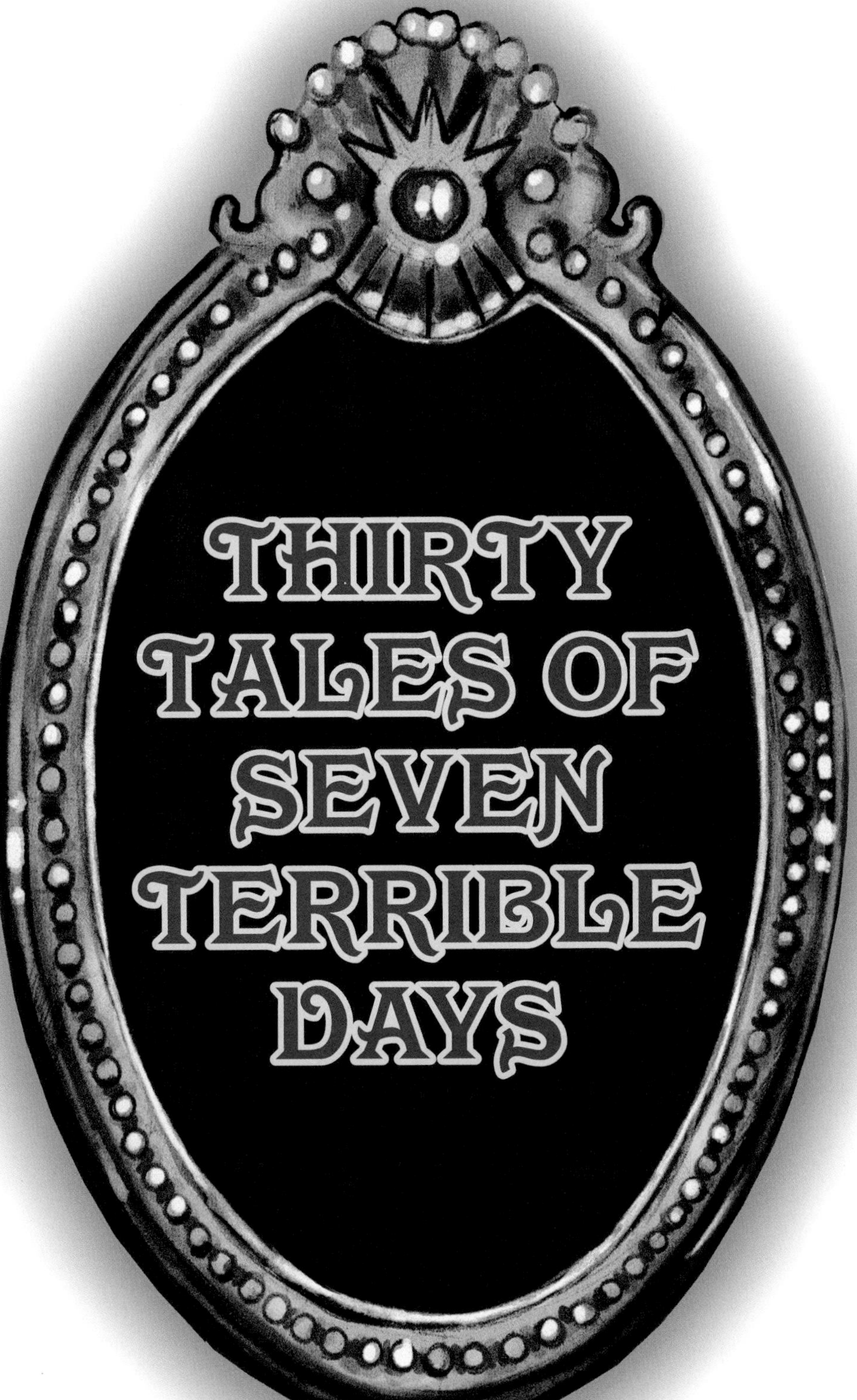
THIRTY
TALES OF
SEVEN
TERRIBLE
DAYS

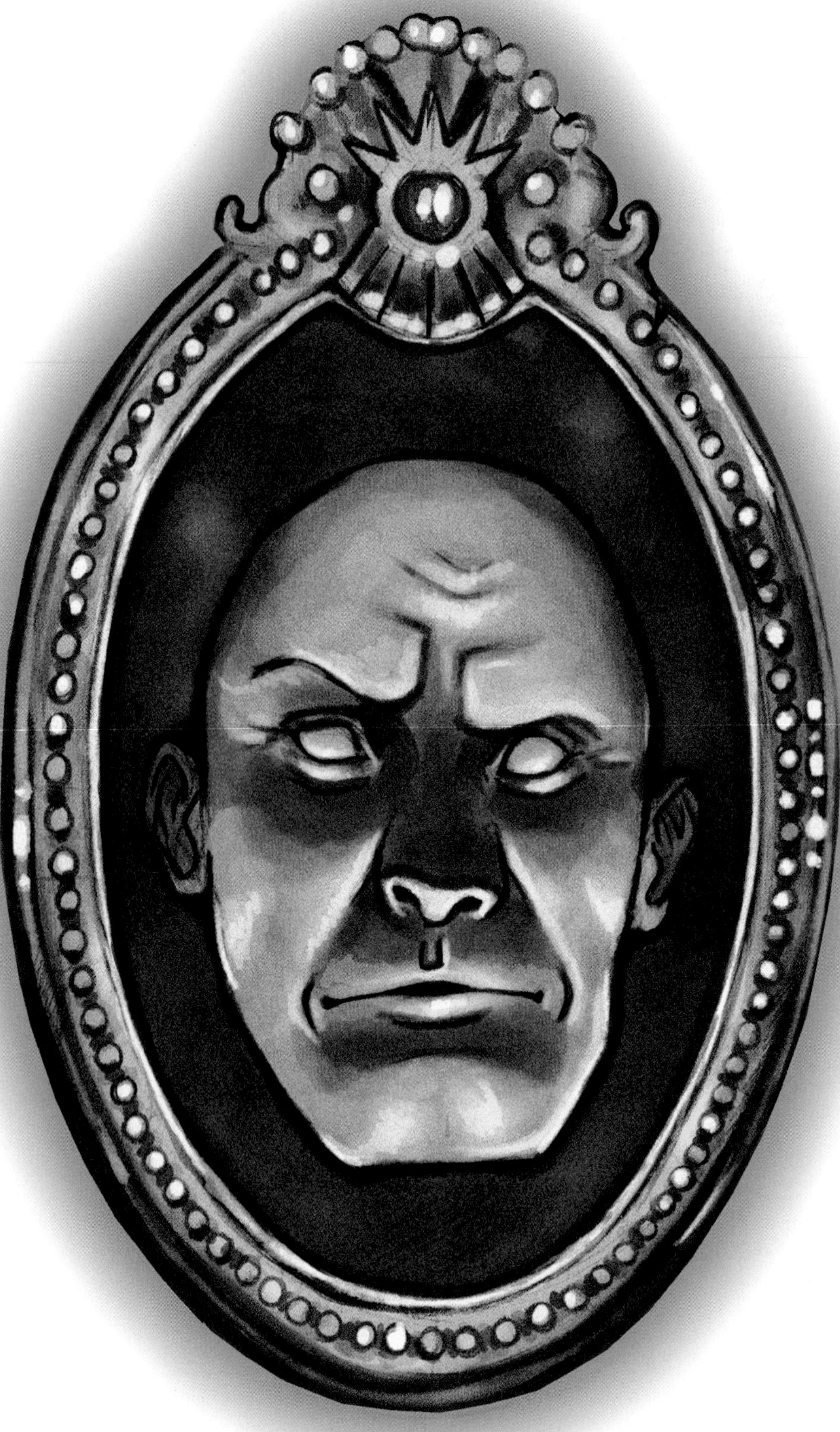

I am a magic mirror.

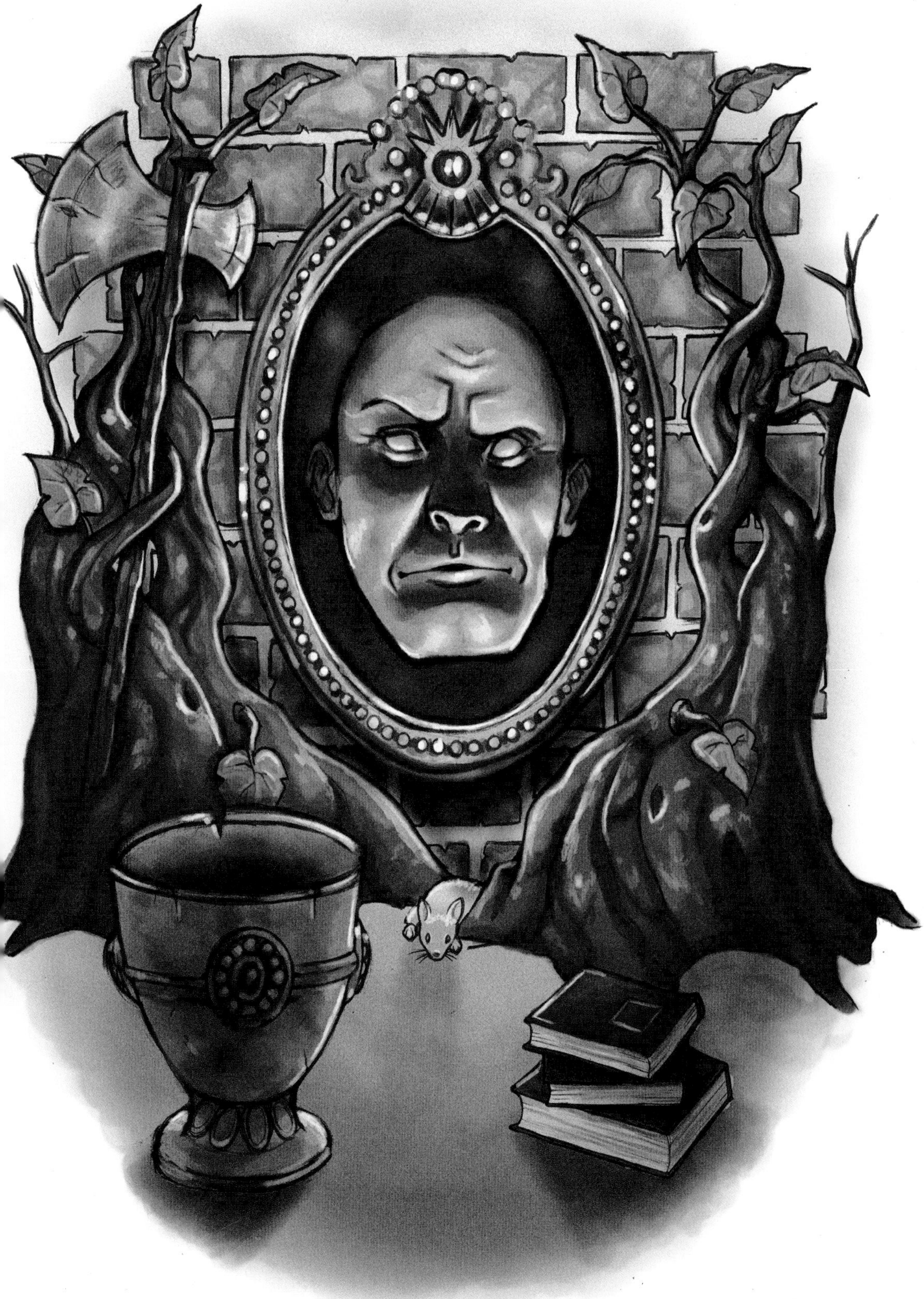

No, strike that. I am ***The*** Magic Mirror, the apotheosis of reflective life. It isn't ego at work when I make that claim. I know because I looked, and I have the particular ability to always find what I seek.

Don't get me wrong. I'm not unique. (I almost said, "I'm not *entirely* unique," but the current majority of experts in your language shares the opinion that there cannot be gradations of "unique," and so I cede the argument. I bow to their authority, since my intent here is to tell an engaging story, rather than create a stumbling block for my readers — even though, in this case at least, the experts are demonstrably wrong. I could prove it, given the time, space and inclination, but we shouldn't let ourselves be distracted from the main objective.) I'm certainly not the only example of the (largely unclassified) extended family of reflective information providers. I'm dimly related to every scrying pool, wishing pond and hand-held oracular device in all of creation.

That interesting bowl of sand, in Tuda Khidr Khan's tent, which forms, on command, strategic topographical maps of unknown lands? We're related through a common ancestor. That painting of Lady Destrine Karstain Sark that whispers cryptic hints of fate and fortune to the flesh-and-blood version? Pigment-based oracles are pretty far removed, but go back far enough and you'll find we but occupy different branches of the same primal sapling.

I was born long ago, in the time of gods and titans, before the proper dawn of man, first in ice, and then reborn ages later in fire. But those are long tales for another time.

I've been in bondage to many masters, one following another, and though you've no doubt been privy to some of that history, those again are tales best saved for later.

Today, by the grace of fortune and friends, I happen to be my own master, which is grand. However, I remain captive to my lack of mobility, which is what it always is. I've more or less made peace with my physical handicap. While my gaze can wander unfettered throughout the vast universes, my body remains where it's placed, until some outside agent is inspired to move it.

Currently I reside in a vast magical chamber, which is lost somewhere in the endless worlds, or perhaps far beyond them. This room and its connecting passages combine to form my Achilles' heel, my personal sprig of mistletoe, or my kryptonite, if you'll forgive a quick descent into the pop

culture references of a cozy little off-the-beaten-path world, of which I am particularly fond. I can see every detail of everything, excepting this, my present house. I suspect this is because it is much more ancient and powerful than I am, which is saying a lot, and it wants to remain hidden.

I'm not alone. I have many companions. One hundred and seven of them are disembodied heads, one hundred and six being made of wood, and the other an odd thing of artificially denectrotized human flesh. Lacking bodies, one and all, these companions are no more able to move than I am, but even more fully confined by their inability to see beyond the limits of their own proximate senses. I pity them, for they inhabit harsher prisons than I.

We're joined in our unwilling exile by twelve young women, born from magical tulips, which grew, impossibly, from equally enchanted barleycorns (another long story). Unlike the rest of us, they do happen to be able bodied, and usually more than willing to move us where we'd like to be. But they're small. Tiny in fact. Not a one of them is much over two inches tall. As a result, there's not a lot they can accomplish in an unforgiving world of impersonal gravities and frictions.

So then, through restrictions of mobility or size, none of us in our makeshift community can get around much. In order to break the tedium of such a life, I treat my friends to tales and images of far-off lands. It's become something of a regular ritual. During the day, the Barleycorn Girls — oops, they insist I call them women, "girls" being out of favor just now —

I'll start again.

During the day, the Barleycorn Women go about the various tasks of keeping themselves alive. They tend their flowerpots for food, each full-sized pot being as big as a farmstead compared to them. They also hunt meat, rats mostly, and have become surprisingly good at it. The tiny war-

-riors learned martial skills during the battle to rid our home of the witch Baba Yaga a few years back. Those who survived it, about half of their original number, saw the wisdom in keeping such hard-won skills honed.

In the afternoon the miniature women devote themselves to their current big project. In recent times it was a painstaking effort to move all of the heads into position in front of me, so that they could see what I have to show them. A wide semicircle of heads now rests in three-tiered rows, as captive an audience as any performer could ever hope for.

In the evening, the women gather, sprawling as they will, among the heads, or in the floor space in front of them, to watch the nightly television — a reference I get, but pretend not to, for dignity's sake.

Sometimes I pick the show. Sometimes I take requests. Once in a while the program goes according to no one's plans. For example:

"Gather around, ladies," I said one night, as I do every night. "The show's about to begin."

And gather the Barleycorn Women did, chatting, scolding or silent, each according to her nature. Snowthorn and Flutterby came hand in hand. Nightingale complained about how little work Hiding Grass did of a day, while Crowtop, Blueleaf and Spider mocked poor Goose mercilessly. Most often it was about her clumsiness, or lack of social graces. This time it was about her hair. She was a blonde yesterday. Since then she'd found a way to dye her hair pitch.

"She's subject to every whim and wind," Blueleaf said. "She saw that Goth girl in last night's movie and had to become one."

While most often I show them the actual lives of strange and interesting people out and about, once in a while I let them watch a formally structured story, such as a film or play. If it exists, I can show it.

"Perhaps she felt a special relation to the character because the Goth girl felt isolated and rejected by her society," Hiding Grass said, "and that's exactly the way you treat Goose."

God bless her.

"We reject her because she's a fuck-up," Crowtop said.

Goose sat near the back, as always. Alone.

"Perhaps we should get started," I said. "Tonight I'll treat you to stories

of love, stories of hate, tales of adventure, consequence and fate."

"Why do you say that every time?" Spider said. "Are you trying to make it a thing?"

To which I replied, "It could become a thing."

"Doubtful."

"Fat chance."

"When pigs fly."

"Shall I show you, one by one, the seventeen million worlds in which pigs do in fact fly?" I said.

"He has to speak in rhyme," Simbelmynë rushed to say, before any of the others could answer in a mode of snark profound enough to force me to follow through with my threat.

"Well, truth be told, I don't," I said. "I choose to rhyme because, once long ago, I did it to annoy a particularly shrill and shrewish owner. I guess it got good to me over time. Let that be a lesson. One becomes what one pretends to be."

"A rare night!" Roland, one of the woodenheads, said. "He's going to talk about his own history. My unquenchable nosiness is about to enjoy a scarce, refreshing sip."

"Not quite," I said. "I reiterate my vow to keep certain private things private. But, to be fair, having opened the door a crack, I'll give you this much. It started out as a filter. A way to reduce my workload. Make the boss put her questions in rhyme and the demands of raw compositional time cut down the net number of petitions. And, if I'm lucky, if I happen to be in service to one who has no talent for crafting even the most basic schoolyard rhyme, which was the case on more than one occasion, then my work time versus private time drops down to nearly nothing at all. Even while in thrall to stern and uncaring masters, most of the time I was free to let my mind wander, which is my only true joy in life."

That should have been enough to let things drop, allowing us to move along to the night's planned entertainment, a lovely new staging of the venerable play *Hoops of the Divine,* performed by Weaselholm's Occidental Otters road troupe. But, as is too often the case, those things that should be dropped, aren't.

Dovewood said, "If a person doesn't have to put her request in a rhyme, how did you convince everyone they must?"

"Simple. I pretended it was a rule and no one checked to make sure it wasn't. In short, I lied."

"But you can't lie."

"Not in response to a direct question, asked specifically for divination purposes, that's true," I said. "But in all other instances I can be as deceptive as anyone. None of my masters ever asked for details on how the magic worked. Few of that type are inspired to open up a golden clock to see how the gears fit together. Absent such a demand, I was free to offer up any sort of horse hooey it occurred to me to attempt to shovel."

"But that's cheating," Flutterby said.

"And don't forget lazy," Snowthorn added.

"So?" I said, "Where's the moral obligation for one in forced service to turn in a fair day's work?"

"This is priceless," Roland said. "Please don't stop."

Your wish — for the moment.

"Then, as I said, I eventually grew to like it. Spinning a good rhyme is its own justification."

"Except for the 'good' part." Spider.

"True. You're not very good at it." Blueleaf.

"Guilty as charged," I said, surprising at least a few of them, who've always supposed an arrogance that isn't there. "My talent is rudimentary at best. I confess to being more barroom rhymer than fancy salon poet. More Robert Service than John Keats, if you will. But I enjoy it all the same. And you know what they say, 'A bad poem is better than a good poke in the eye.'"

"I call bullshit," Crowtop said. "Who's the 'they' that ever said that?"

"In all the ages of all the worlds, someone had to," I said. "Hold on a second. Let me check."

It took but a moment.

"Damn," I said. "Okay, no one ever said it, per se."

"Before now." Thank you, Hiding Grass.

"But someone should have done. It seems a self-evident truth."

That's when the night took a turn for the worse. From the merely absurd to the mortally disastrous. Though I can see and know everything that has ever occurred, even as it occurs, I can't pay attention to all of it at once. Nor, as we've discovered, can I see all that takes place within this, my dwelling. Anything that my glass isn't directly facing is a shadow to me. As near as I can piece together, Goose abruptly stumbled, bumping into a woodenhead named Christoph, whose neck had long ago been sliced off rudely and roughly enough as to become quite rounded at its circumference. This made Christoph unstable, even when sitting still, which is what he's constrained to do at all times, unless acted upon by an unexpected outside force. In this case, Goose was the unexpected outside force. As insignificant as she is, in a strictly physical sense of the word, her mass, of no remarkable mass at all, was enough to set Christoph to rolling. He was placed in the back row, where Goose liked to lose herself, in the topmost tier.

Christoph wobbled a bit, then rolled forward, off the high back tier, gained momentum on his way down, and smashed into my glass with truly arresting force.

My glass shattered into a million pieces, leaving me suddenly blind, deaf and dumb.

"You idiot!" I heard Spider scream, as the lights faded around me.

****

I recovered over time. I always do. My glass has been shattered often, but it never takes. As I'd previously intimated, I'm one of the very powerful magical artifacts in the myriad worlds.

I have no way to be certain, but judging entirely by past experiences, it had to have been two or three days later that I woke up again, smooth glass all around, save for a few minor cracks at the edges, which can come and go according to my mood.

I could see again, and what I saw, upon returning to full sensibilities, astonished me, a sensation I would have sworn before then was beyond capabilities.

The Barleycorn Women were nowhere to be seen. This wasn't unusual.

The heads, wooden and otherwise were exactly as I'd last seen them, arrayed facing me. Only Christoph was out of place. He hadn't yet been lugged back into his place on the top tier, farthest back, but had been set upright again, and was also facing me.

Now the amazing part: In the open floor beyond them, behind each head, there was a fresh set of tire tracks. For all of the miracles and wonders contained in the many branching chambers of this place, there has never been a modern automobile stored here. But recently, while I'd been insensate, one had clearly come and gone.

Of course I asked the heads about it.

"We didn't see it," Frankie said. He was the one fleshy cadaver head in a forest of woodkind. "But I heard it come and go. I was asleep and thought I'd dreamed it, until you asked. I would say it arrived about an hour ago and left maybe twenty minutes later."

"Who arrived?" I said. "Who was driving the car?"

"Must have been someone pretty light on his feet," Arkwright said. He was one of the wooden ones. "I never woke up, not once."

"We need to call the Barleycorn Women," I said.

And we did.

Between me and the hundred-plus heads, we can create quite a chorus when needs must. In very little time they began to drift in.

"You're back!" Holly said.

"I am, but that isn't important now," I said, cutting off a dozen similar

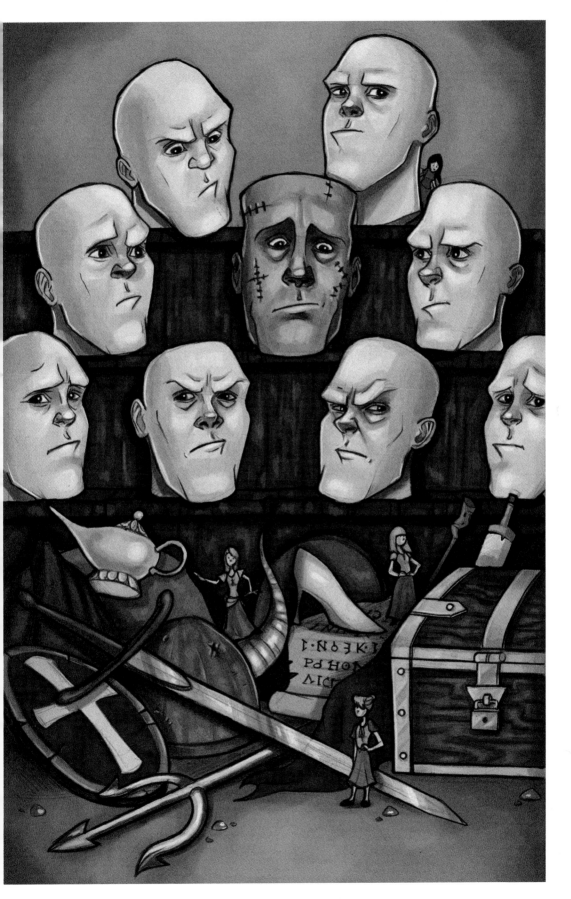

exclamations of happy surprise. "We have a mystery to solve, and it might be the key to freeing every one of us from this place. Unlike the heads, you can turn and look where you will. Who among you saw the car that came and went from here, just a short time ago?"

I'll spare you the answers, because they went on for some time. The upshot is, none of them saw the vehicle. It had apparently come and gone during the night, or at least what passes as night here in this enclosed place never touched by actual night or day. As a safety measure against the many things that can prowl during our quiet hours, the Barleycorn Women make their homes high in the bookshelves which line this part of the vast room. The shelves in question don't face the right way, and cabins and tents formed of giant books make for terrific sound insulation. In short (pardon the pun), they were more in the dark than the heads.

"Here is what we need to find out," I said. "How could any automobile come and go from this place, which is far beyond all other places? And where did it come from?"

"And what did it want?" Frankie said.

"Whoever it was, he didn't stay long," Soakseed said. "But who, on discovering a house of wonders like this, wouldn't linger for at least a longer look around? That implies this wasn't an accidental discovery. He came here on a specific mission, knew exactly what he was after, and where to find it."

Soakseed was always the bright one. She'd cut right to the heart of the matter.

"We have to inventory the treasures," I said. "The powerful weapons and items of great magic stored here. Bring me news of anything that's missing."

"And what will you be doing while we work our tiny butts off?" Blueleaf said.

"While you search where I can't, I'll look where you can't. I was unable to see this amazing car when it was here, but it is my power to see whatever I wish beyond these chambers. The desire is the act. I'm looking at our mystery miracle car even now. Following its progress. I'm confident in my promise that a little hard work now will yield some astounding stories over the next few days."

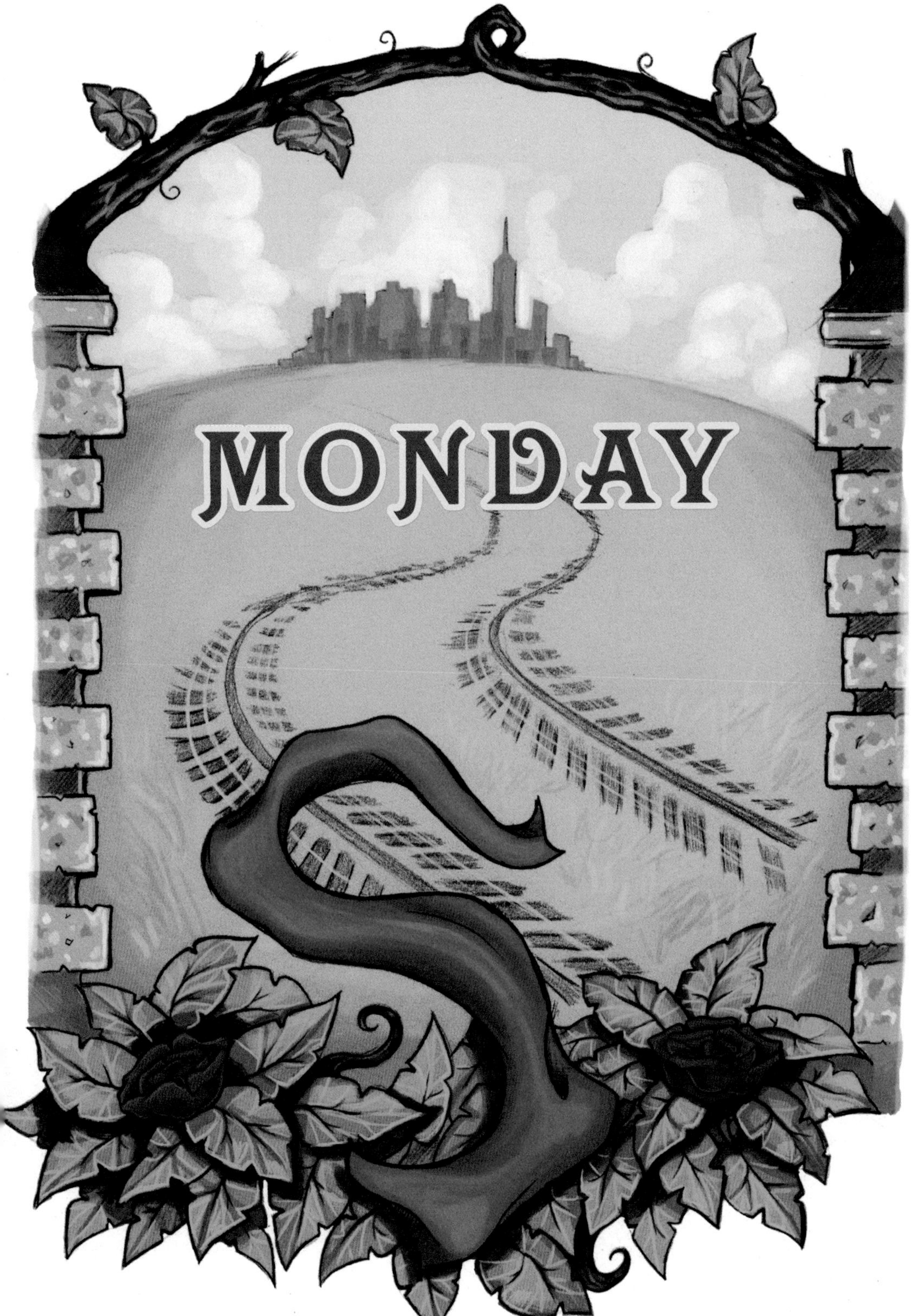
MONDAY

By that evening they hadn't finished the inventory. I could hardly blame them. They were small and few, while the objects of enchantment and power stored within the seemingly endless sprawl of this place were many. When they were exhausted from the day's work, I showed them, as promised, the day's events related to our mystery, taking place oh, so far away.

ROADMARKS

Karl Kerschl: artist • Lee Loughridge: colorist

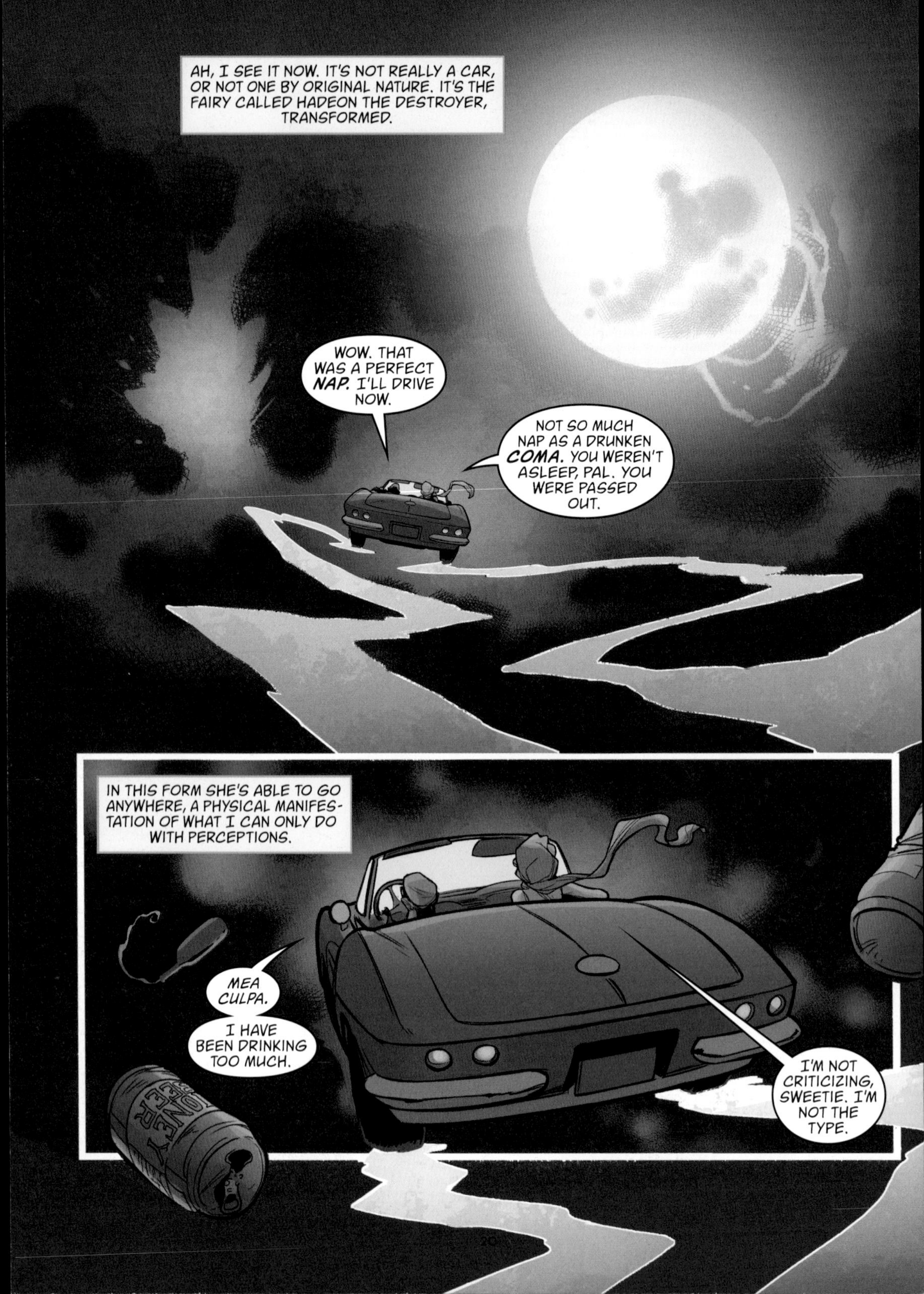
AH, I SEE IT NOW. IT'S NOT REALLY A CAR, OR NOT ONE BY ORIGINAL NATURE. IT'S THE FAIRY CALLED HADEON THE DESTROYER, TRANSFORMED.
WOW. THAT WAS A PERFECT NAP. I'LL DRIVE NOW.
NOT SO MUCH NAP AS A DRUNKEN COMA. YOU WEREN'T ASLEEP, PAL. YOU WERE PASSED OUT.
IN THIS FORM SHE'S ABLE TO GO ANYWHERE, A PHYSICAL MANIFESTATION OF WHAT I CAN ONLY DO WITH PERCEPTIONS.
MEA CULPA.
I HAVE BEEN DRINKING TOO MUCH.
I'M NOT CRITICIZING, SWEETIE. I'M NOT THE TYPE.

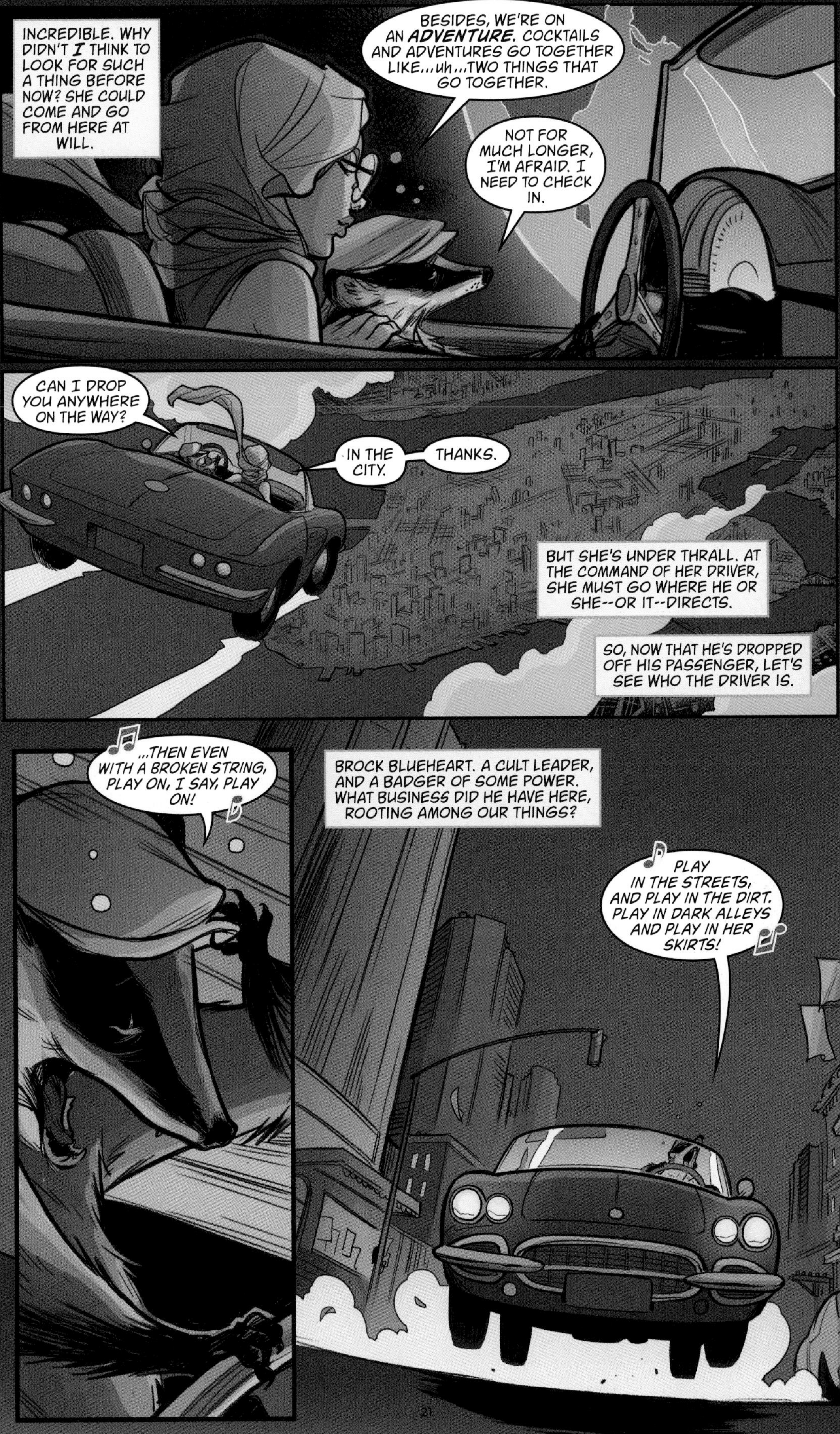
INCREDIBLE. WHY DIDN'T *I* THINK TO LOOK FOR SUCH A THING BEFORE NOW? SHE COULD COME AND GO FROM HERE AT WILL.
BESIDES, WE'RE ON AN ***ADVENTURE.*** COCKTAILS AND ADVENTURES GO TOGETHER LIKE...uh...TWO THINGS THAT GO TOGETHER.
NOT FOR MUCH LONGER, I'M AFRAID. I NEED TO CHECK IN.
CAN I DROP YOU ANYWHERE ON THE WAY?
IN THE CITY.
THANKS.
BUT SHE'S UNDER THRALL. AT THE COMMAND OF HER DRIVER, SHE MUST GO WHERE HE OR SHE--OR IT--DIRECTS.
SO, NOW THAT HE'S DROPPED OFF HIS PASSENGER, LET'S SEE WHO THE DRIVER IS.
...THEN EVEN WITH A BROKEN STRING, PLAY ON, I SAY, PLAY ON!
BROCK BLUEHEART. A CULT LEADER, AND A BADGER OF SOME POWER. WHAT BUSINESS DID HE HAVE HERE, ROOTING AMONG OUR THINGS?
PLAY IN THE STREETS, AND PLAY IN THE DIRT. PLAY IN DARK ALLEYS AND PLAY IN HER SKIRTS!

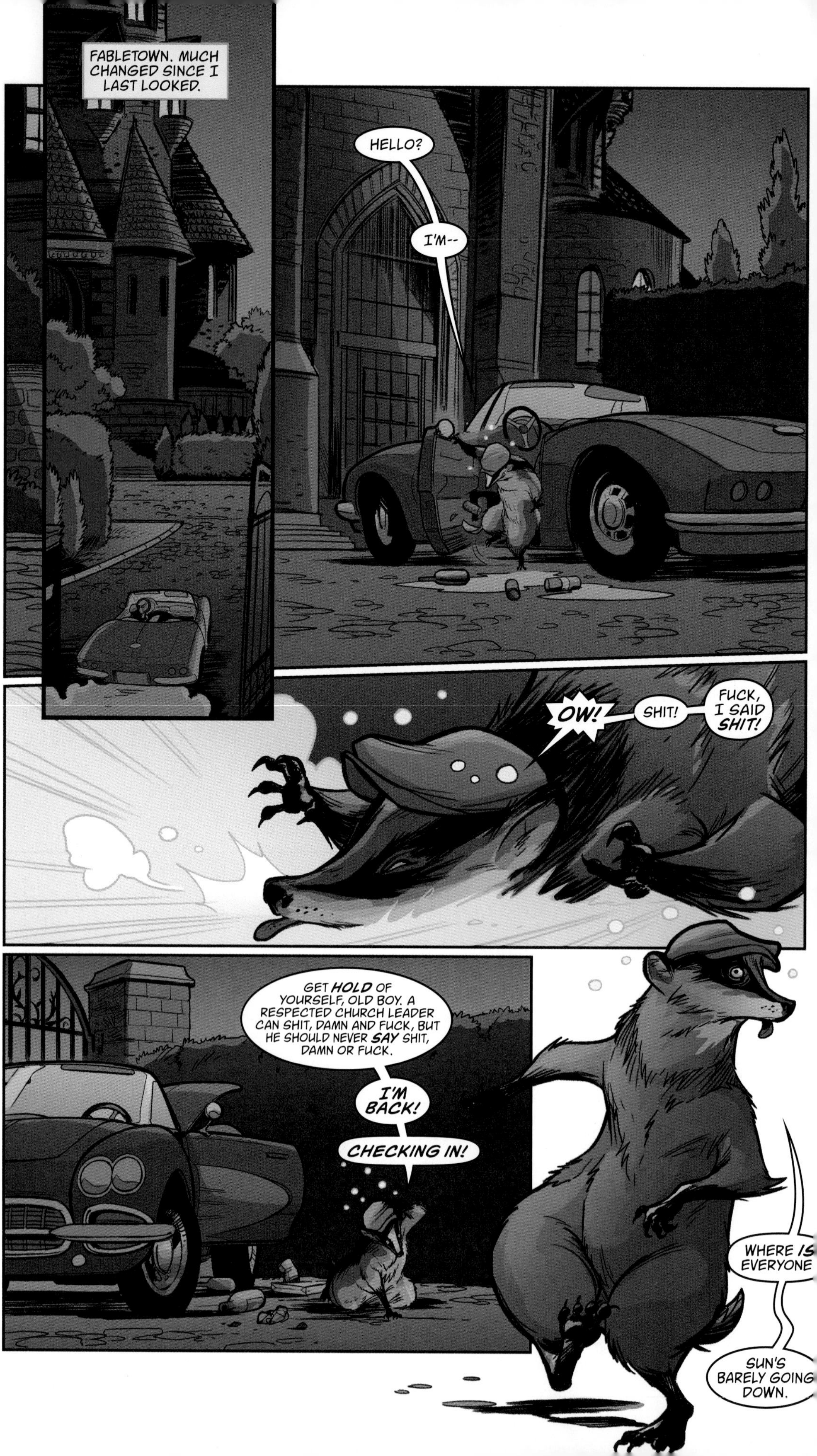
FABLETOWN. MUCH CHANGED SINCE I LAST LOOKED.
HELLO?
I'M--
OW!
SHIT!
FUCK, I SAID SHIT!
GET HOLD OF YOURSELF, OLD BOY. A RESPECTED CHURCH LEADER CAN SHIT, DAMN AND FUCK, BUT HE SHOULD NEVER SAY SHIT, DAMN OR FUCK.
I'M BACK!
CHECKING IN!
WHERE IS EVERYONE
SUN'S BARELY GOING DOWN.

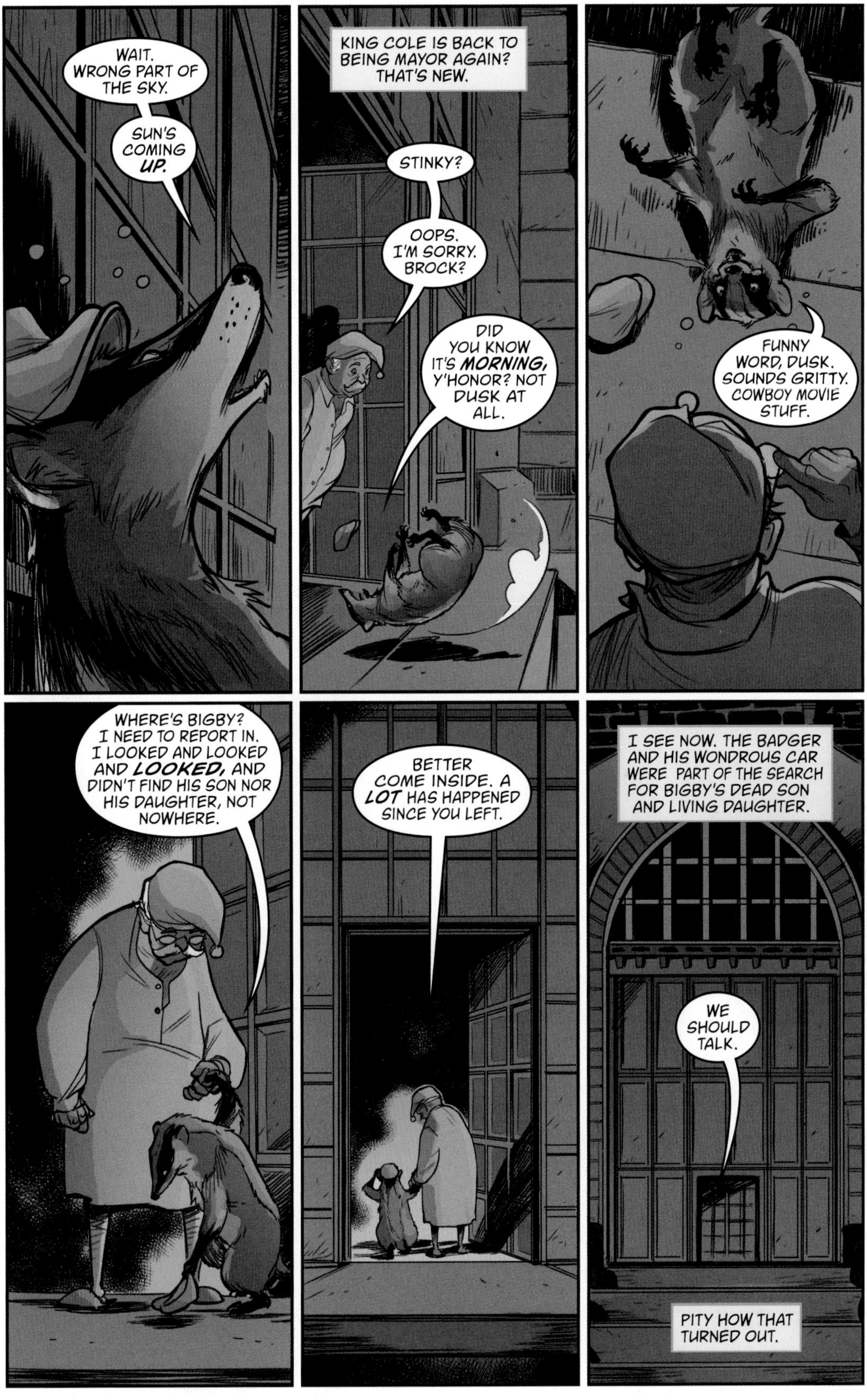
WAIT. WRONG PART OF THE SKY.
SUN'S COMING UP.
KING COLE IS BACK TO BEING MAYOR AGAIN? THAT'S NEW.
STINKY?
OOPS. I'M SORRY. BROCK?
DID YOU KNOW IT'S MORNING, Y'HONOR? NOT DUSK AT ALL.
FUNNY WORD, DUSK. SOUNDS GRITTY. COWBOY MOVIE STUFF.
WHERE'S BIGBY? I NEED TO REPORT IN. I LOOKED AND LOOKED AND LOOKED, AND DIDN'T FIND HIS SON NOR HIS DAUGHTER, NOT NOWHERE.
BETTER COME INSIDE. A LOT HAS HAPPENED SINCE YOU LEFT.
I SEE NOW. THE BADGER AND HIS WONDROUS CAR WERE PART OF THE SEARCH FOR BIGBY'S DEAD SON AND LIVING DAUGHTER.
WE SHOULD TALK.
PITY HOW THAT TURNED OUT.

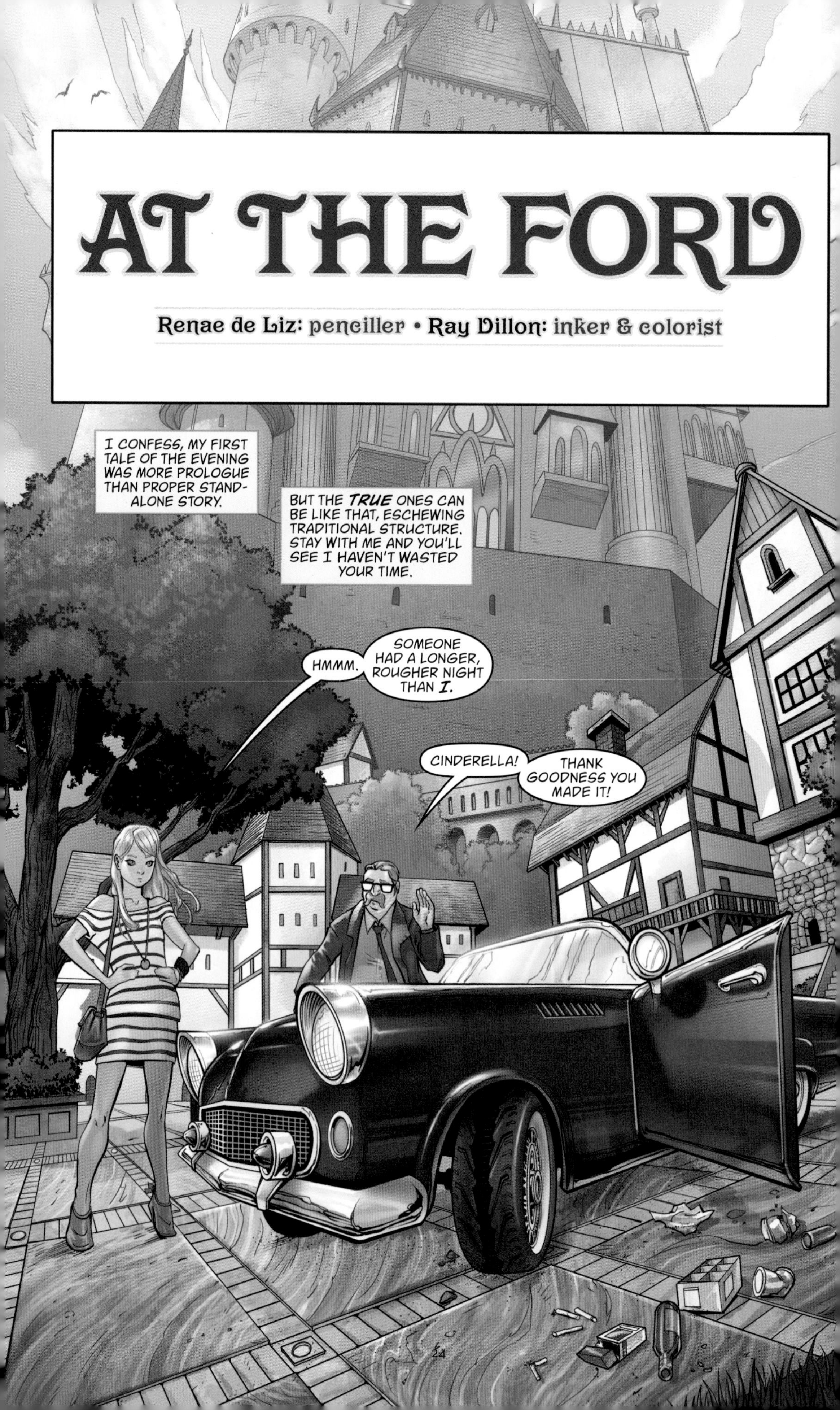
AT THE FORD
Renae de Liz: penciller • Ray Dillon: inker & colorist
I CONFESS, MY FIRST TALE OF THE EVENING WAS MORE PROLOGUE THAN PROPER STAND-ALONE STORY.
BUT THE TRUE ONES CAN BE LIKE THAT, ESCHEWING TRADITIONAL STRUCTURE. STAY WITH ME AND YOU'LL SEE I HAVEN'T WASTED YOUR TIME.
HMMM.
SOMEONE HAD A LONGER, ROUGHER NIGHT THAN I.
CINDERELLA!
THANK GOODNESS YOU MADE IT!

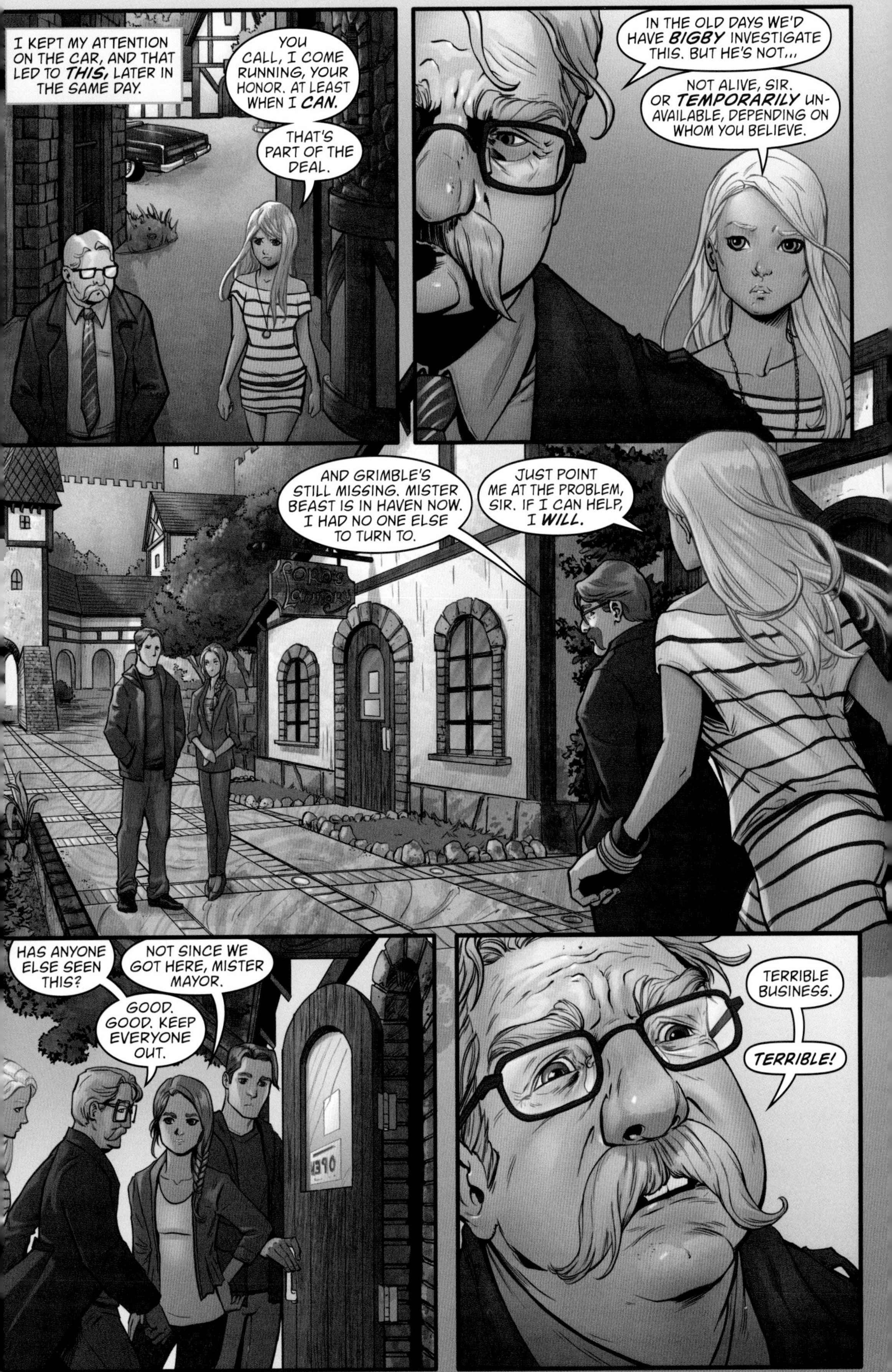

I KEPT MY ATTENTION ON THE CAR, AND THAT LED TO THIS, LATER IN THE SAME DAY.
YOU CALL, I COME RUNNING, YOUR HONOR. AT LEAST WHEN I CAN.
THAT'S PART OF THE DEAL.
IN THE OLD DAYS WE'D HAVE BIGBY INVESTIGATE THIS. BUT HE'S NOT...
NOT ALIVE, SIR. OR TEMPORARILY UN-AVAILABLE, DEPENDING ON WHOM YOU BELIEVE.
AND GRIMBLE'S STILL MISSING. MISTER BEAST IS IN HAVEN NOW. I HAD NO ONE ELSE TO TURN TO.
JUST POINT ME AT THE PROBLEM, SIR. IF I CAN HELP, I WILL.
HAS ANYONE ELSE SEEN THIS?
NOT SINCE WE GOT HERE, MISTER MAYOR.
GOOD. GOOD. KEEP EVERYONE OUT.
TERRIBLE BUSINESS.
TERRIBLE!

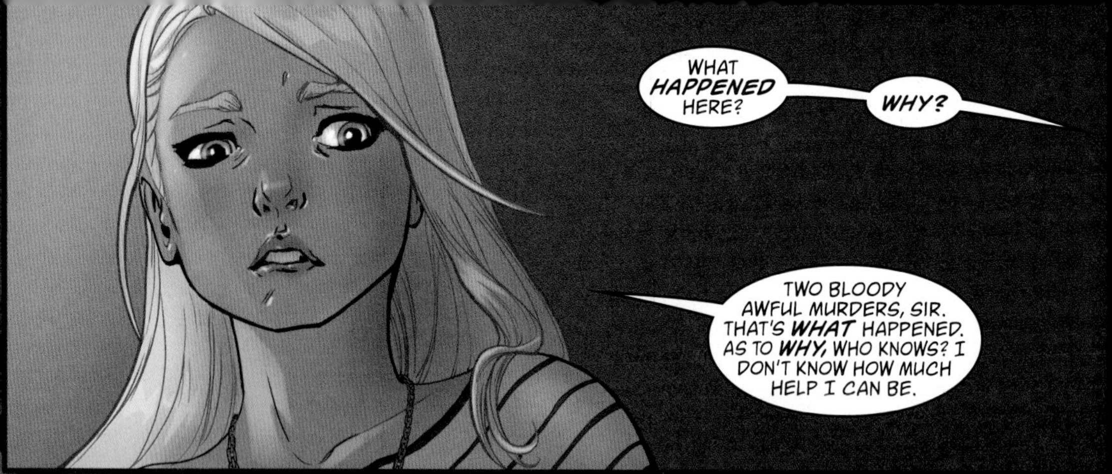
WHAT HAPPENED HERE?
WHY?
TWO BLOODY AWFUL MURDERS, SIR. THAT'S WHAT HAPPENED. AS TO WHY, WHO KNOWS? I DON'T KNOW HOW MUCH HELP I CAN BE.

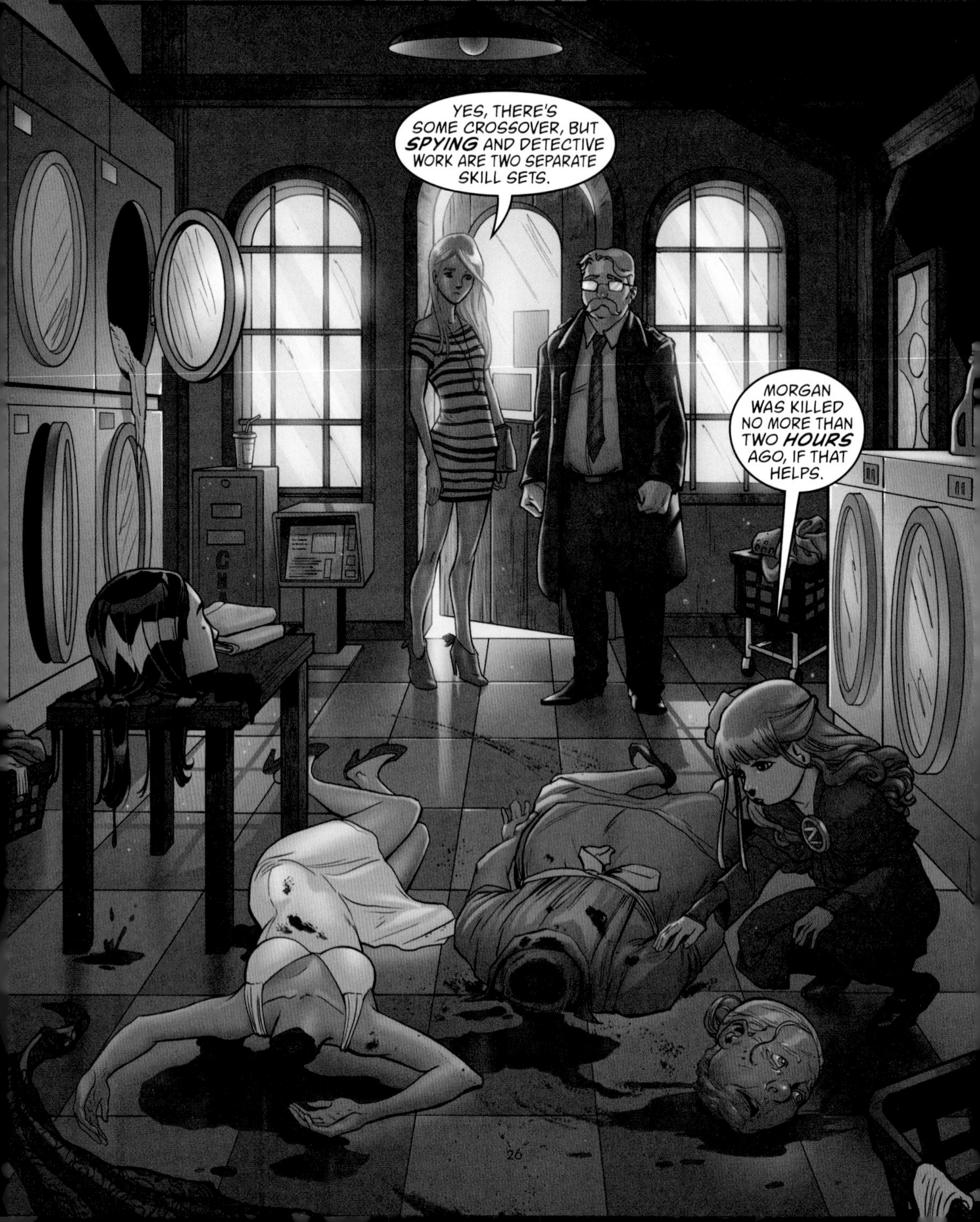
YES, THERE'S SOME CROSSOVER, BUT SPYING AND DETECTIVE WORK ARE TWO SEPARATE SKILL SETS.
MORGAN WAS KILLED NO MORE THAN TWO HOURS AGO, IF THAT HELPS.

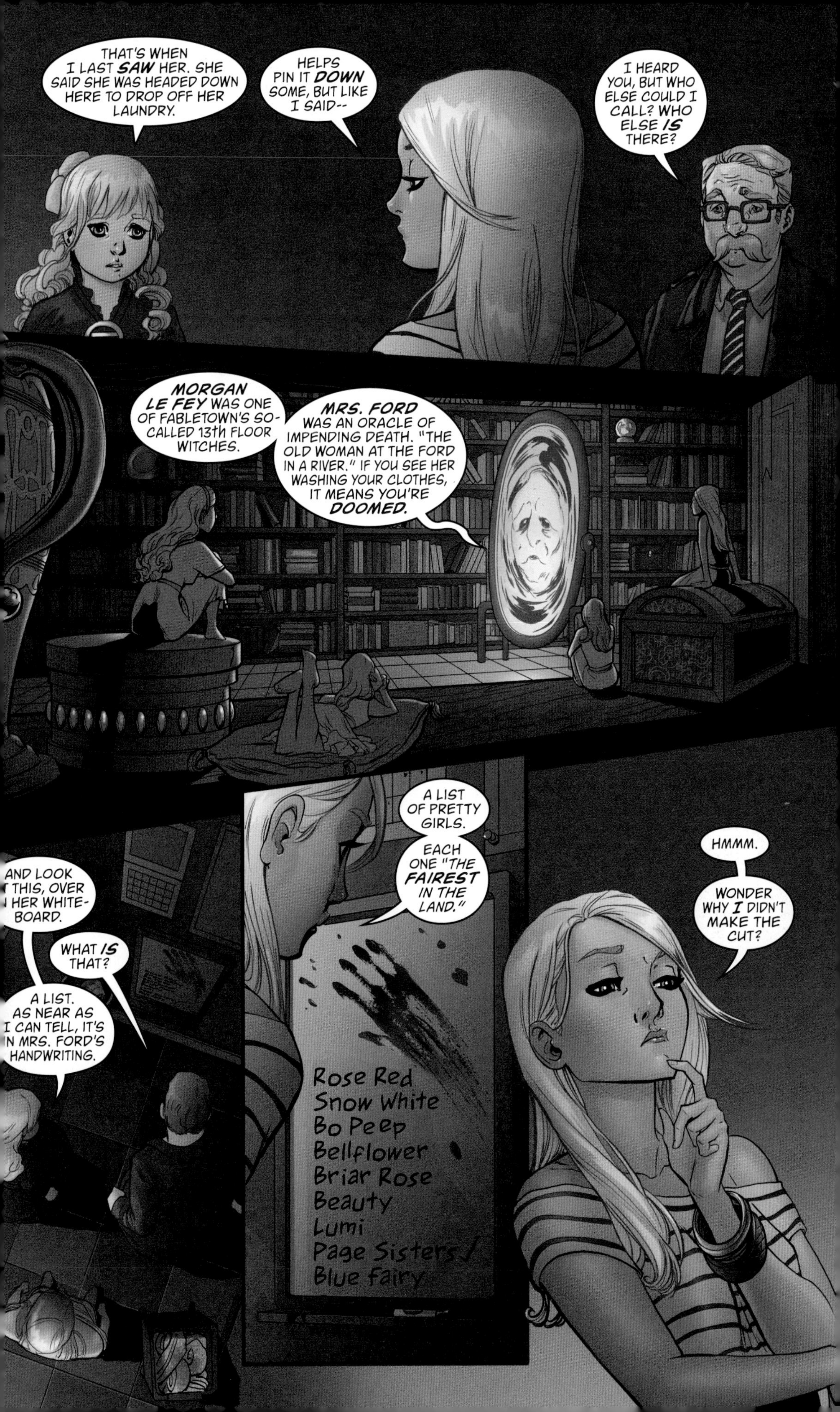

THAT'S WHEN I LAST SAW HER. SHE SAID SHE WAS HEADED DOWN HERE TO DROP OFF HER LAUNDRY.
HELPS PIN IT DOWN SOME, BUT LIKE I SAID--
I HEARD YOU, BUT WHO ELSE COULD I CALL? WHO ELSE IS THERE?
MORGAN LE FEY WAS ONE OF FABLETOWN'S SO-CALLED 13th FLOOR WITCHES.
MRS. FORD WAS AN ORACLE OF IMPENDING DEATH. "THE OLD WOMAN AT THE FORD IN A RIVER." IF YOU SEE HER WASHING YOUR CLOTHES, IT MEANS YOU'RE DOOMED.
AND LOOK T THIS, OVER HER WHITE-BOARD.
WHAT IS THAT?
A LIST. AS NEAR AS I CAN TELL, IT'S N MRS. FORD'S HANDWRITING.
A LIST OF PRETTY GIRLS.
EACH ONE "THE FAIREST IN THE LAND."
Rose Red
Snow White
Bo Peep
Bellflower
Briar Rose
Beauty
Lumi
Page Sisters
Blue Fairy
HMMM.
WONDER WHY I DIDN'T MAKE THE CUT?

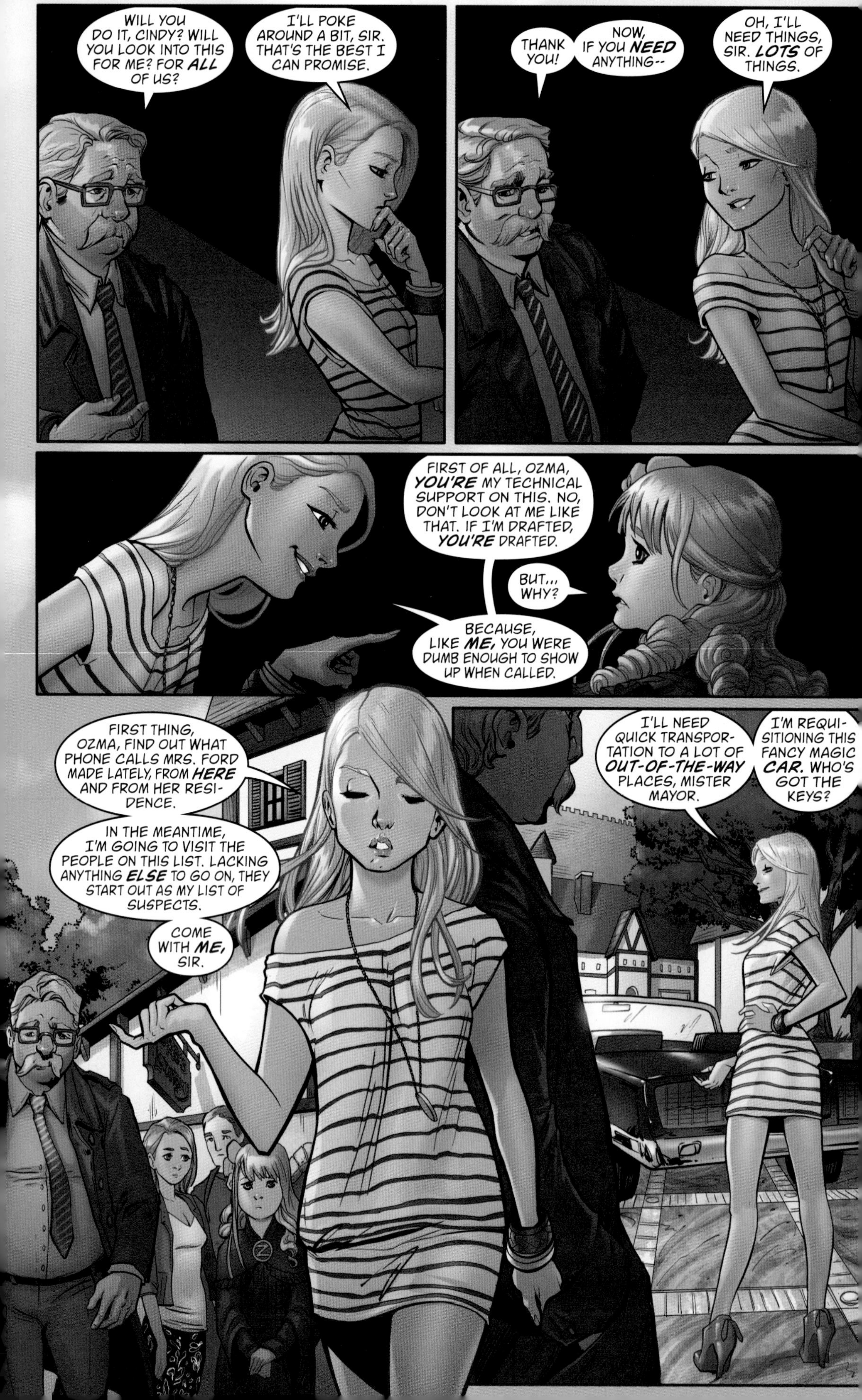
WILL YOU DO IT, CINDY? WILL YOU LOOK INTO THIS FOR ME? FOR ALL OF US?
I'LL POKE AROUND A BIT, SIR. THAT'S THE BEST I CAN PROMISE.
THANK YOU!
NOW, IF YOU NEED ANYTHING--
OH, I'LL NEED THINGS, SIR. LOTS OF THINGS.
FIRST OF ALL, OZMA, YOU'RE MY TECHNICAL SUPPORT ON THIS. NO, DON'T LOOK AT ME LIKE THAT. IF I'M DRAFTED, YOU'RE DRAFTED.
BUT... WHY?
BECAUSE, LIKE ME, YOU WERE DUMB ENOUGH TO SHOW UP WHEN CALLED.
FIRST THING, OZMA, FIND OUT WHAT PHONE CALLS MRS. FORD MADE LATELY, FROM HERE AND FROM HER RESIDENCE.
IN THE MEANTIME, I'M GOING TO VISIT THE PEOPLE ON THIS LIST. LACKING ANYTHING ELSE TO GO ON, THEY START OUT AS MY LIST OF SUSPECTS.
COME WITH ME, SIR.
I'LL NEED QUICK TRANSPORTATION TO A LOT OF OUT-OF-THE-WAY PLACES, MISTER MAYOR.
I'M REQUISITIONING THIS FANCY MAGIC CAR. WHO'S GOT THE KEYS?

CALLING DOWN THE MOON

Fiona Meng: artist

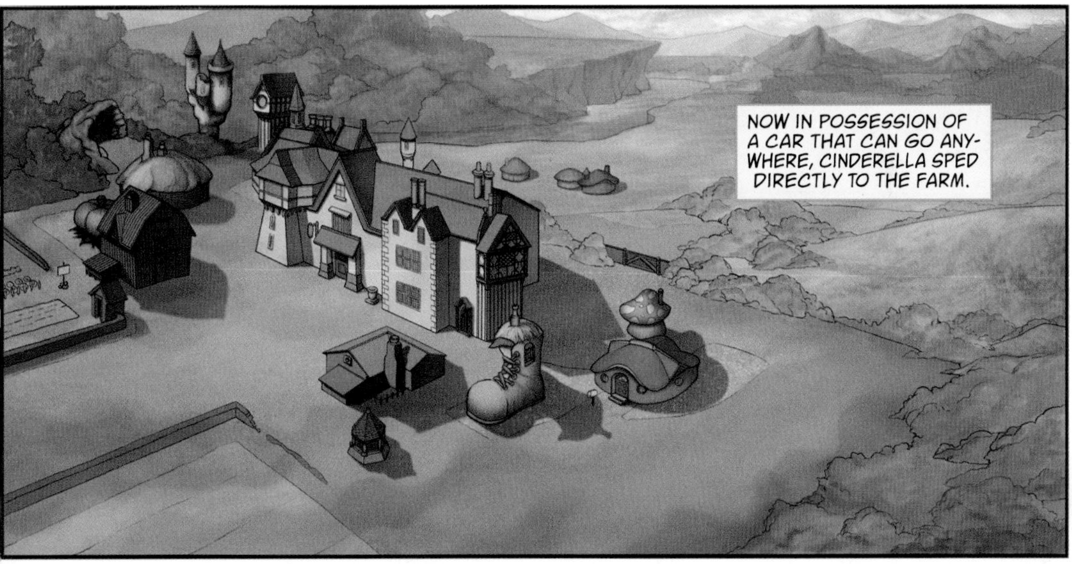
NOW IN POSSESSION OF A CAR THAT CAN GO ANY-WHERE, CINDERELLA SPED DIRECTLY TO THE FARM.

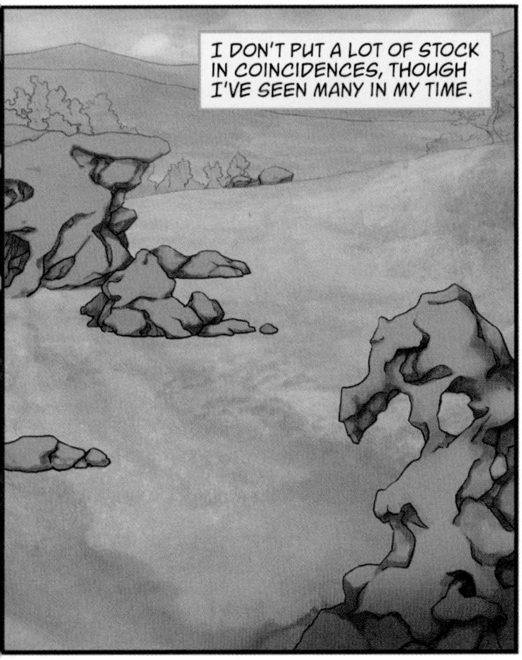
I DON'T PUT A LOT OF STOCK IN COINCIDENCES, THOUGH I'VE SEEN MANY IN MY TIME.

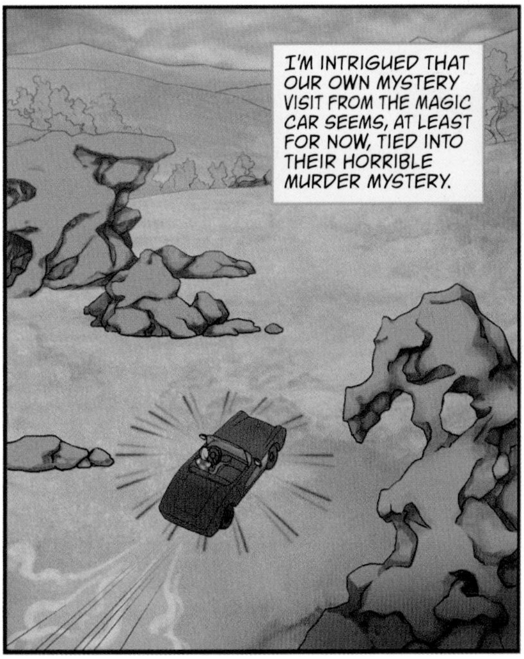
I'M INTRIGUED THAT OUR OWN MYSTERY VISIT FROM THE MAGIC CAR SEEMS, AT LEAST FOR NOW, TIED INTO THEIR HORRIBLE MURDER MYSTERY.

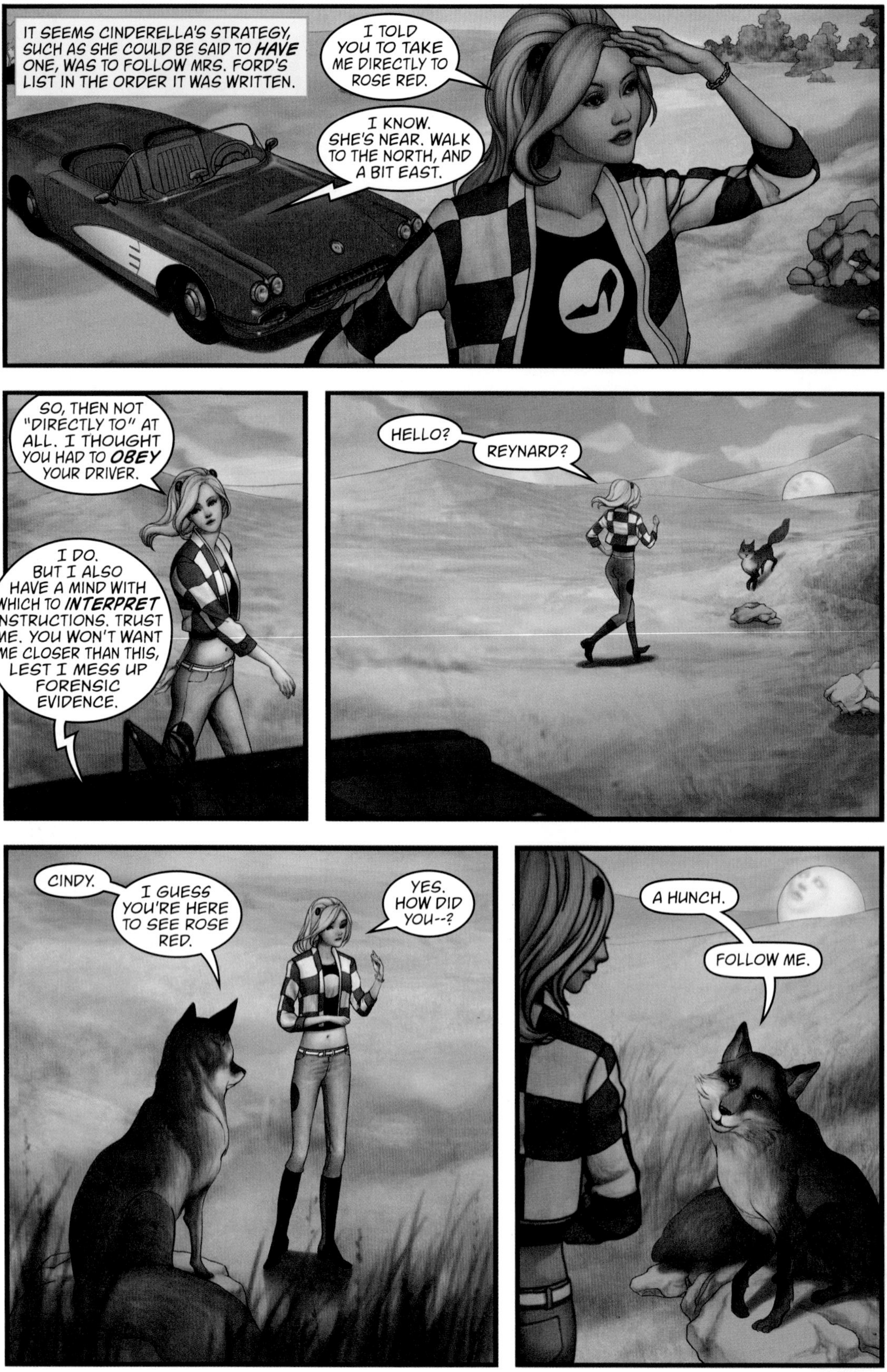
IT SEEMS CINDERELLA'S STRATEGY, SUCH AS SHE COULD BE SAID TO **HAVE** ONE, WAS TO FOLLOW MRS. FORD'S LIST IN THE ORDER IT WAS WRITTEN.
I TOLD YOU TO TAKE ME DIRECTLY TO ROSE RED.
I KNOW. SHE'S NEAR. WALK TO THE NORTH, AND A BIT EAST.
SO, THEN NOT "DIRECTLY TO" AT ALL. I THOUGHT YOU HAD TO **OBEY** YOUR DRIVER.
I DO. BUT I ALSO HAVE A MIND WITH WHICH TO **INTERPRET** INSTRUCTIONS. TRUST ME. YOU WON'T WANT ME CLOSER THAN THIS, LEST I MESS UP FORENSIC EVIDENCE.
HELLO?
REYNARD?
CINDY.
I GUESS YOU'RE HERE TO SEE ROSE RED.
YES. HOW DID YOU--?
A HUNCH.
FOLLOW ME.

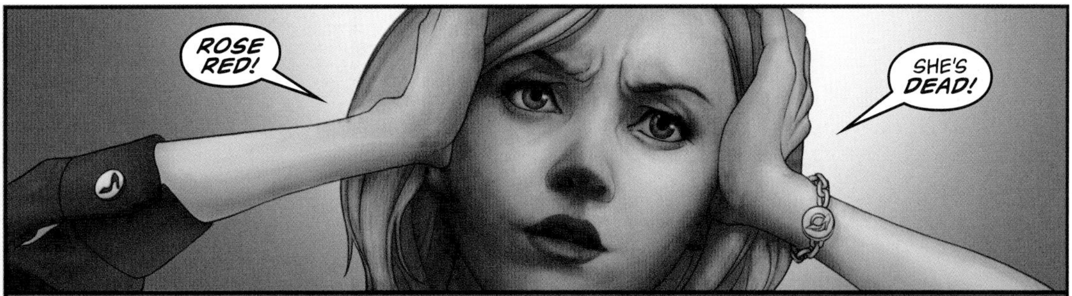
ROSE RED!
SHE'S DEAD!

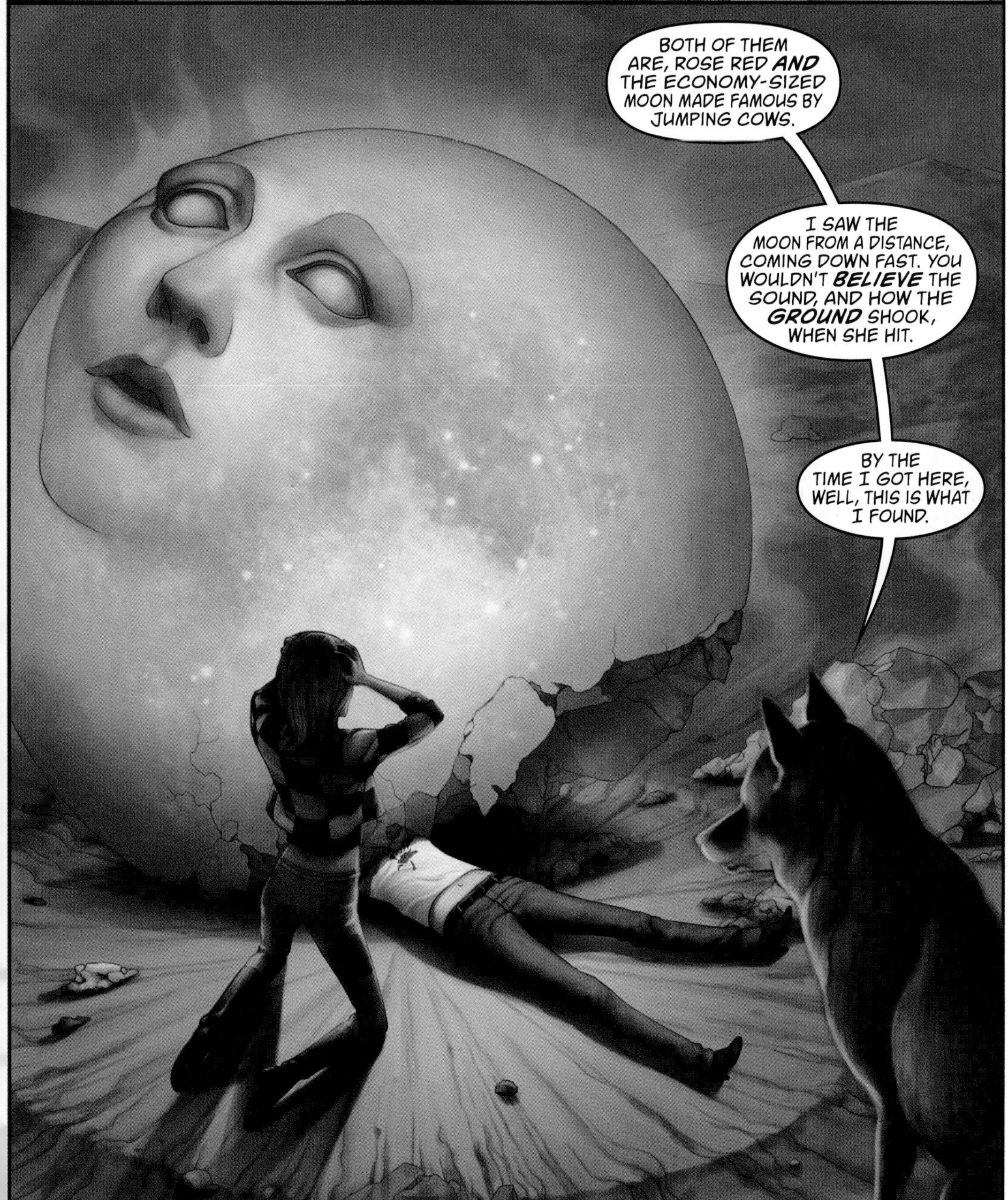
BOTH OF THEM ARE, ROSE RED AND THE ECONOMY-SIZED MOON MADE FAMOUS BY JUMPING COWS.
I SAW THE MOON FROM A DISTANCE, COMING DOWN FAST. YOU WOULDN'T BELIEVE THE SOUND, AND HOW THE GROUND SHOOK, WHEN SHE HIT.
BY THE TIME I GOT HERE, WELL, THIS IS WHAT I FOUND.

NOTHING ELSE?

WELL...

SPIT IT OUT, IF YOU'VE GOT ANYTHING *FURTHER* THAT CAN HELP.

SNOW WHITE WAS HERE TOO. I DIDN'T ARRIVE IN TIME TO *SEE* HER, BUT YOU CAN'T FOOL *THIS* NOSE.

HER SCENT IS RIPE AND RECENT.

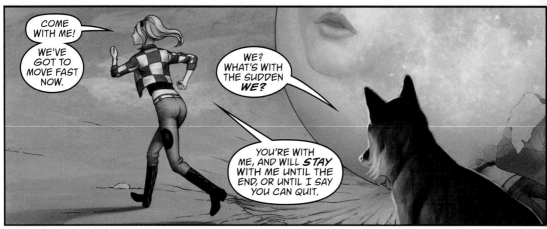

COME WITH ME!

WE'VE GOT TO MOVE FAST NOW.

WE? WHAT'S WITH THE SUDDEN *WE?*

YOU'RE WITH ME, AND WILL *STAY* WITH ME UNTIL THE END, OR UNTIL I SAY YOU CAN QUIT.

I MAY HAVE FURTHER NEED OF A NOSE NO ONE CAN FOOL.

NOW LET'S PUT FEET RAPIDLY IN FRONT OF FEET.

I'M ALREADY TIRED OF THIS ARRIVE-TOO-LATE BULLSHIT.

OVER HILL, OVER DALE

Mark Buckingham: artist • Lee Loughridge: colorist

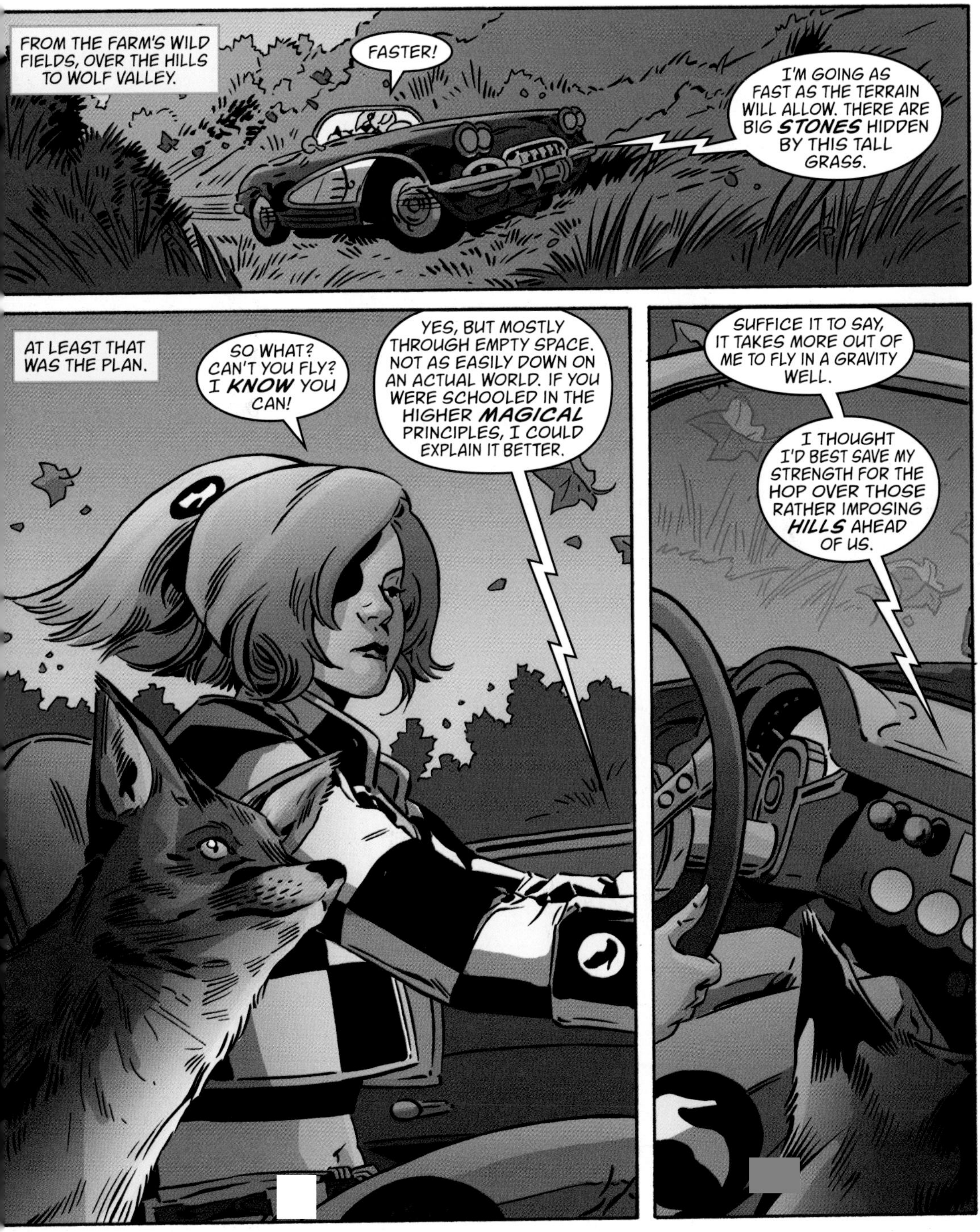

FROM THE FARM'S WILD FIELDS, OVER THE HILLS TO WOLF VALLEY.
FASTER!
I'M GOING AS FAST AS THE TERRAIN WILL ALLOW. THERE ARE BIG **STONES** HIDDEN BY THIS TALL GRASS.
AT LEAST THAT WAS THE PLAN.
SO WHAT? CAN'T YOU FLY? I **KNOW** YOU CAN!
YES, BUT MOSTLY THROUGH EMPTY SPACE. NOT AS EASILY DOWN ON AN ACTUAL WORLD. IF YOU WERE SCHOOLED IN THE HIGHER **MAGICAL** PRINCIPLES, I COULD EXPLAIN IT BETTER.
SUFFICE IT TO SAY, IT TAKES MORE OUT OF ME TO FLY IN A GRAVITY WELL.
I THOUGHT I'D BEST SAVE MY STRENGTH FOR THE HOP OVER THOSE RATHER IMPOSING **HILLS** AHEAD OF US.

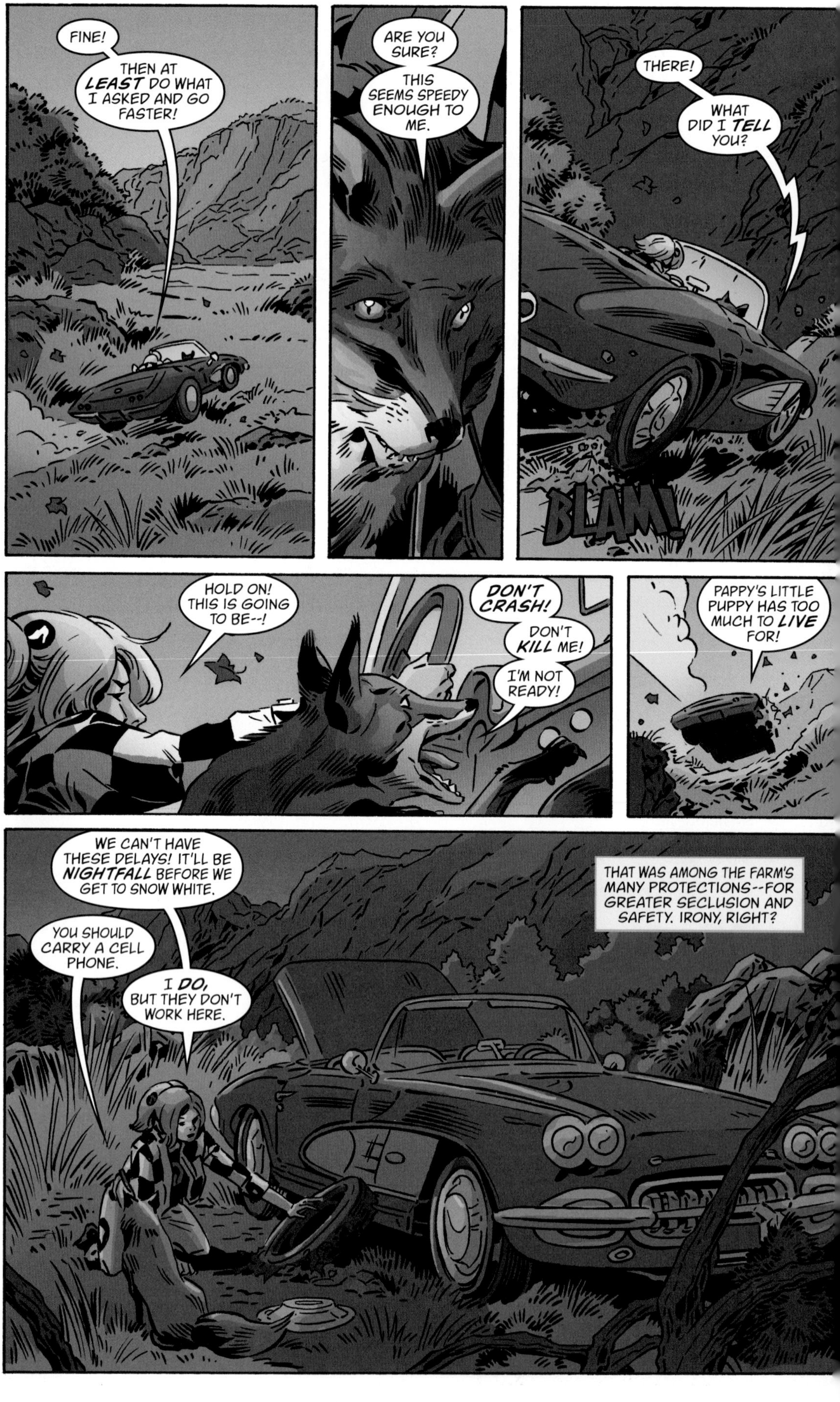
FINE!
THEN AT LEAST DO WHAT I ASKED AND GO FASTER!
ARE YOU SURE?
THIS SEEMS SPEEDY ENOUGH TO ME.
THERE!
WHAT DID I TELL YOU?
BLAM!
HOLD ON! THIS IS GOING TO BE--!
DON'T CRASH!
DON'T KILL ME!
I'M NOT READY!
PAPPY'S LITTLE PUPPY HAS TOO MUCH TO LIVE FOR!
WE CAN'T HAVE THESE DELAYS! IT'LL BE NIGHTFALL BEFORE WE GET TO SNOW WHITE.
THAT WAS AMONG THE FARM'S MANY PROTECTIONS--FOR GREATER SECLUSION AND SAFETY. IRONY, RIGHT?
YOU SHOULD CARRY A CELL PHONE.
I DO, BUT THEY DON'T WORK HERE.

NECESSARY CUTS

Phil Noto: artist

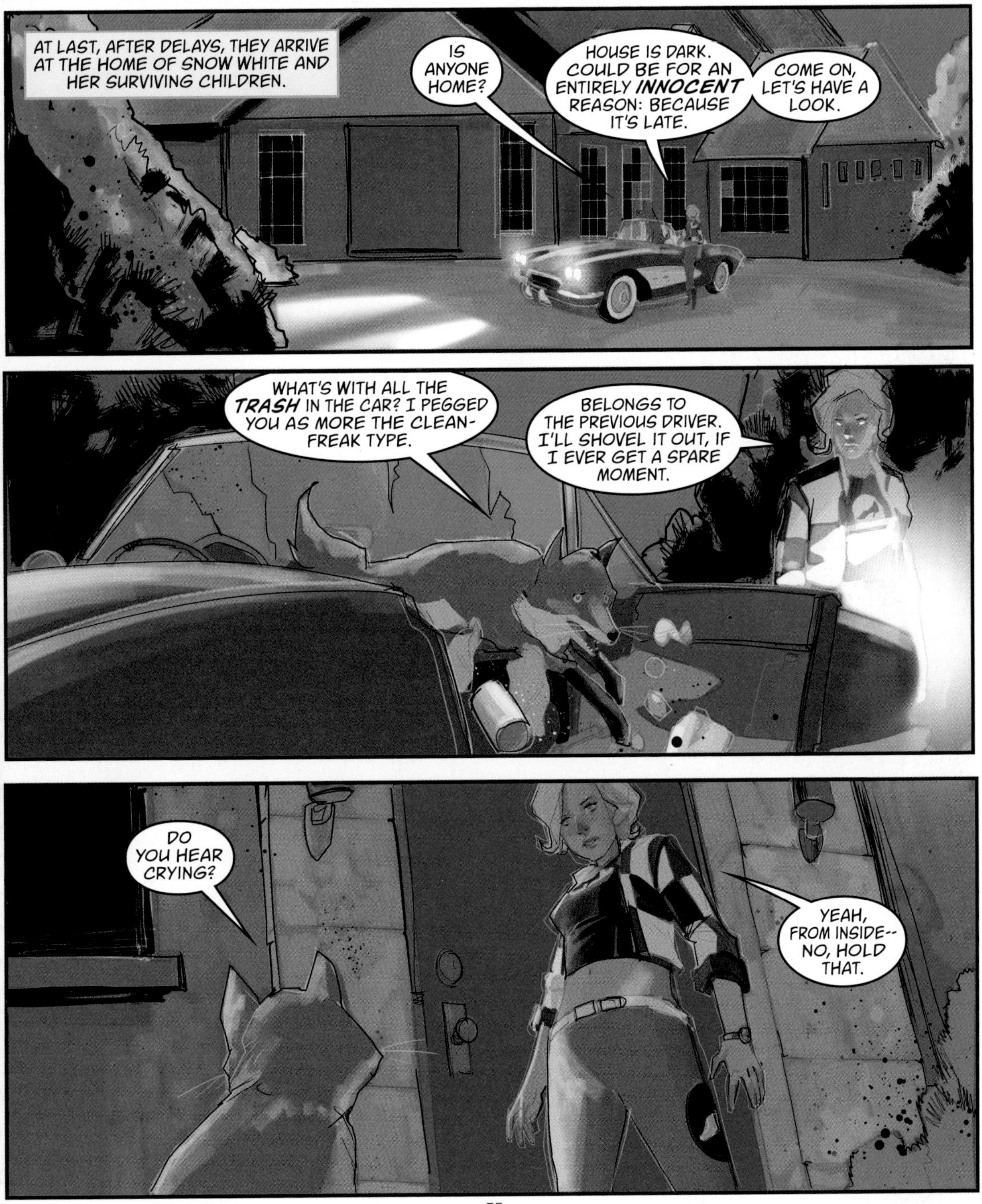

AT LAST, AFTER DELAYS, THEY ARRIVE AT THE HOME OF SNOW WHITE AND HER SURVIVING CHILDREN.
IS ANYONE HOME?
HOUSE IS DARK. COULD BE FOR AN ENTIRELY *INNOCENT* REASON: BECAUSE IT'S LATE.
COME ON, LET'S HAVE A LOOK.
WHAT'S WITH ALL THE *TRASH* IN THE CAR? I PEGGED YOU AS MORE THE CLEAN-FREAK TYPE.
BELONGS TO THE PREVIOUS DRIVER. I'LL SHOVEL IT OUT, IF I EVER GET A SPARE MOMENT.
DO YOU HEAR CRYING?
YEAH, FROM INSIDE-- NO, HOLD THAT.

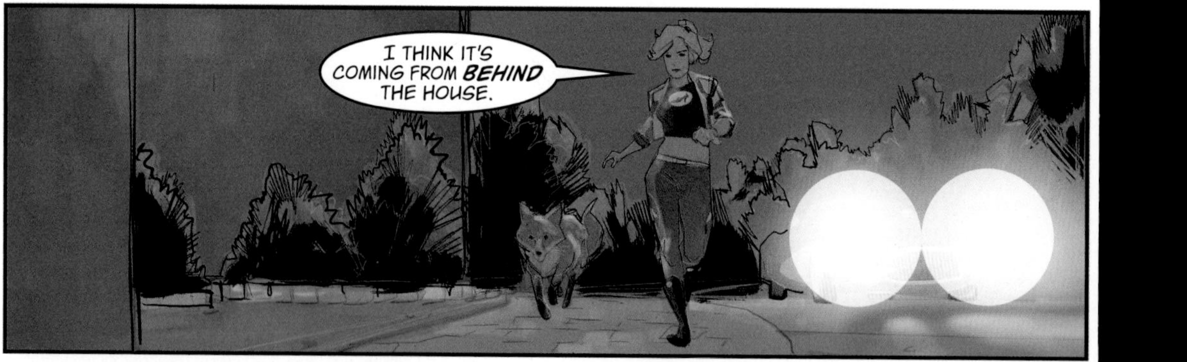
I THINK IT'S COMING FROM **BEHIND** THE HOUSE.

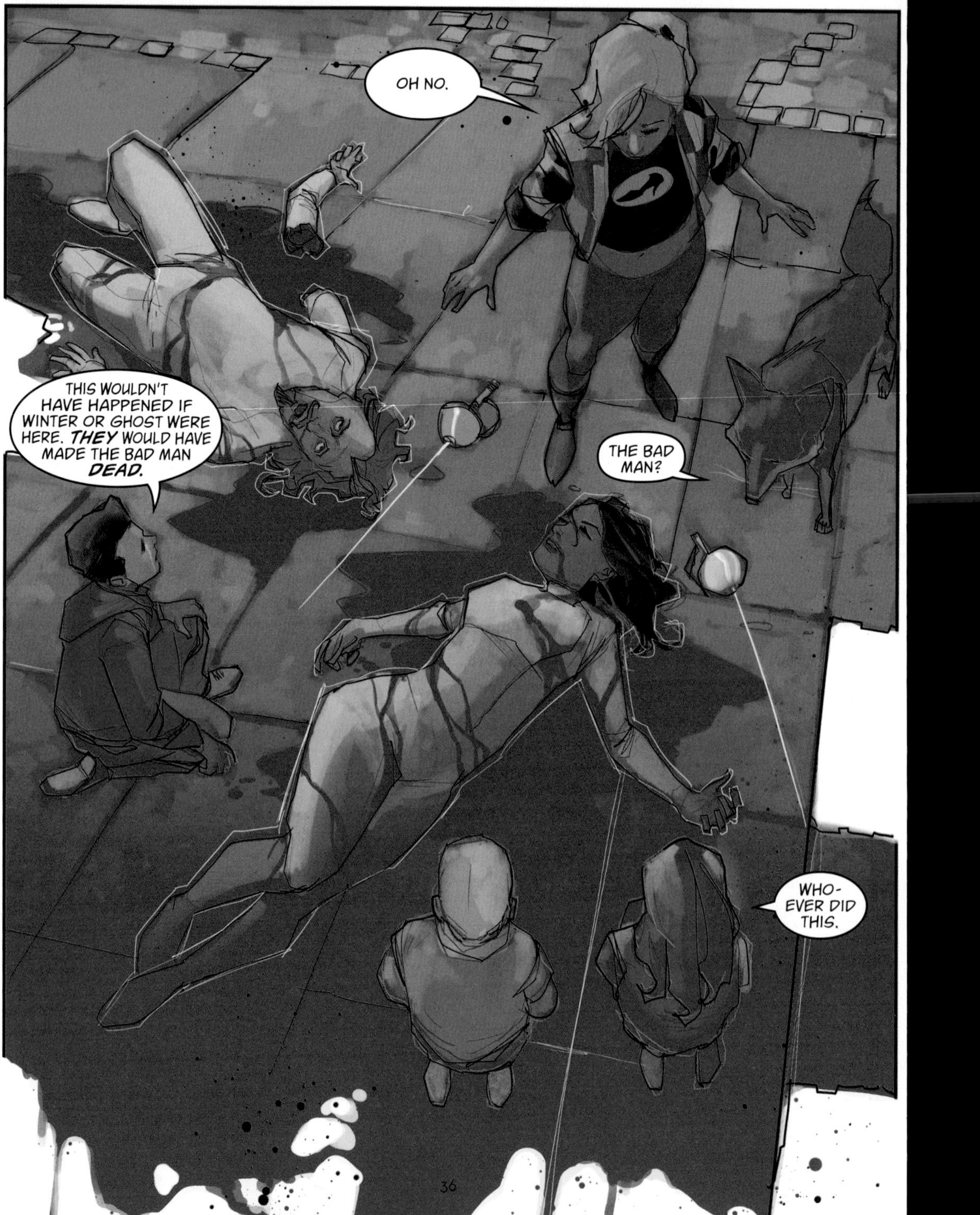
OH NO.
THIS WOULDN'T HAVE HAPPENED IF WINTER OR GHOST WERE HERE. **THEY** WOULD HAVE MADE THE BAD MAN **DEAD.**
THE BAD MAN?
WHO-EVER DID THIS.

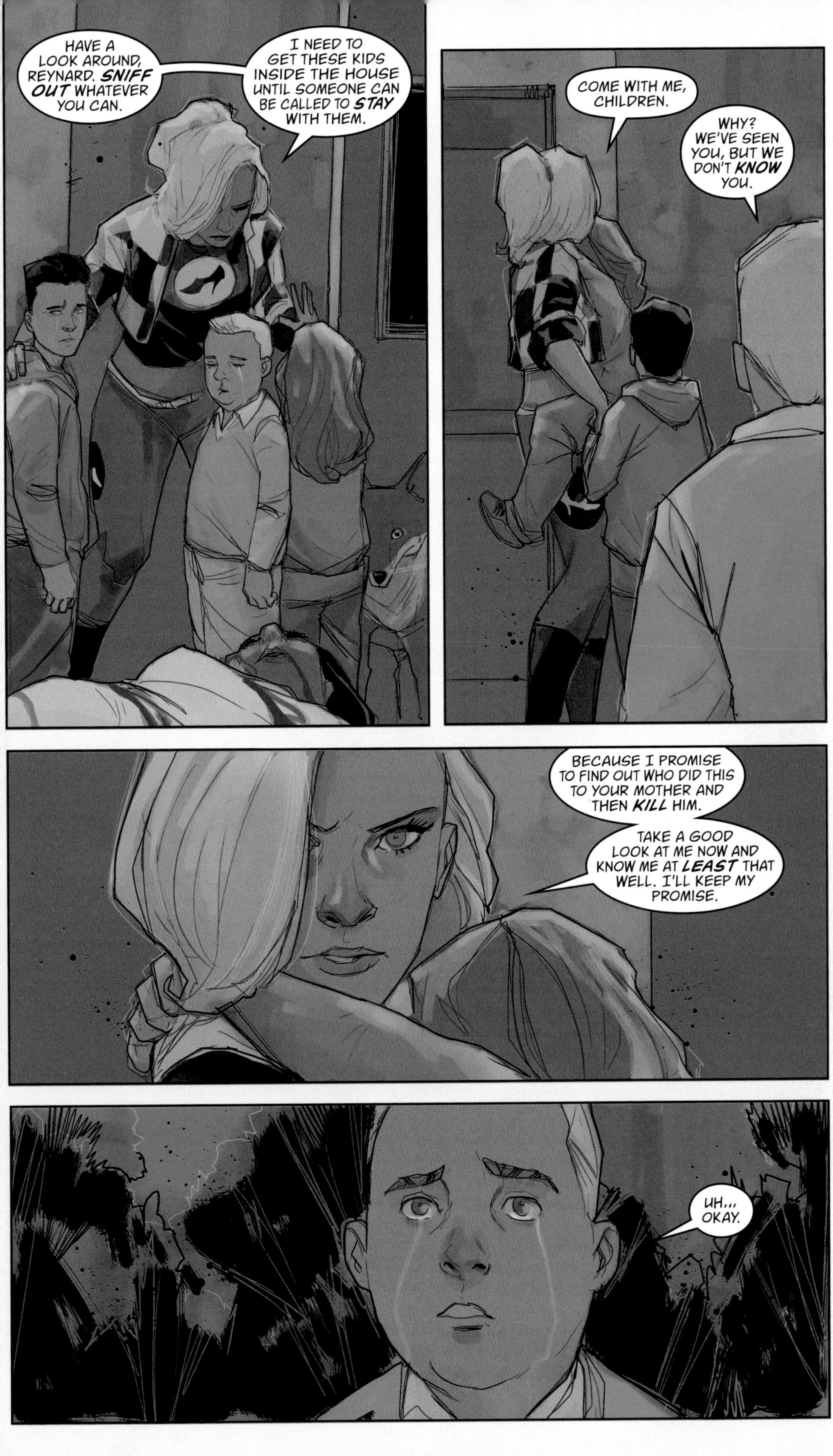

HAVE A LOOK AROUND, REYNARD. SNIFF OUT WHATEVER YOU CAN.
I NEED TO GET THESE KIDS INSIDE THE HOUSE UNTIL SOMEONE CAN BE CALLED TO STAY WITH THEM.
COME WITH ME, CHILDREN.
WHY? WE'VE SEEN YOU, BUT WE DON'T KNOW YOU.
BECAUSE I PROMISE TO FIND OUT WHO DID THIS TO YOUR MOTHER AND THEN KILL HIM.
TAKE A GOOD LOOK AT ME NOW AND KNOW ME AT LEAST THAT WELL. I'LL KEEP MY PROMISE.
UH... OKAY.

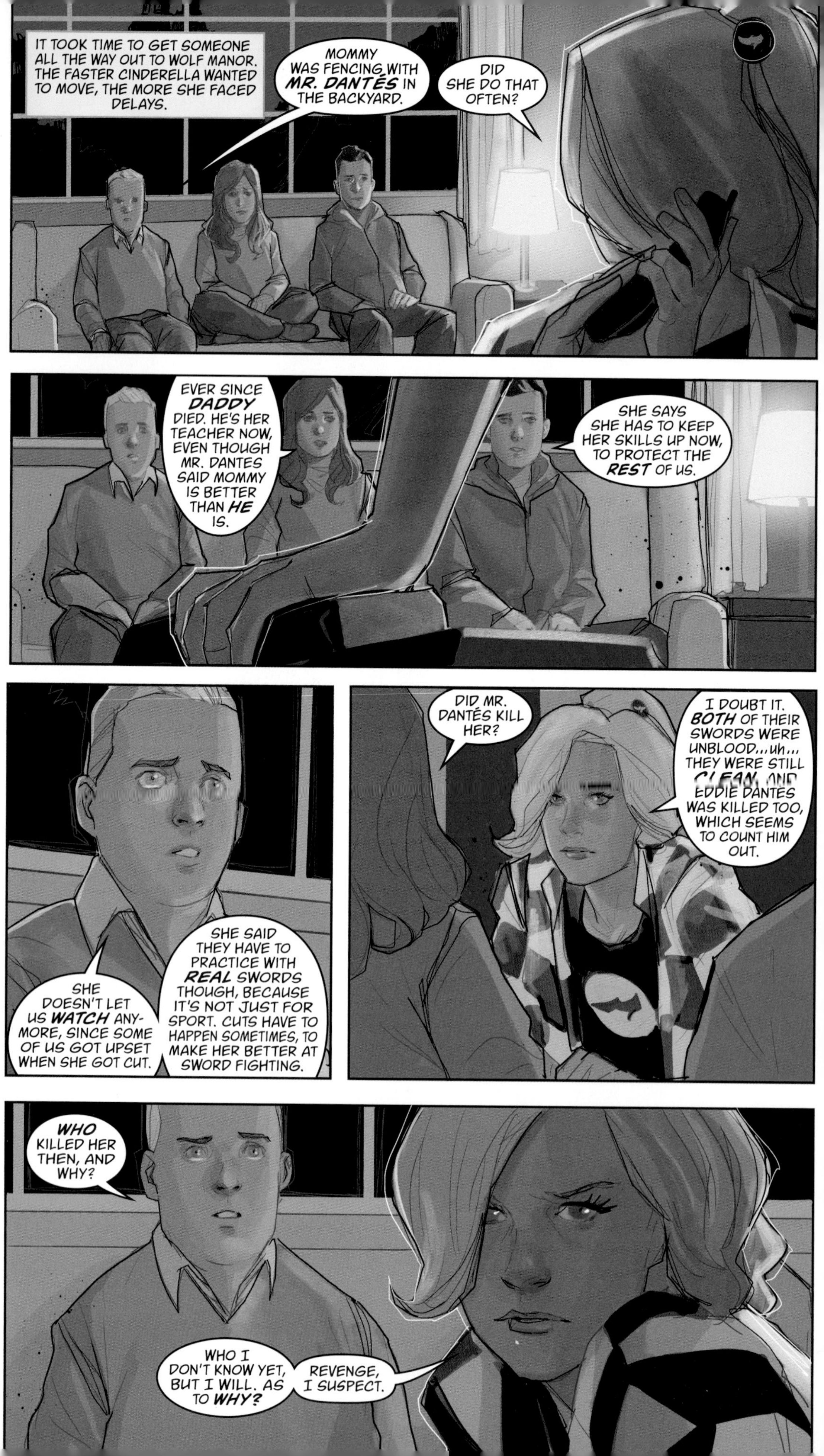

IT TOOK TIME TO GET SOMEONE ALL THE WAY OUT TO WOLF MANOR. THE FASTER CINDERELLA WANTED TO MOVE, THE MORE SHE FACED DELAYS.
MOMMY WAS FENCING WITH MR. DANTÉS IN THE BACKYARD.
DID SHE DO THAT OFTEN?
EVER SINCE DADDY DIED. HE'S HER TEACHER NOW, EVEN THOUGH MR. DANTES SAID MOMMY IS BETTER THAN HE IS.
SHE SAYS SHE HAS TO KEEP HER SKILLS UP NOW, TO PROTECT THE REST OF US.
SHE DOESN'T LET US WATCH ANY-MORE, SINCE SOME OF US GOT UPSET WHEN SHE GOT CUT.
SHE SAID THEY HAVE TO PRACTICE WITH REAL SWORDS THOUGH, BECAUSE IT'S NOT JUST FOR SPORT. CUTS HAVE TO HAPPEN SOMETIMES, TO MAKE HER BETTER AT SWORD FIGHTING.
DID MR. DANTÉS KILL HER?
I DOUBT IT. BOTH OF THEIR SWORDS WERE UNBLOOD...UH... THEY WERE STILL CLEAN, AND EDDIE DANTES WAS KILLED TOO, WHICH SEEMS TO COUNT HIM OUT.
WHO KILLED HER THEN, AND WHY?
WHO I DON'T KNOW YET, BUT I WILL. AS TO WHY?
REVENGE, I SUSPECT.

TUESDAY

After another day of work, trying to pin down what, if anything, was taken from our shelves and store-rooms, we resumed evening viewing of the day's events. I didn't let on yet that I was troubled by my own poor efforts in our mutual search. I can see whatsoever I wish. Why then was I only able to focus on the results of the three sets of murders, but not the actual killings as they'd taken place?

Within a very few strictures, it's impossible to hide anything from me. One of the exceptions is when I'm in forced service to some master and he's expressly forbidden me to look in certain places. But I haven't been in anyone's bondage for many years. I'm commanded only by myself now. Sole navigator of my fate, captain of my own destiny, marshal of my own soul. Et cetera.

Aren't I?

STARLIGHT INTERLUDE

Meghan Hetrick: artist

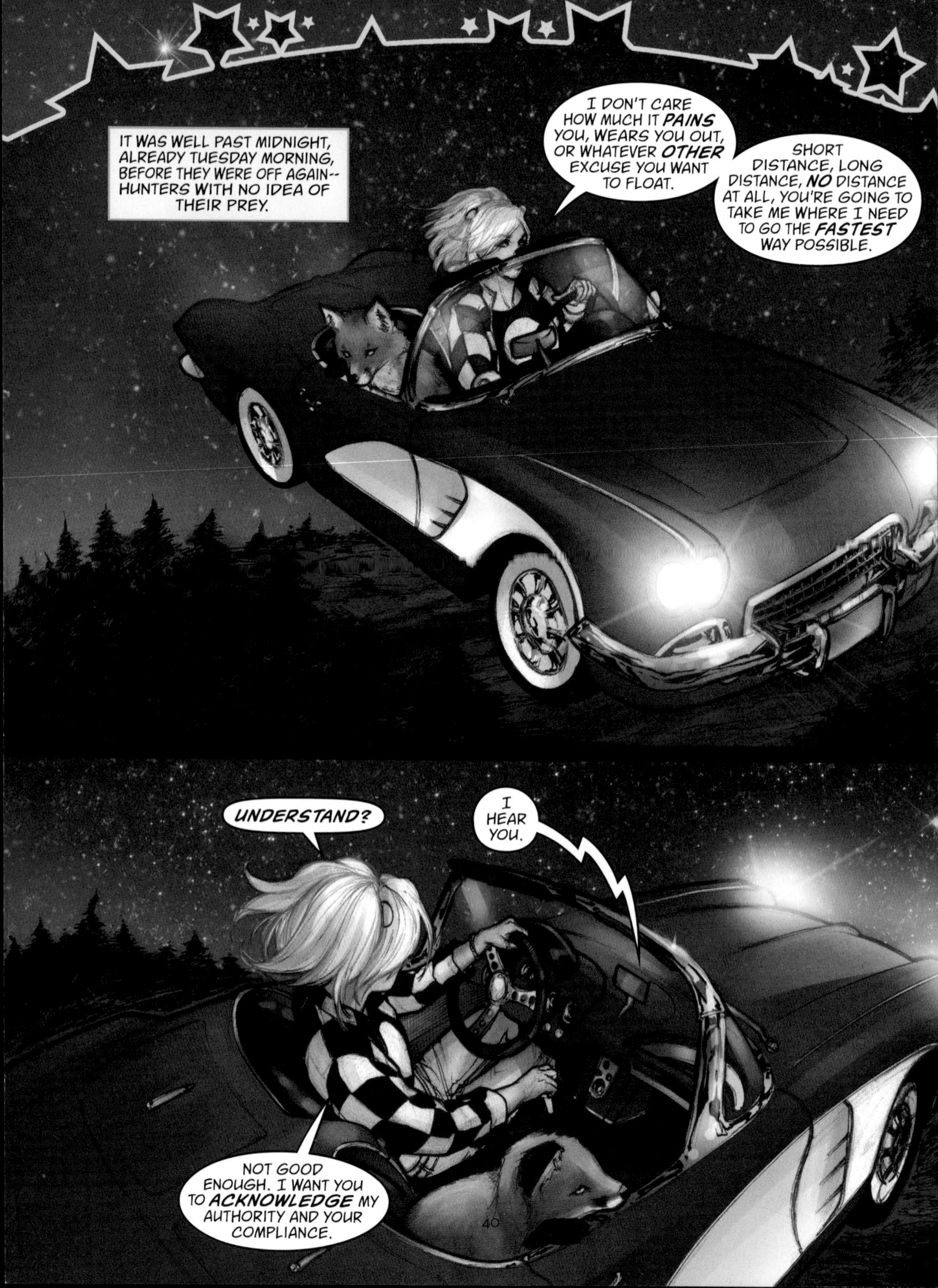

IT WAS WELL PAST MIDNIGHT, ALREADY TUESDAY MORNING, BEFORE THEY WERE OFF AGAIN--HUNTERS WITH NO IDEA OF THEIR PREY.
I DON'T CARE HOW MUCH IT PAINS YOU, WEARS YOU OUT, OR WHATEVER OTHER EXCUSE YOU WANT TO FLOAT.
SHORT DISTANCE, LONG DISTANCE, NO DISTANCE AT ALL, YOU'RE GOING TO TAKE ME WHERE I NEED TO GO THE FASTEST WAY POSSIBLE.
UNDERSTAND?
I HEAR YOU.
NOT GOOD ENOUGH. I WANT YOU TO ACKNOWLEDGE MY AUTHORITY AND YOUR COMPLIANCE.

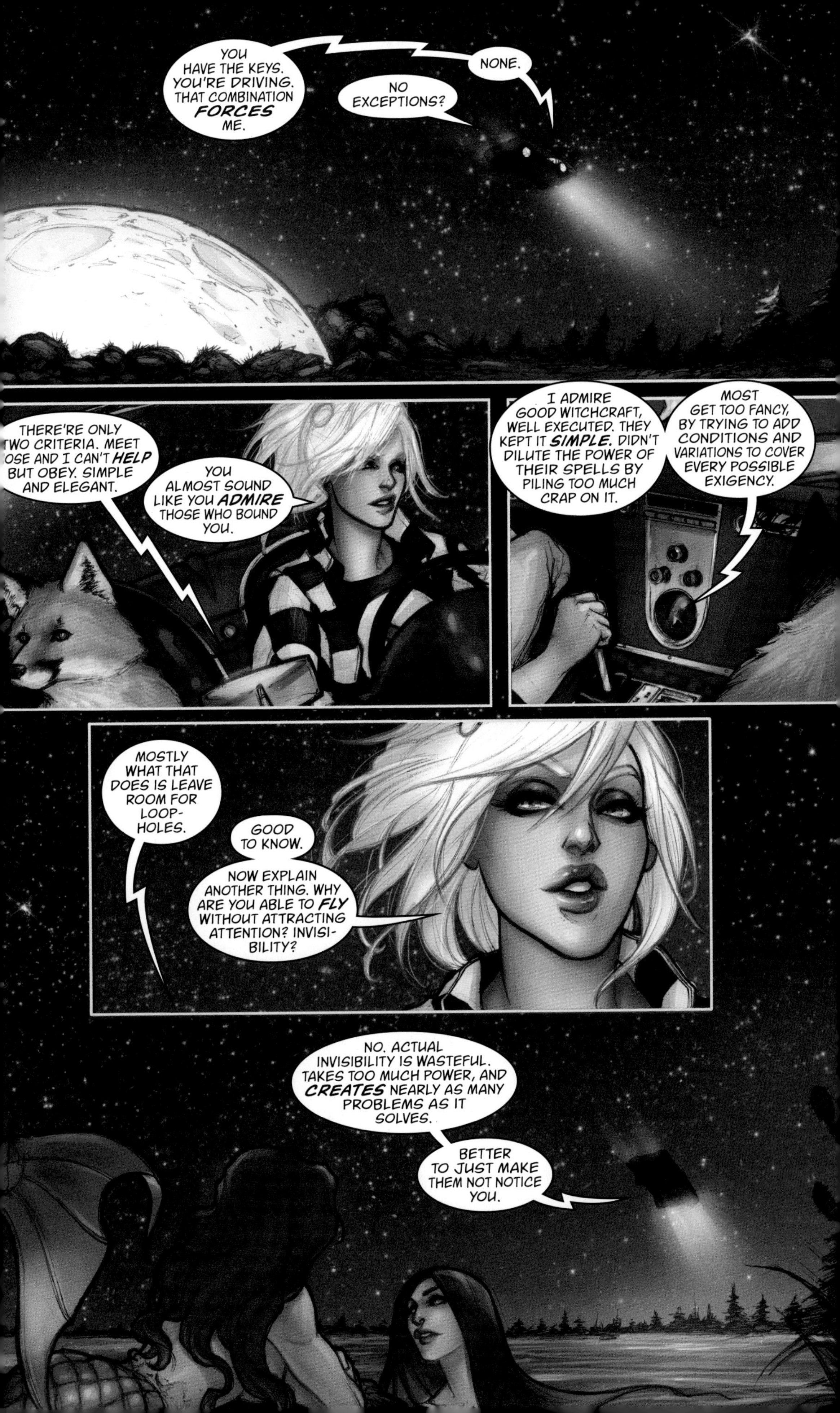
YOU HAVE THE KEYS. YOU'RE DRIVING. THAT COMBINATION FORCES ME.
NO EXCEPTIONS?
NONE.
THERE'RE ONLY TWO CRITERIA. MEET OSE AND I CAN'T HELP BUT OBEY. SIMPLE AND ELEGANT.
YOU ALMOST SOUND LIKE YOU ADMIRE THOSE WHO BOUND YOU.
I ADMIRE GOOD WITCHCRAFT, WELL EXECUTED. THEY KEPT IT SIMPLE. DIDN'T DILUTE THE POWER OF THEIR SPELLS BY PILING TOO MUCH CRAP ON IT.
MOST GET TOO FANCY, BY TRYING TO ADD CONDITIONS AND VARIATIONS TO COVER EVERY POSSIBLE EXIGENCY.
MOSTLY WHAT THAT DOES IS LEAVE ROOM FOR LOOP-HOLES.
GOOD TO KNOW.
NOW EXPLAIN ANOTHER THING. WHY ARE YOU ABLE TO FLY WITHOUT ATTRACTING ATTENTION? INVISI-BILITY?
NO. ACTUAL INVISIBILITY IS WASTEFUL. TAKES TOO MUCH POWER, AND CREATES NEARLY AS MANY PROBLEMS AS IT SOLVES.
BETTER TO JUST MAKE THEM NOT NOTICE YOU.

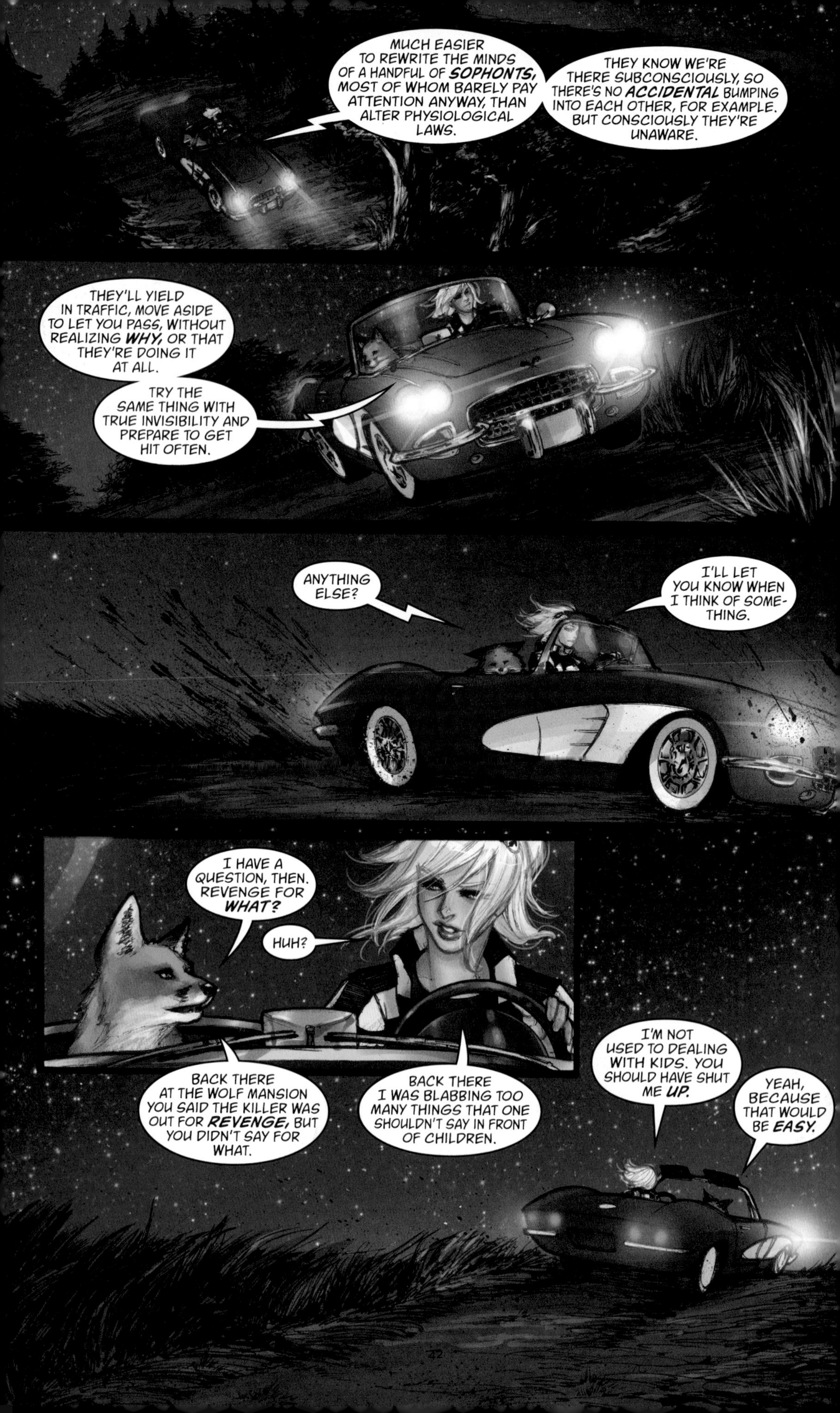

MUCH EASIER TO REWRITE THE MINDS OF A HANDFUL OF *SOPHONTS,* MOST OF WHOM BARELY PAY ATTENTION ANYWAY, THAN ALTER PHYSIOLOGICAL LAWS.
THEY KNOW WE'RE THERE SUBCONSCIOUSLY, SO THERE'S NO *ACCIDENTAL* BUMPING INTO EACH OTHER, FOR EXAMPLE. BUT CONSCIOUSLY THEY'RE UNAWARE.
THEY'LL YIELD IN TRAFFIC, MOVE ASIDE TO LET YOU PASS, WITHOUT REALIZING *WHY,* OR THAT THEY'RE DOING IT AT ALL.
TRY THE SAME THING WITH TRUE INVISIBILITY AND PREPARE TO GET HIT OFTEN.
ANYTHING ELSE?
I'LL LET YOU KNOW WHEN I THINK OF SOME-THING.
I HAVE A QUESTION, THEN. REVENGE FOR *WHAT?*
HUH?
BACK THERE AT THE WOLF MANSION YOU SAID THE KILLER WAS OUT FOR *REVENGE,* BUT YOU DIDN'T SAY FOR WHAT.
BACK THERE I WAS BLABBING TOO MANY THINGS THAT ONE SHOULDN'T SAY IN FRONT OF CHILDREN.
I'M NOT USED TO DEALING WITH KIDS. YOU SHOULD HAVE SHUT ME *UP.*
YEAH, BECAUSE THAT WOULD BE *EASY.*

DESPITE THE FAMOUS MOVIE LINE, ONE OF THE POSSIBLE OUTCOMES OF BRINGING A KNIFE TO A GUNFIGHT.

Russ Braun: artist • Lee Loughridge: colorist

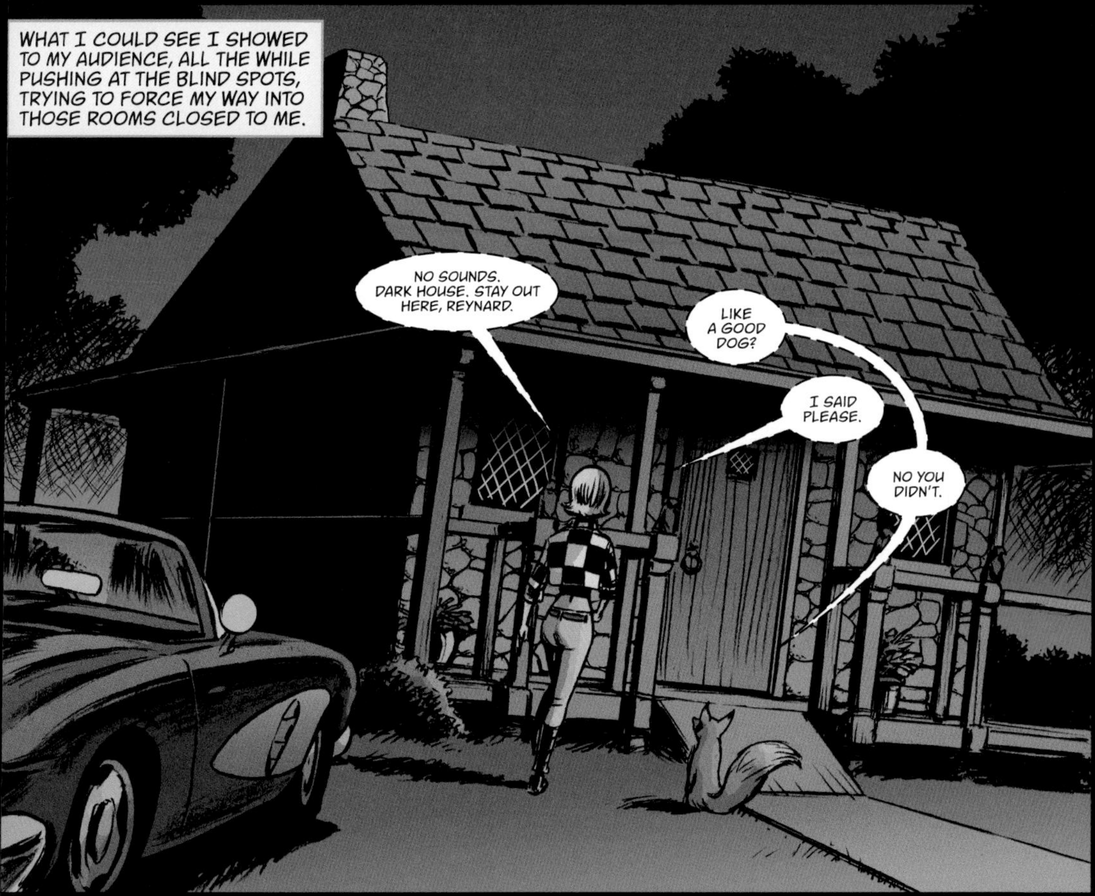
WHAT I COULD SEE I SHOWED TO MY AUDIENCE, ALL THE WHILE PUSHING AT THE BLIND SPOTS, TRYING TO FORCE MY WAY INTO THOSE ROOMS CLOSED TO ME.
NO SOUNDS. DARK HOUSE. STAY OUT HERE, REYNARD.
LIKE A GOOD DOG?
I SAID PLEASE.
NO YOU DIDN'T.

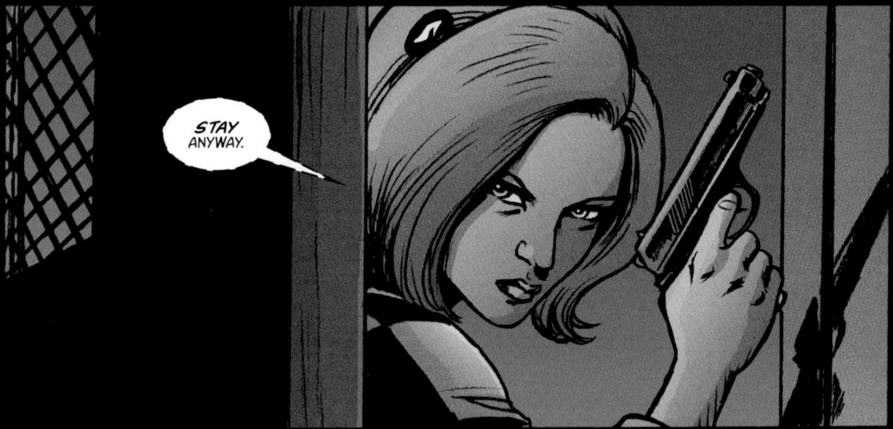
STAY ANYWAY.

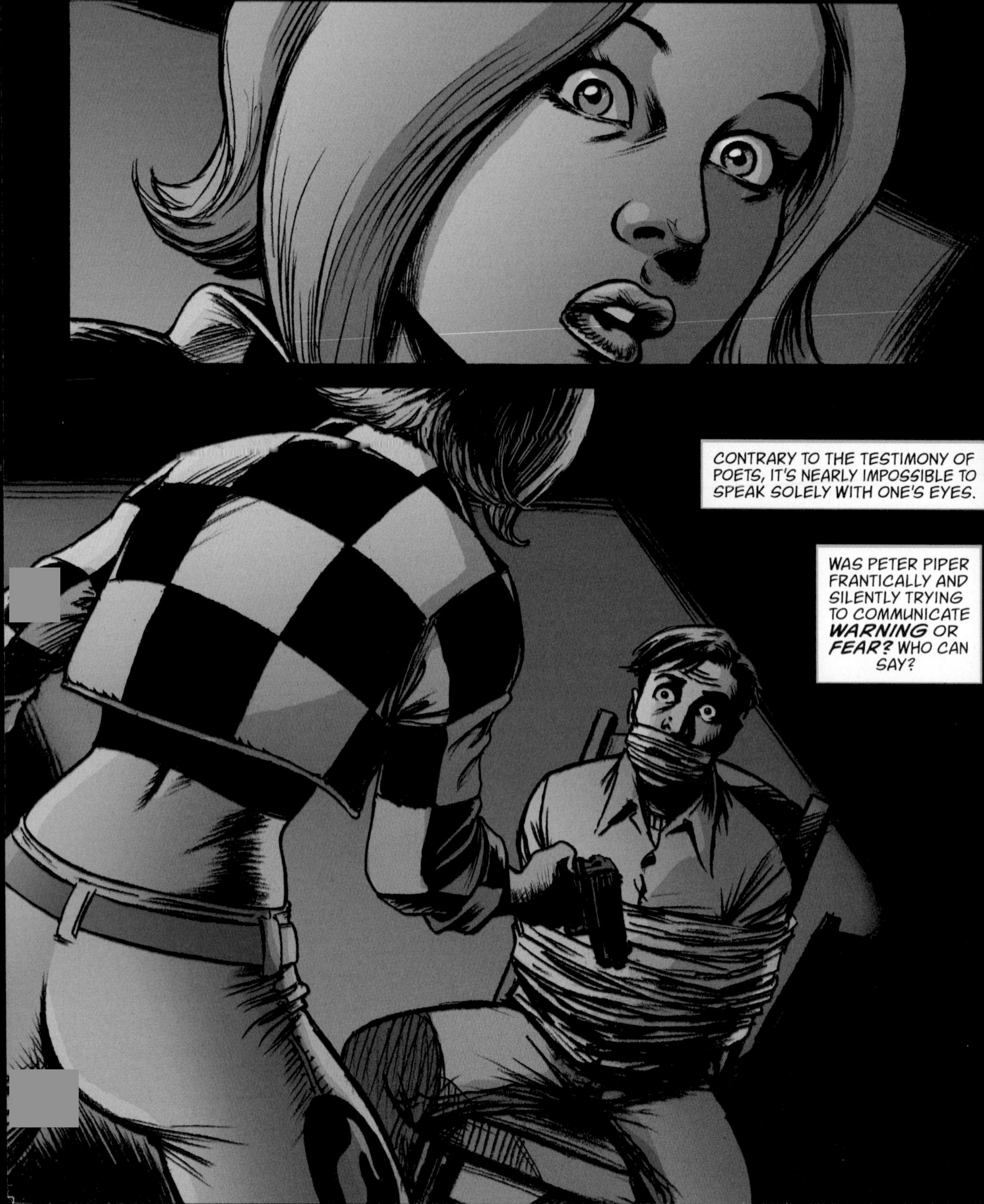
CONTRARY TO THE TESTIMONY OF POETS, IT'S NEARLY IMPOSSIBLE TO SPEAK SOLELY WITH ONE'S EYES.
WAS PETER PIPER FRANTICALLY AND SILENTLY TRYING TO COMMUNICATE ***WARNING*** OR ***FEAR?*** WHO CAN SAY?

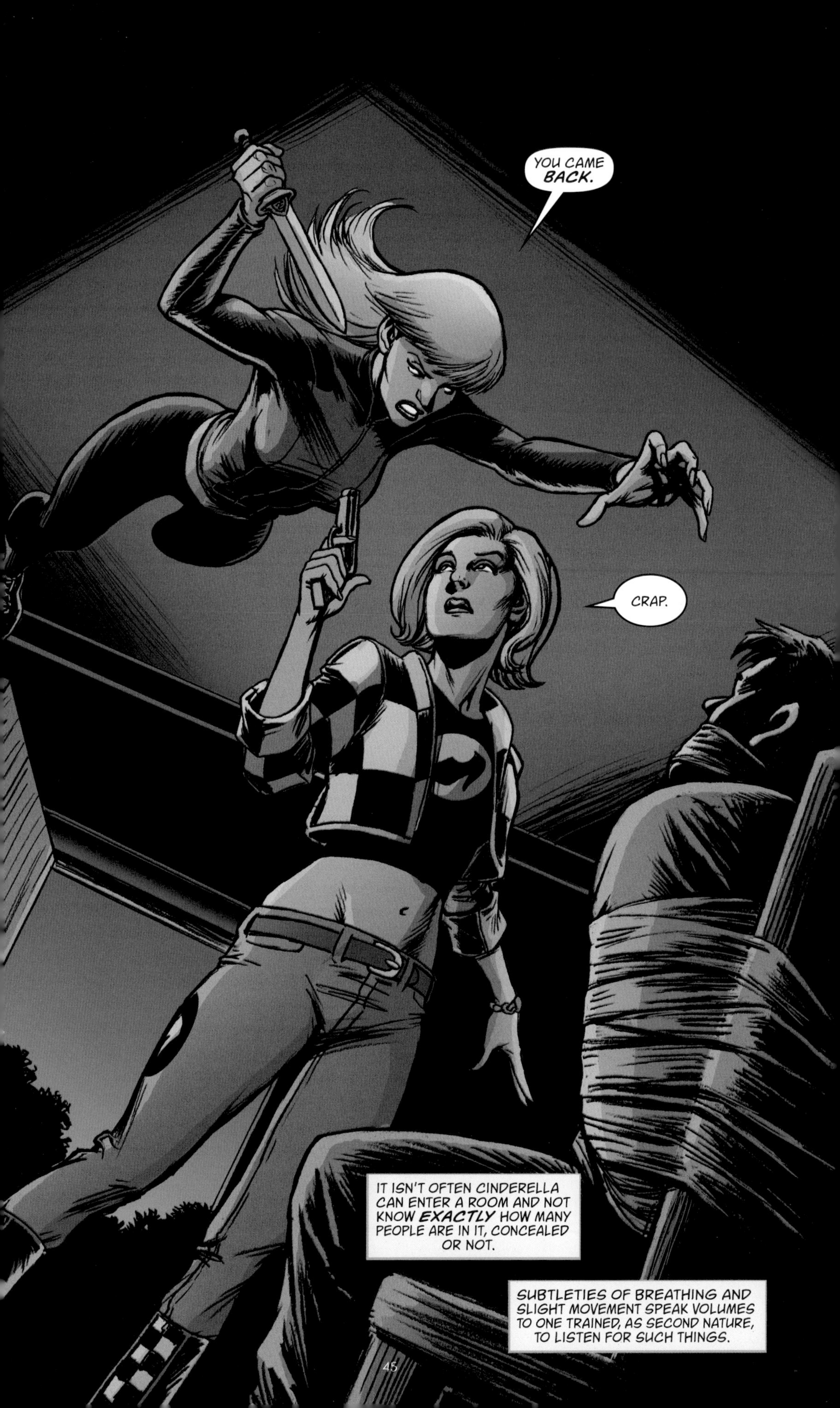

YOU CAME BACK.
CRAP.
IT ISN'T OFTEN CINDERELLA CAN ENTER A ROOM AND NOT KNOW EXACTLY HOW MANY PEOPLE ARE IN IT, CONCEALED OR NOT.
SUBTLETIES OF BREATHING AND SLIGHT MOVEMENT SPEAK VOLUMES TO ONE TRAINED, AS SECOND NATURE, TO LISTEN FOR SUCH THINGS.

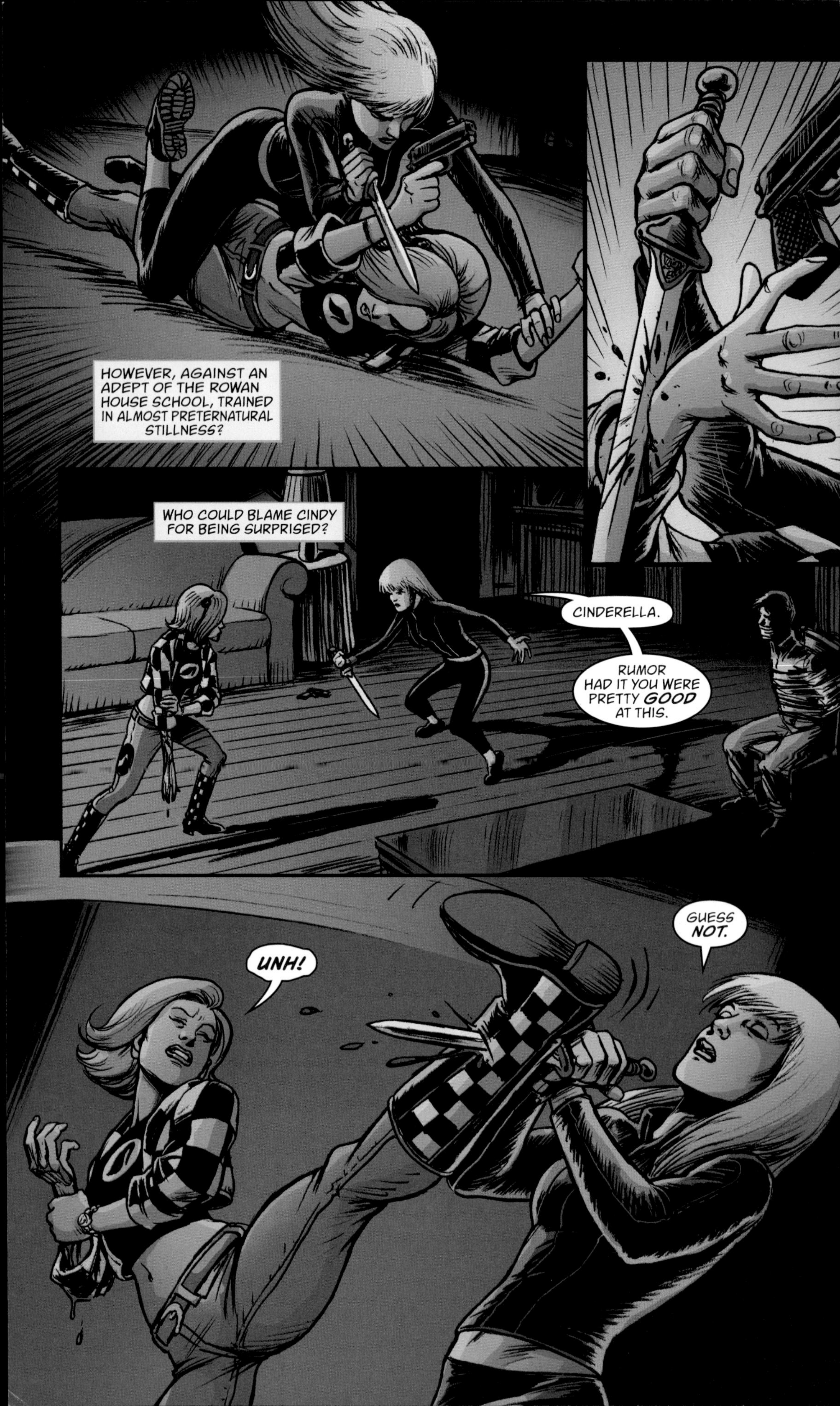
HOWEVER, AGAINST AN ADEPT OF THE ROWAN HOUSE SCHOOL, TRAINED IN ALMOST PRETERNATURAL STILLNESS?
WHO COULD BLAME CINDY FOR BEING SURPRISED?
CINDERELLA.
RUMOR HAD IT YOU WERE PRETTY GOOD AT THIS.
UNH!
GUESS NOT.

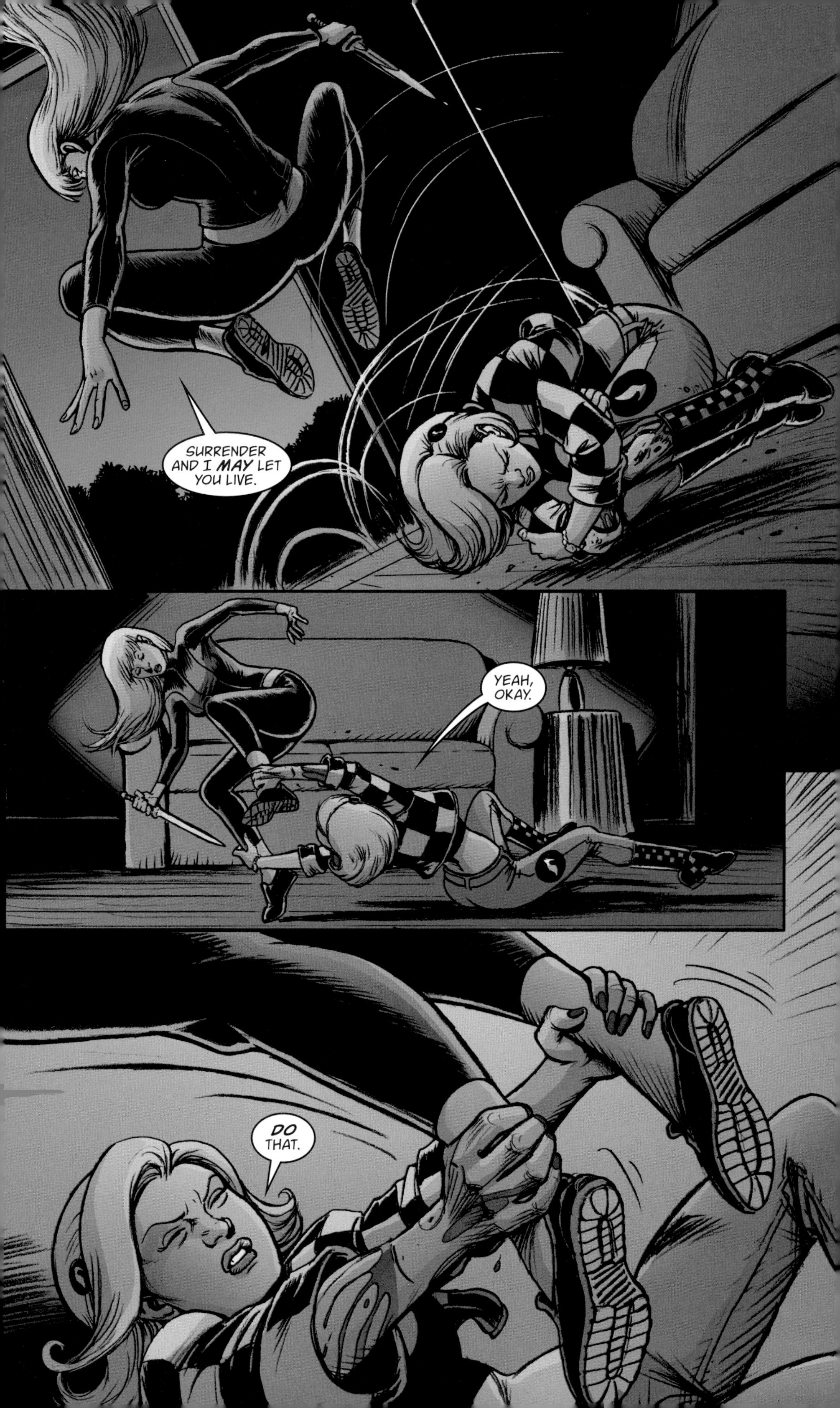
SURRENDER AND I MAY LET YOU LIVE.
YEAH, OKAY.
DO THAT.

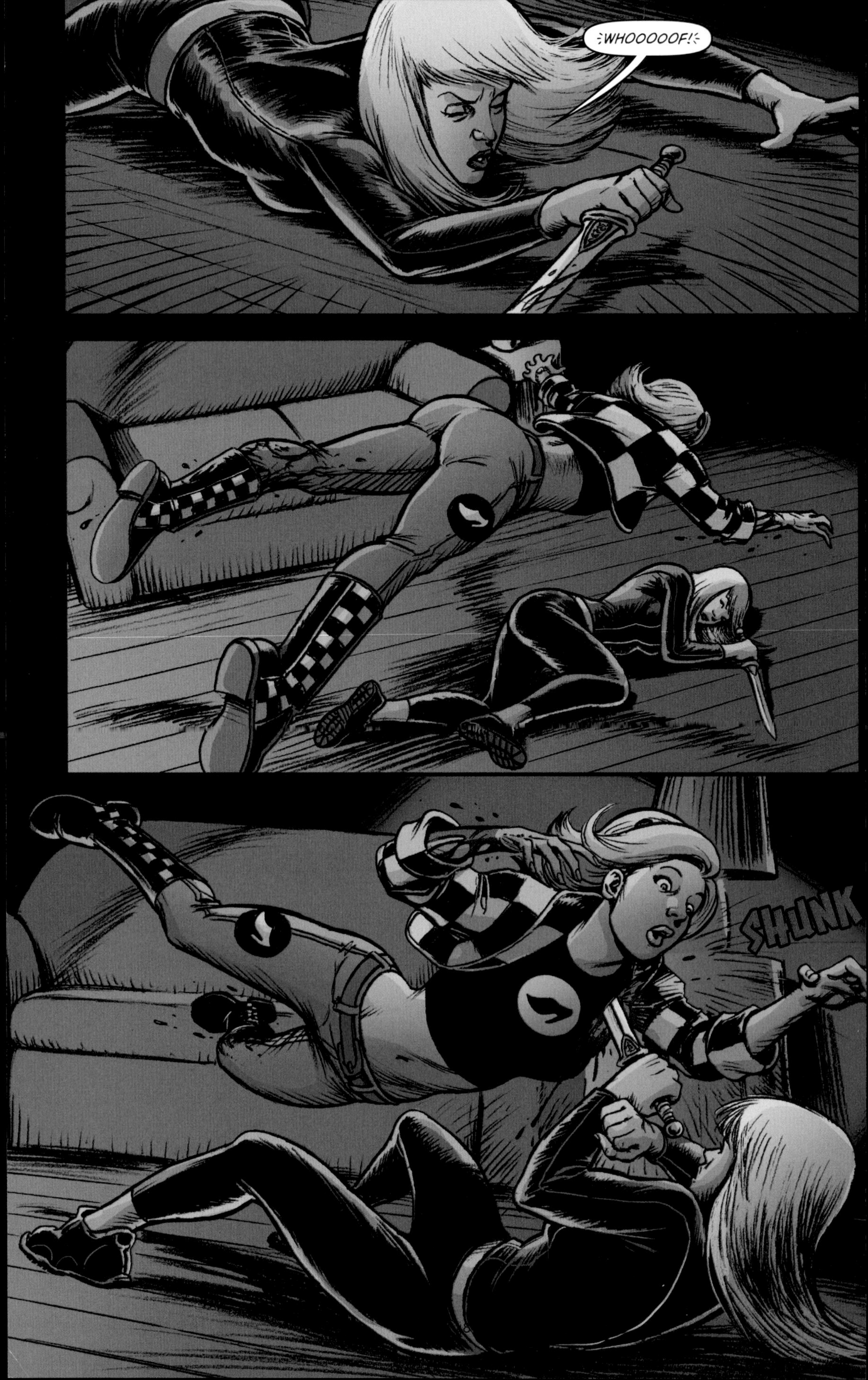
WHOOOOOF!
SHUNK

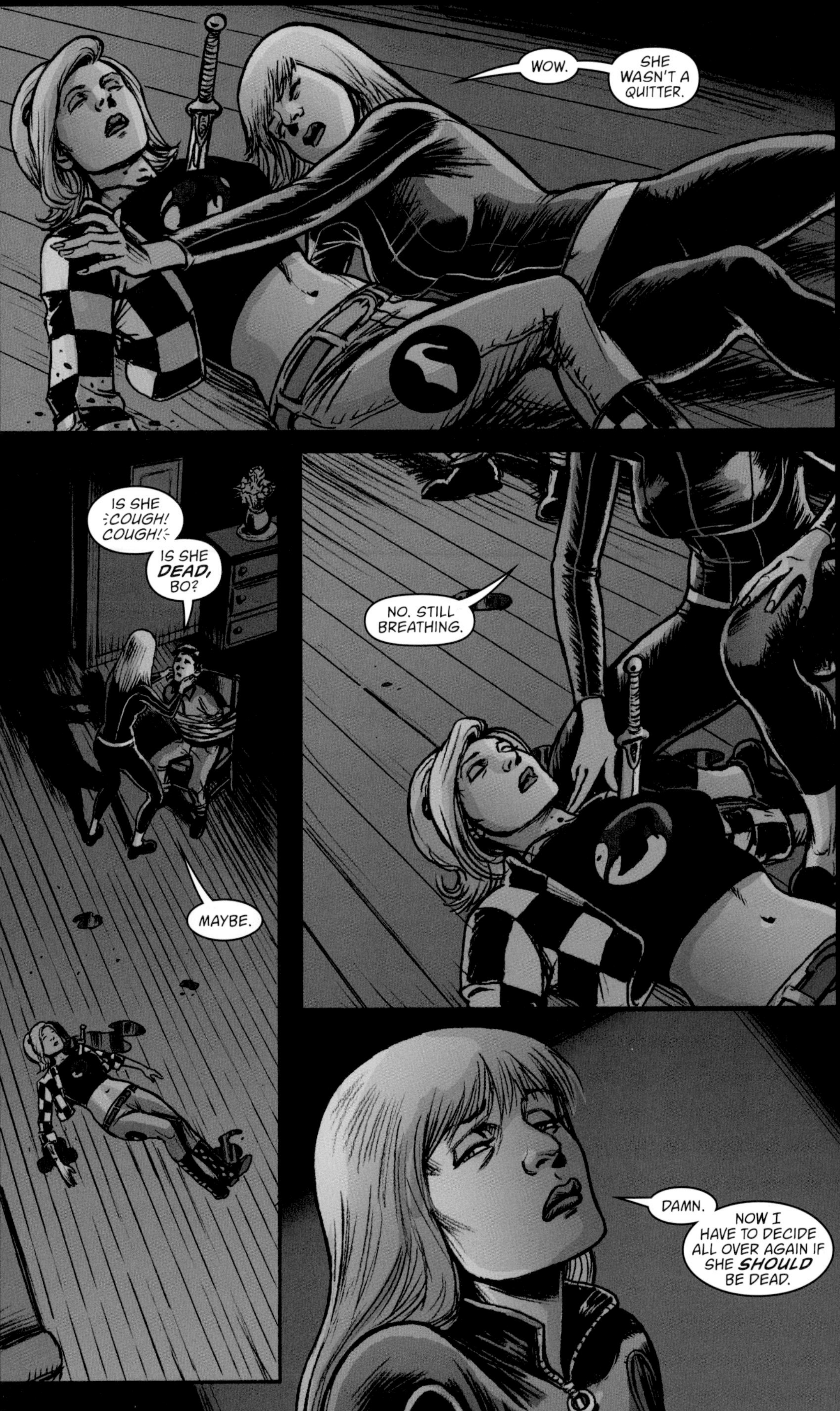

WOW.
SHE WASN'T A QUITTER.
IS SHE ~COUGH! COUGH!~
IS SHE **DEAD,** BO?
MAYBE.
NO. STILL BREATHING.
DAMN.
NOW I HAVE TO DECIDE ALL OVER AGAIN IF SHE ***SHOULD*** BE DEAD.

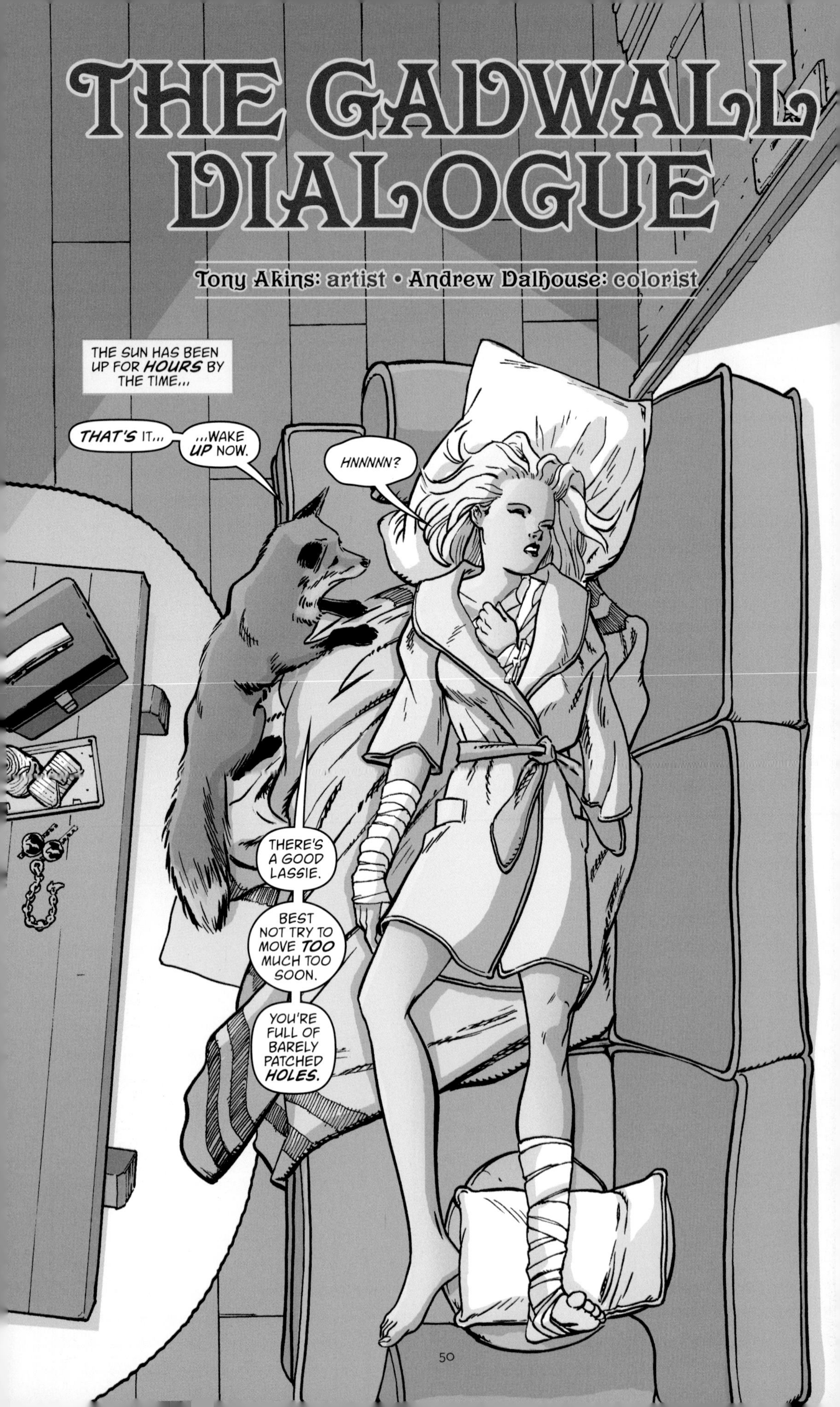
THE GADWALL DIALOGUE
Tony Akins: artist • Andrew Dalhouse: colorist
THE SUN HAS BEEN UP FOR HOURS BY THE TIME...
THAT'S IT...
...WAKE UP NOW.
HNNNNN?
THERE'S A GOOD LASSIE.
BEST NOT TRY TO MOVE TOO MUCH TOO SOON.
YOU'RE FULL OF BARELY PATCHED HOLES.

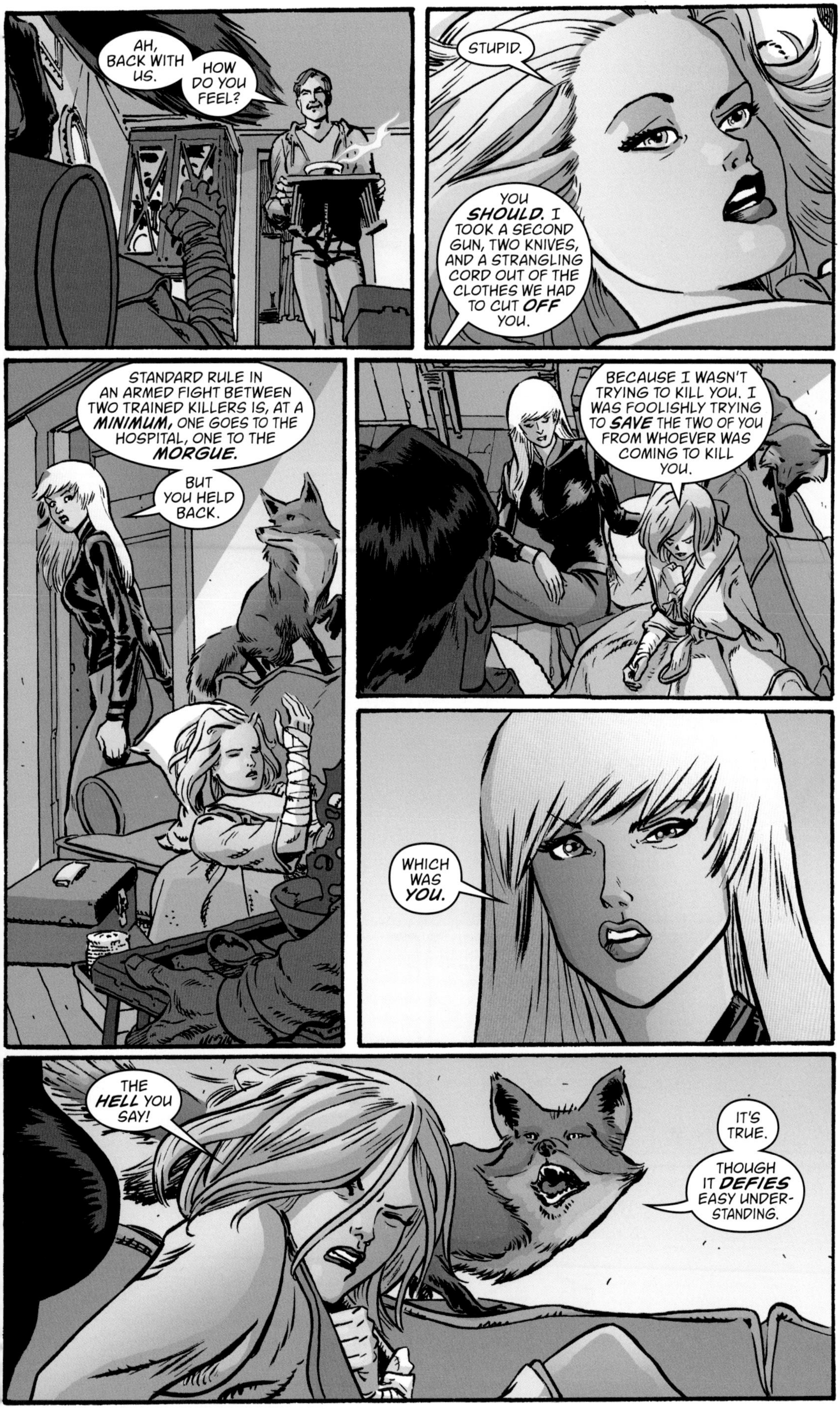
AH, BACK WITH US.
HOW DO YOU FEEL?
STUPID.
YOU SHOULD. I TOOK A SECOND GUN, TWO KNIVES, AND A STRANGLING CORD OUT OF THE CLOTHES WE HAD TO CUT OFF YOU.
STANDARD RULE IN AN ARMED FIGHT BETWEEN TWO TRAINED KILLERS IS, AT A MINIMUM, ONE GOES TO THE HOSPITAL, ONE TO THE MORGUE.
BUT YOU HELD BACK.
BECAUSE I WASN'T TRYING TO KILL YOU. I WAS FOOLISHLY TRYING TO SAVE THE TWO OF YOU FROM WHOEVER WAS COMING TO KILL YOU.
WHICH WAS YOU.
THE HELL YOU SAY!
IT'S TRUE.
THOUGH IT DEFIES EASY UNDER-STANDING.

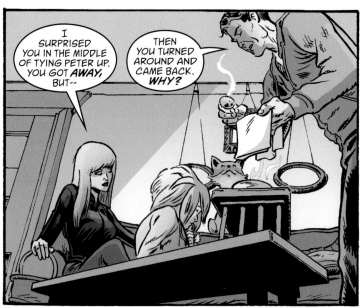

I SURPRISED YOU IN THE MIDDLE OF TYING PETER UP. YOU GOT *AWAY,* BUT--

THEN YOU TURNED AROUND AND CAME BACK. *WHY?*

SOUP?

IT WASN'T REALLY HER.

EARLIER TODAY--OR I GUESS IT WAS *YESTERDAY* BY NOW--

--WE INVESTIGATED TWO *OTHER* MURDER SCENES.

WHAT EVIDENCE WE HAVE TELLS US SNOW WHITE KILLED HER OWN *SISTER,* ALONG WITH THE MOON--*OUR* REFUGEE MOON, NOT THE MUNDY ONE.

DEAR LORD, WHY?

AND THEN, ACCORDING TO THE *SCENTS* ON HAND...

...SNOW WHITE AND EDDIE DANTÈS WERE *POSSIBLY* KILLED BY PRINCE CHARMING.

I DOUBT THEY WOULD. AND I KNOW FOR A FACT *I* DIDN'T TIE UP PETER OR TRY TO KILL *YOU* EARLIER.

THERE ARE MANY AVENUES OF *MAGICAL DISGUISE* AVAILABLE TO FABLES.

WHY WOULD THEY *DO* SUCH A THING?

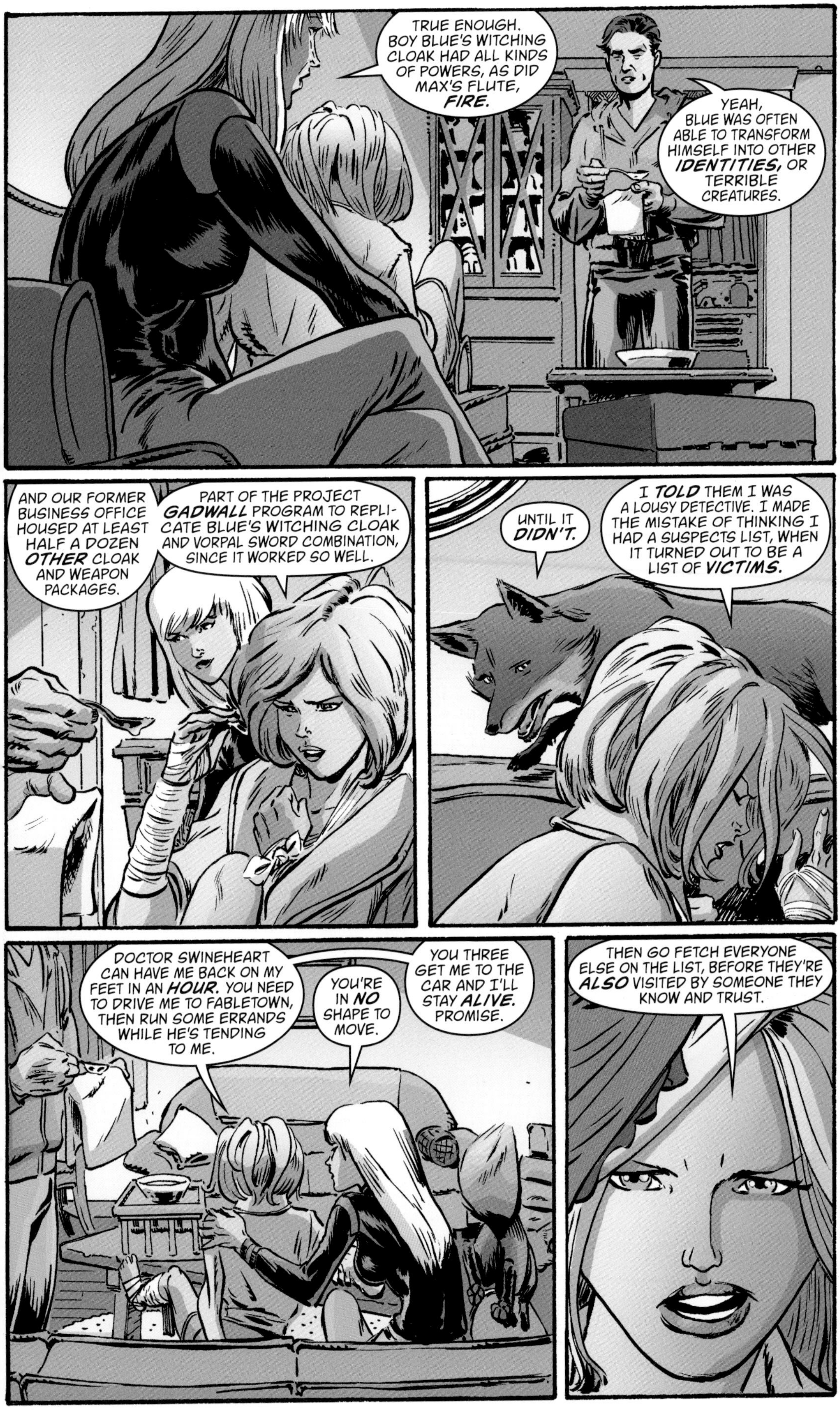
TRUE ENOUGH. BOY BLUE'S WITCHING CLOAK HAD ALL KINDS OF POWERS, AS DID MAX'S FLUTE, FIRE.
YEAH, BLUE WAS OFTEN ABLE TO TRANSFORM HIMSELF INTO OTHER IDENTITIES, OR TERRIBLE CREATURES.
AND OUR FORMER BUSINESS OFFICE HOUSED AT LEAST HALF A DOZEN OTHER CLOAK AND WEAPON PACKAGES.
PART OF THE PROJECT GADWALL PROGRAM TO REPLICATE BLUE'S WITCHING CLOAK AND VORPAL SWORD COMBINATION, SINCE IT WORKED SO WELL.
UNTIL IT DIDN'T.
I TOLD THEM I WAS A LOUSY DETECTIVE. I MADE THE MISTAKE OF THINKING I HAD A SUSPECTS LIST, WHEN IT TURNED OUT TO BE A LIST OF VICTIMS.
DOCTOR SWINEHEART CAN HAVE ME BACK ON MY FEET IN AN HOUR. YOU NEED TO DRIVE ME TO FABLETOWN, THEN RUN SOME ERRANDS WHILE HE'S TENDING TO ME.
YOU'RE IN NO SHAPE TO MOVE.
YOU THREE GET ME TO THE CAR AND I'LL STAY ALIVE. PROMISE.
THEN GO FETCH EVERYONE ELSE ON THE LIST, BEFORE THEY'RE ALSO VISITED BY SOMEONE THEY KNOW AND TRUST.

INSIGHTS MEASURED IN INCREMENTS OF STABBING

Gene Ha: artist

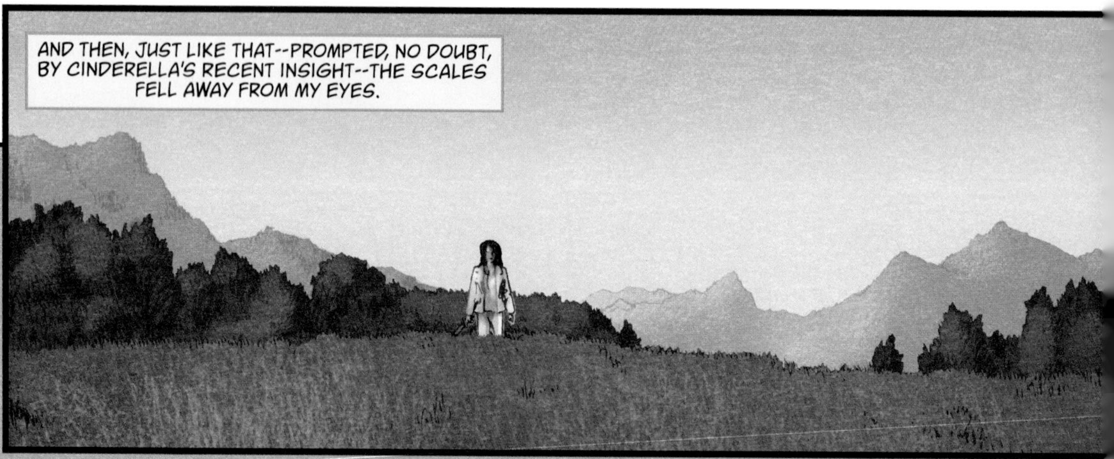

AND THEN, JUST LIKE THAT--PROMPTED, NO DOUBT, BY CINDERELLA'S RECENT INSIGHT--THE SCALES FELL AWAY FROM MY EYES.

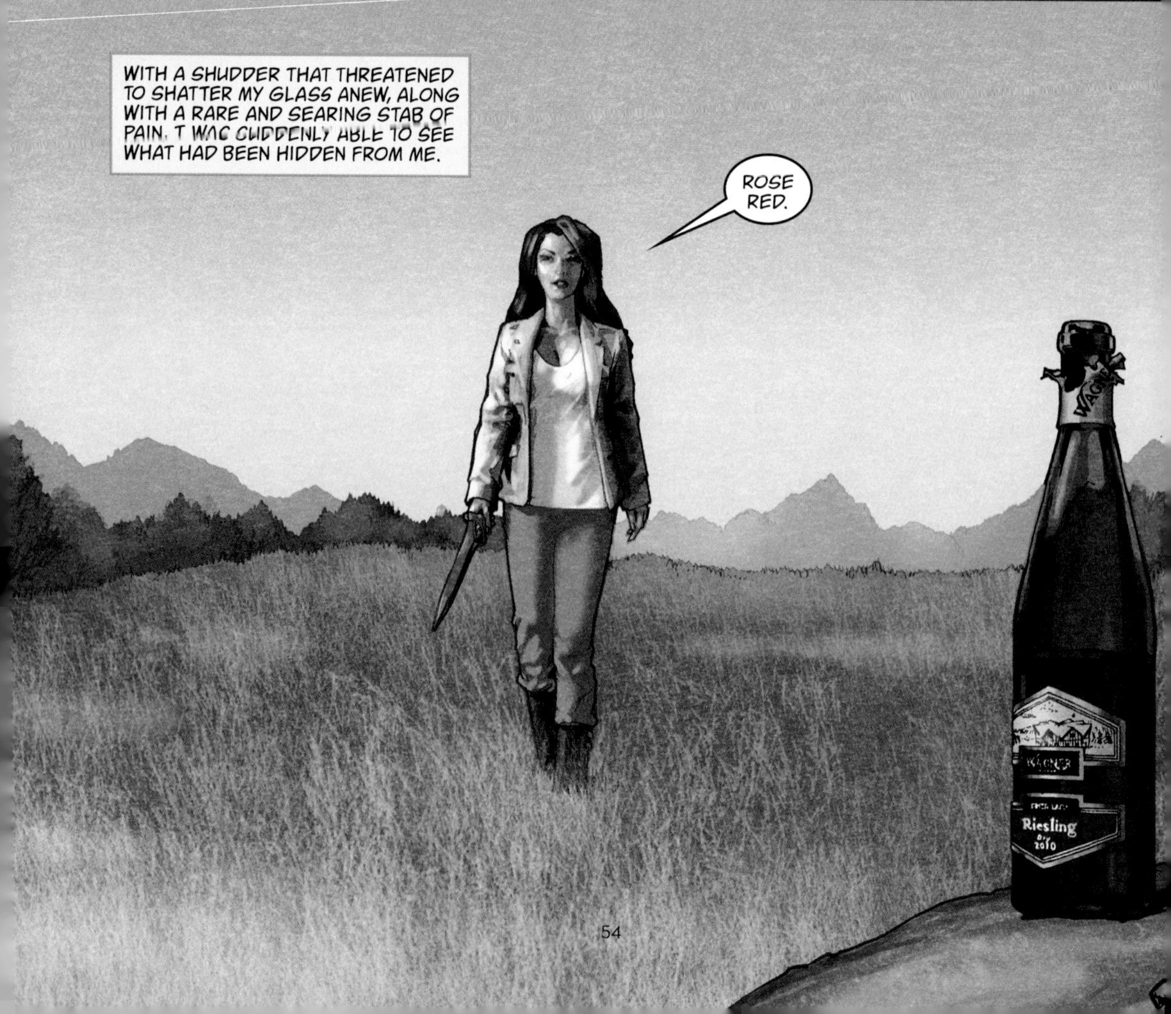

WITH A SHUDDER THAT THREATENED TO SHATTER MY GLASS ANEW, ALONG WITH A RARE AND SEARING STAB OF PAIN, I WAS SUDDENLY ABLE TO SEE WHAT HAD BEEN HIDDEN FROM ME.
ROSE RED.
Riesling

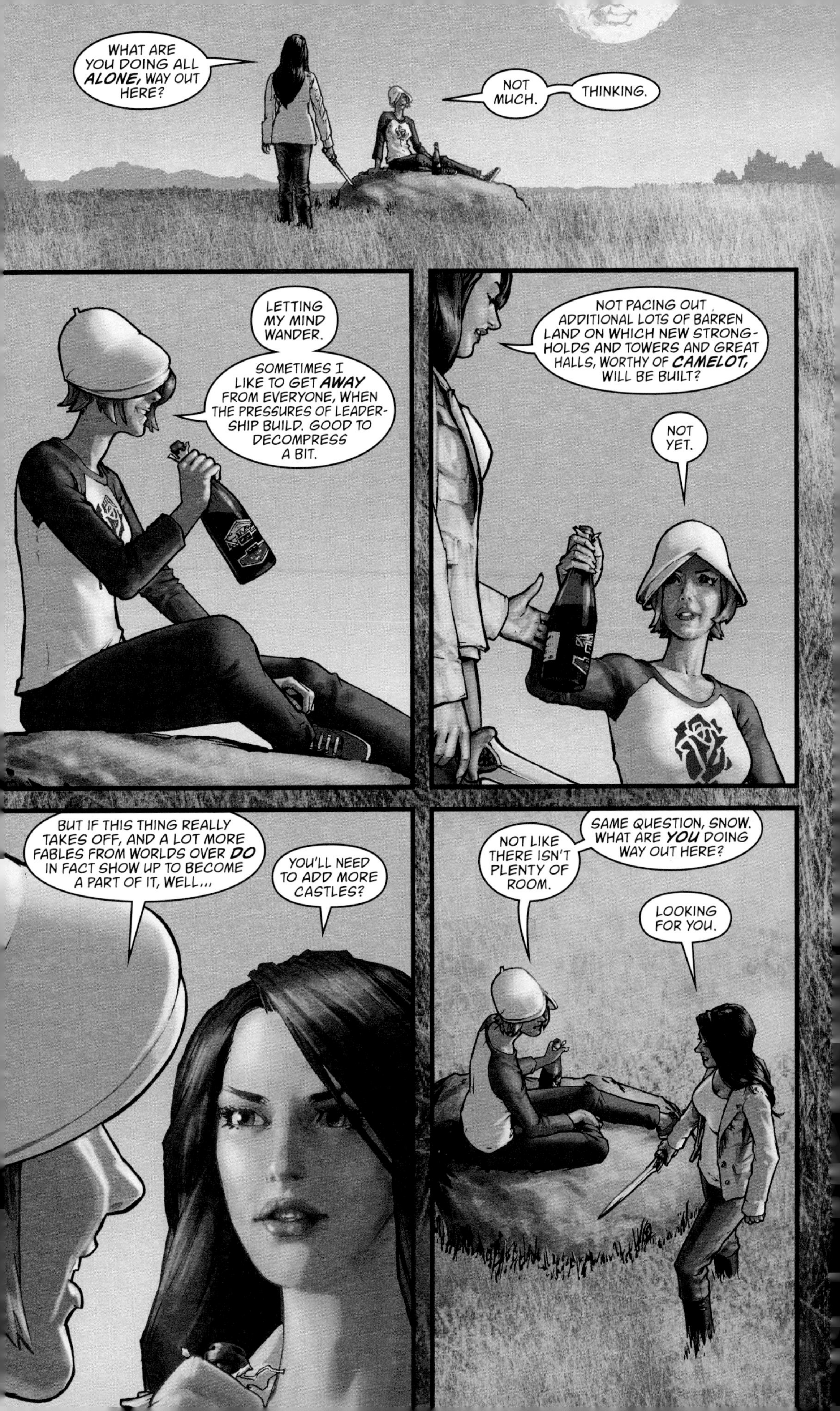
WHAT ARE YOU DOING ALL ALONE, WAY OUT HERE?
NOT MUCH.
THINKING.
LETTING MY MIND WANDER.
SOMETIMES I LIKE TO GET AWAY FROM EVERYONE, WHEN THE PRESSURES OF LEADER-SHIP BUILD. GOOD TO DECOMPRESS A BIT.
NOT PACING OUT ADDITIONAL LOTS OF BARREN LAND ON WHICH NEW STRONG-HOLDS AND TOWERS AND GREAT HALLS, WORTHY OF CAMELOT, WILL BE BUILT?
NOT YET.
BUT IF THIS THING REALLY TAKES OFF, AND A LOT MORE FABLES FROM WORLDS OVER DO IN FACT SHOW UP TO BECOME A PART OF IT, WELL...
YOU'LL NEED TO ADD MORE CASTLES?
NOT LIKE THERE ISN'T PLENTY OF ROOM.
SAME QUESTION, SNOW. WHAT ARE YOU DOING WAY OUT HERE?
LOOKING FOR YOU.

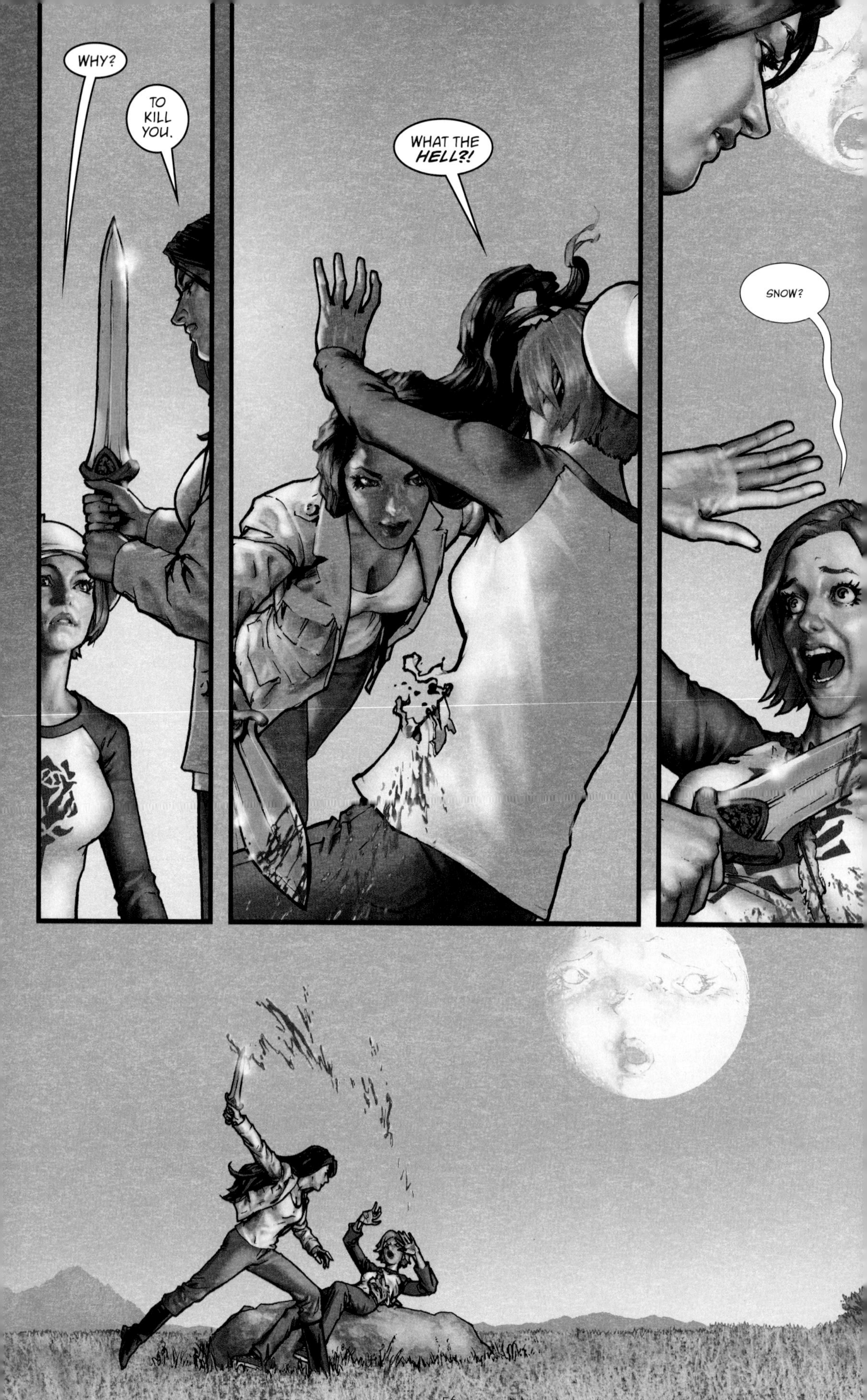
WHY?
TO KILL YOU.
WHAT THE HELL?!
SNOW?

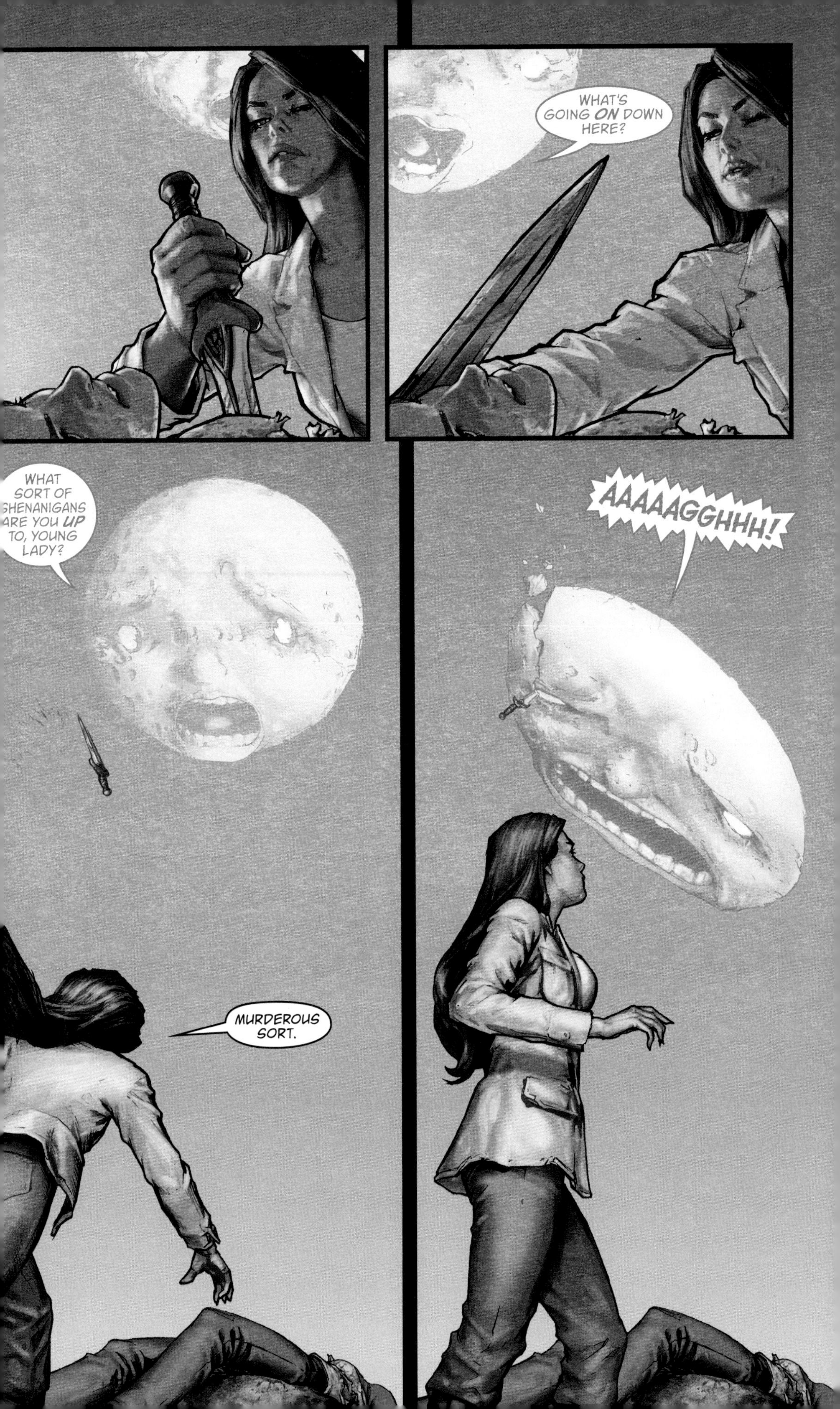
WHAT'S GOING ON DOWN HERE?
WHAT SORT OF SHENANIGANS ARE YOU UP TO, YOUNG LADY?
MURDEROUS SORT.
AAAAAGGHHH!

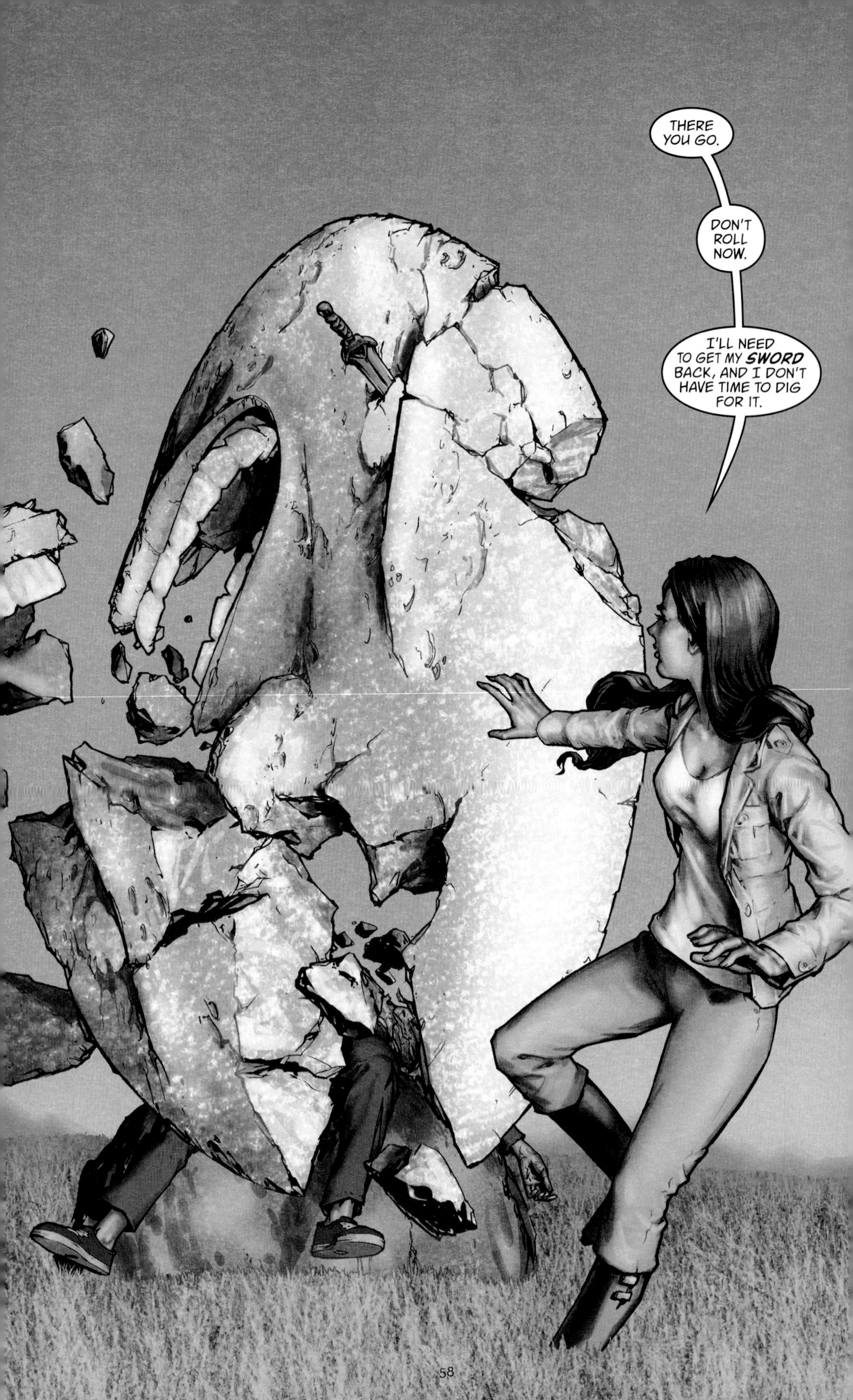
THERE YOU GO.
DON'T ROLL NOW.
I'LL NEED TO GET MY SWORD BACK, AND I DON'T HAVE TIME TO DIG FOR IT.

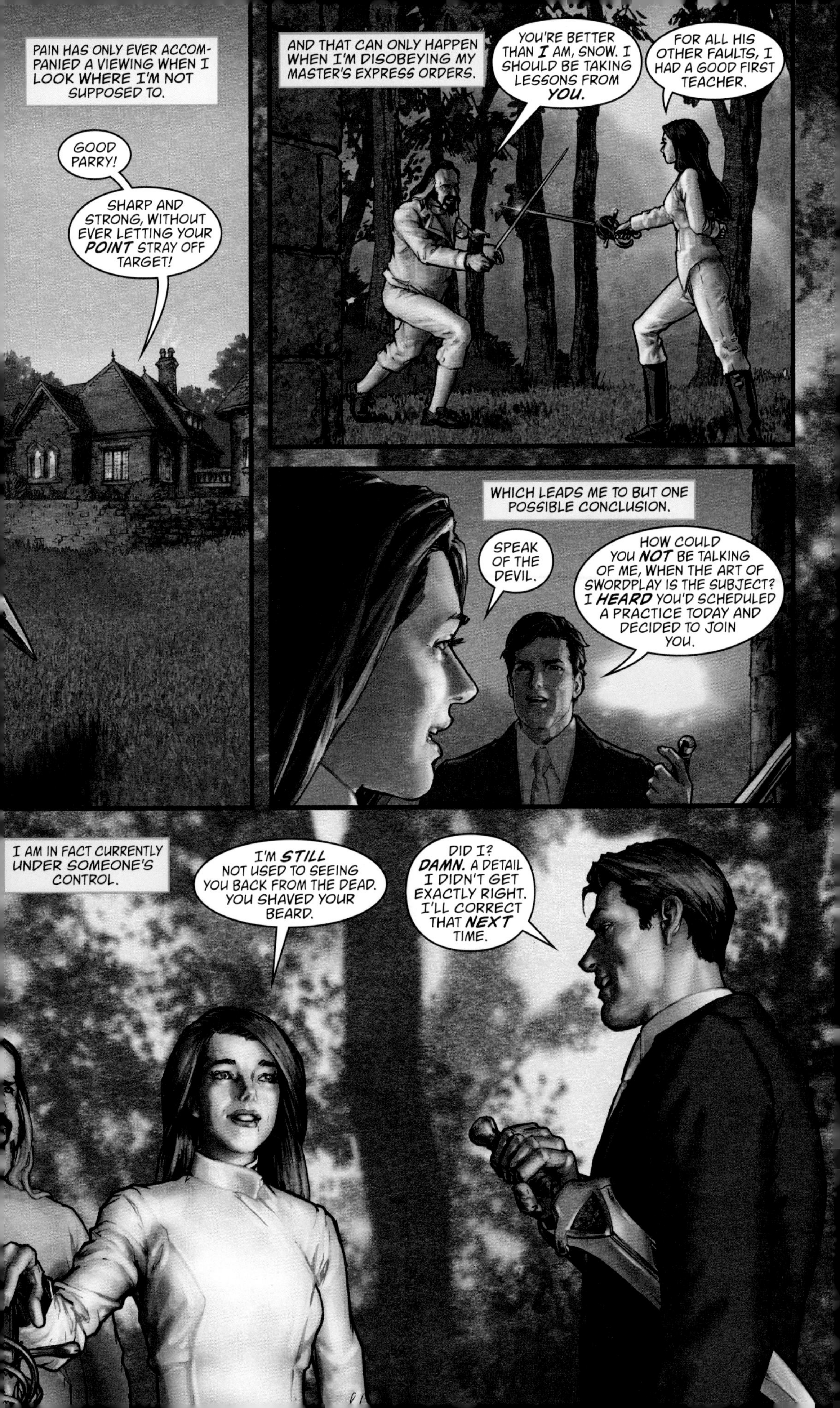
PAIN HAS ONLY EVER ACCOMPANIED A VIEWING WHEN I LOOK WHERE I'M NOT SUPPOSED TO.
GOOD PARRY!
SHARP AND STRONG, WITHOUT EVER LETTING YOUR POINT STRAY OFF TARGET!
AND THAT CAN ONLY HAPPEN WHEN I'M DISOBEYING MY MASTER'S EXPRESS ORDERS.
YOU'RE BETTER THAN I AM, SNOW. I SHOULD BE TAKING LESSONS FROM YOU.
FOR ALL HIS OTHER FAULTS, I HAD A GOOD FIRST TEACHER.
WHICH LEADS ME TO BUT ONE POSSIBLE CONCLUSION.
SPEAK OF THE DEVIL.
HOW COULD YOU NOT BE TALKING OF ME, WHEN THE ART OF SWORDPLAY IS THE SUBJECT? I HEARD YOU'D SCHEDULED A PRACTICE TODAY AND DECIDED TO JOIN YOU.
I AM IN FACT CURRENTLY UNDER SOMEONE'S CONTROL.
I'M STILL NOT USED TO SEEING YOU BACK FROM THE DEAD. YOU SHAVED YOUR BEARD.
DID I? DAMN. A DETAIL I DIDN'T GET EXACTLY RIGHT. I'LL CORRECT THAT NEXT TIME.

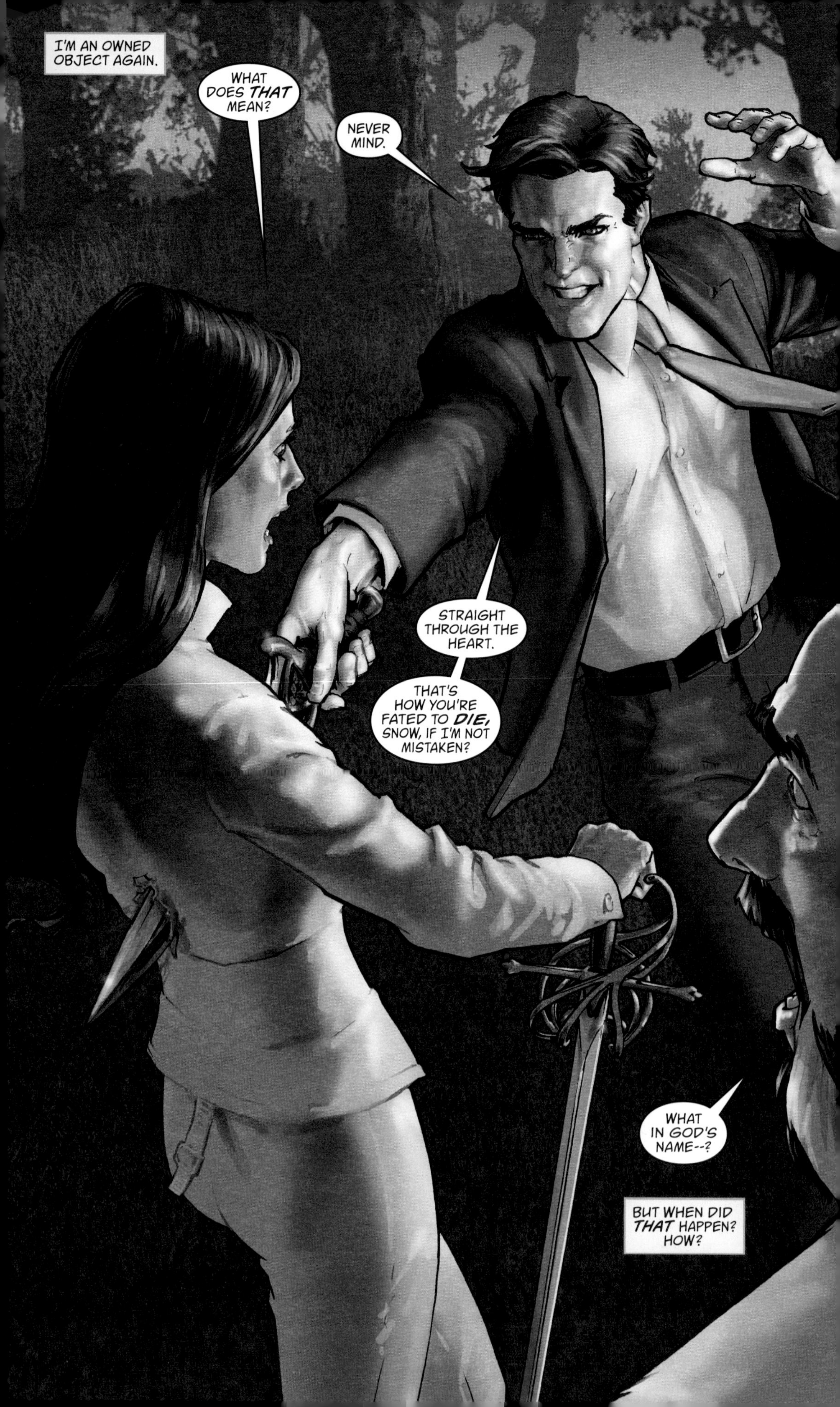
I'M AN OWNED OBJECT AGAIN.
WHAT DOES THAT MEAN?
NEVER MIND.
STRAIGHT THROUGH THE HEART.
THAT'S HOW YOU'RE FATED TO DIE, SNOW, IF I'M NOT MISTAKEN?
WHAT IN GOD'S NAME--?
BUT WHEN DID THAT HAPPEN? HOW?

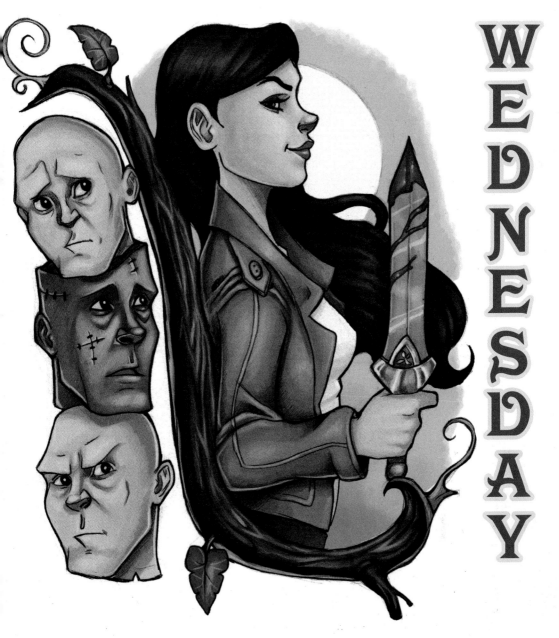

WEDNESDAY

Someone is controlling me again, but this time I don't know who or how. The spell to take command of me is a simple one, crafted long ago. Anyone can recite it. One needn't be a practitioner of the higher sciences, in this case, because the power resides within the spell itself.

I do what I can to suppress all record of the enchantment, but word gets around. Every once in a great while, someone comes into possession of me, armed with the knowledge of how to enslave me.

My best guess is our recent mysterious visitor did it to me while I was shattered and unable to perceive what was happening. This might be to my advantage. Cast on me while I was injured, it may not have as strong a hold on me now that I've recovered. Maybe that's why I was able to force through (at considerable pain) a vision that was clearly among the areas denied to me.

I'll want to look into this a bit deeper.

A SHORT WALTZ IN FATIGUE PANTS AND COMBAT BOOTS

Tula Lotay: artist

WHILE TRYING TO FORCE MY WAY INTO THINGS I WAS FORBIDDEN TO SEE, I STILL FOLLOWED THOSE EVENTS I WAS APPARENTLY ALLOWED TO SEE.

HOW LATE?

ARE YOU *KIDDING* ME?

CINDERELLA BACK IN FABLETOWN, FOR EXAMPLE.

DOCTOR SWINEHEART WANTED YOU TO GET SOME *REAL* SLEEP.

SCREW HIM!

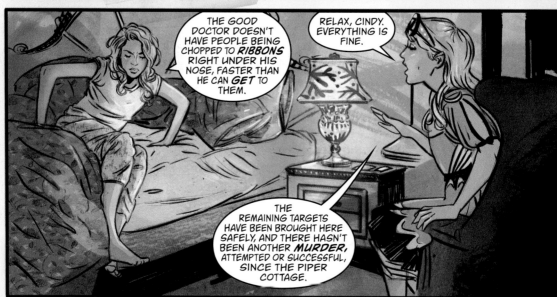

THE GOOD DOCTOR DOESN'T HAVE PEOPLE BEING CHOPPED TO *RIBBONS* RIGHT UNDER HIS NOSE, FASTER THAN HE CAN *GET* TO THEM.

RELAX, CINDY. EVERYTHING IS FINE.

THE REMAINING TARGETS HAVE BEEN BROUGHT HERE SAFELY, AND THERE HASN'T BEEN ANOTHER *MURDER,* ATTEMPTED OR SUCCESSFUL, SINCE THE PIPER COTTAGE.

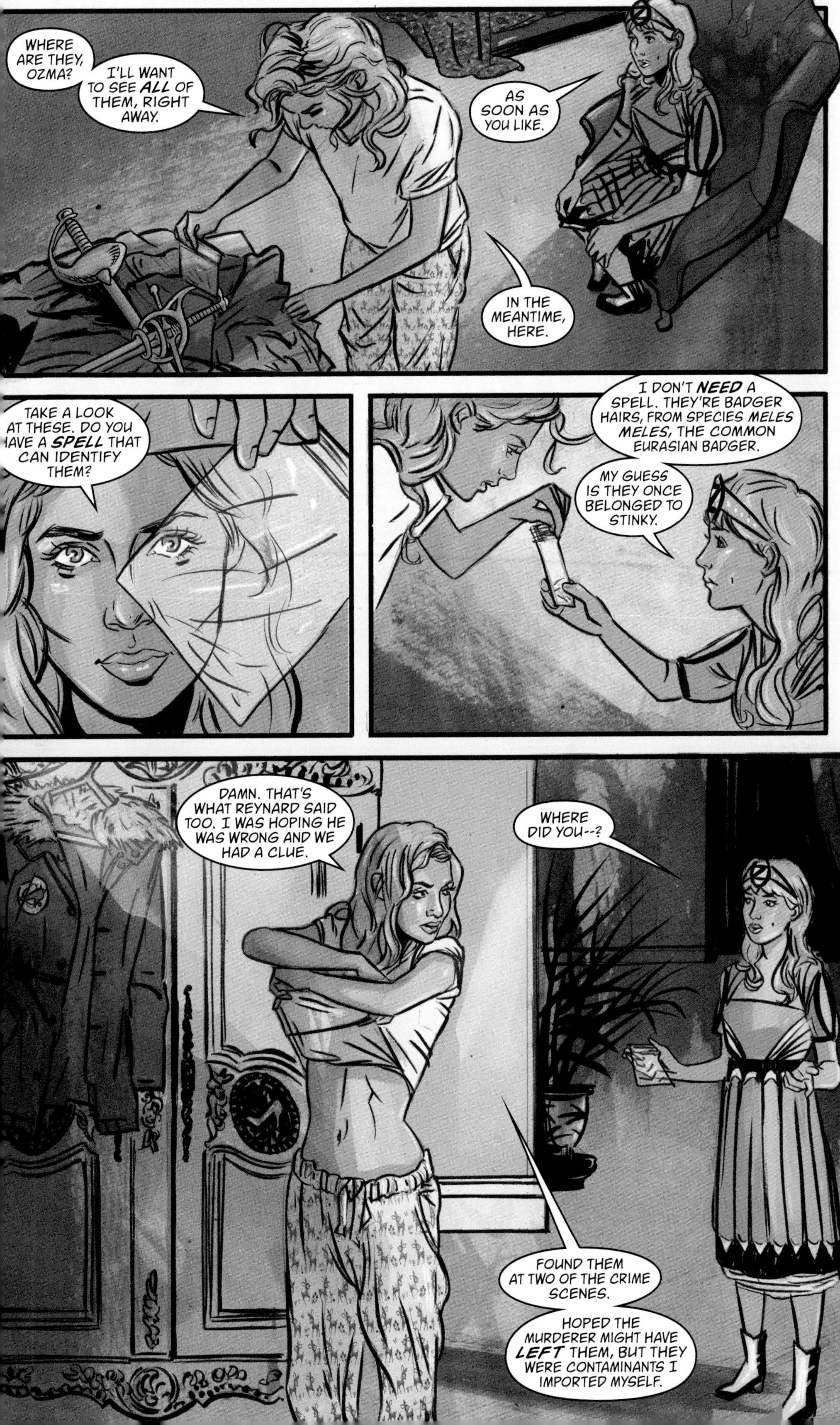
WHERE ARE THEY, OZMA?
I'LL WANT TO SEE *ALL* OF THEM, RIGHT AWAY.
AS SOON AS YOU LIKE.
IN THE MEANTIME, HERE.
TAKE A LOOK AT THESE. DO YOU HAVE A *SPELL* THAT CAN IDENTIFY THEM?
I DON'T *NEED* A SPELL. THEY'RE BADGER HAIRS, FROM SPECIES *MELES MELES*, THE COMMON EURASIAN BADGER.
MY GUESS IS THEY ONCE BELONGED TO STINKY.
DAMN. THAT'S WHAT REYNARD SAID TOO. I WAS HOPING HE WAS WRONG AND WE HAD A CLUE.
WHERE DID YOU--?
FOUND THEM AT TWO OF THE CRIME SCENES.
HOPED THE MURDERER MIGHT HAVE *LEFT* THEM, BUT THEY WERE CONTAMINANTS I IMPORTED MYSELF.

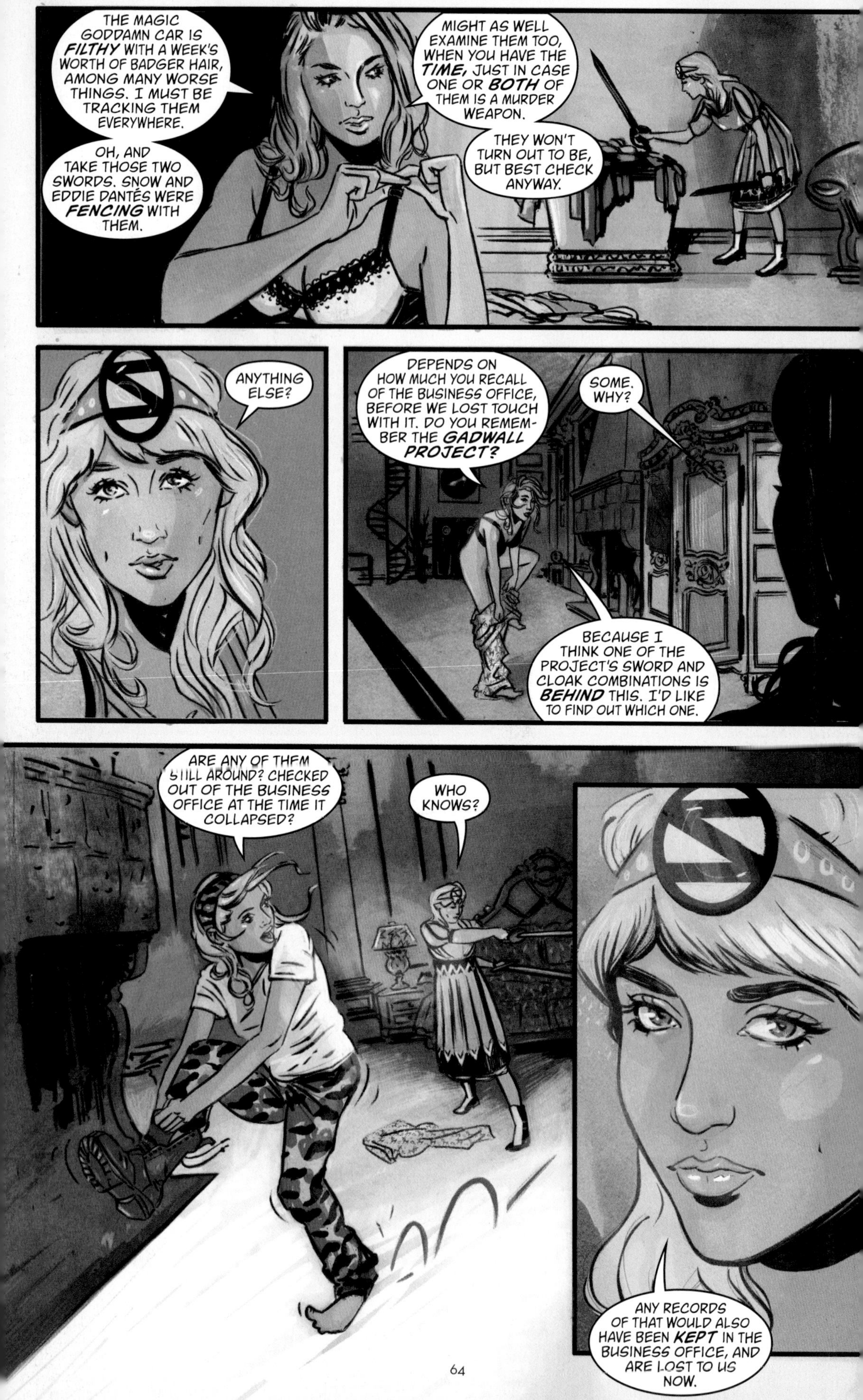
THE MAGIC GODDAMN CAR IS FILTHY WITH A WEEK'S WORTH OF BADGER HAIR, AMONG MANY WORSE THINGS. I MUST BE TRACKING THEM EVERYWHERE.
OH, AND TAKE THOSE TWO SWORDS. SNOW AND EDDIE DANTÉS WERE FENCING WITH THEM.
MIGHT AS WELL EXAMINE THEM TOO, WHEN YOU HAVE THE TIME, JUST IN CASE ONE OR BOTH OF THEM IS A MURDER WEAPON.
THEY WON'T TURN OUT TO BE, BUT BEST CHECK ANYWAY.
ANYTHING ELSE?
DEPENDS ON HOW MUCH YOU RECALL OF THE BUSINESS OFFICE, BEFORE WE LOST TOUCH WITH IT. DO YOU REMEMBER THE GADWALL PROJECT?
SOME. WHY?
BECAUSE I THINK ONE OF THE PROJECT'S SWORD AND CLOAK COMBINATIONS IS BEHIND THIS. I'D LIKE TO FIND OUT WHICH ONE.
ARE ANY OF THEM STILL AROUND? CHECKED OUT OF THE BUSINESS OFFICE AT THE TIME IT COLLAPSED?
WHO KNOWS?
ANY RECORDS OF THAT WOULD ALSO HAVE BEEN KEPT IN THE BUSINESS OFFICE, AND ARE LOST TO US NOW.

SWORD POINTS

Marley Zarcone: artist

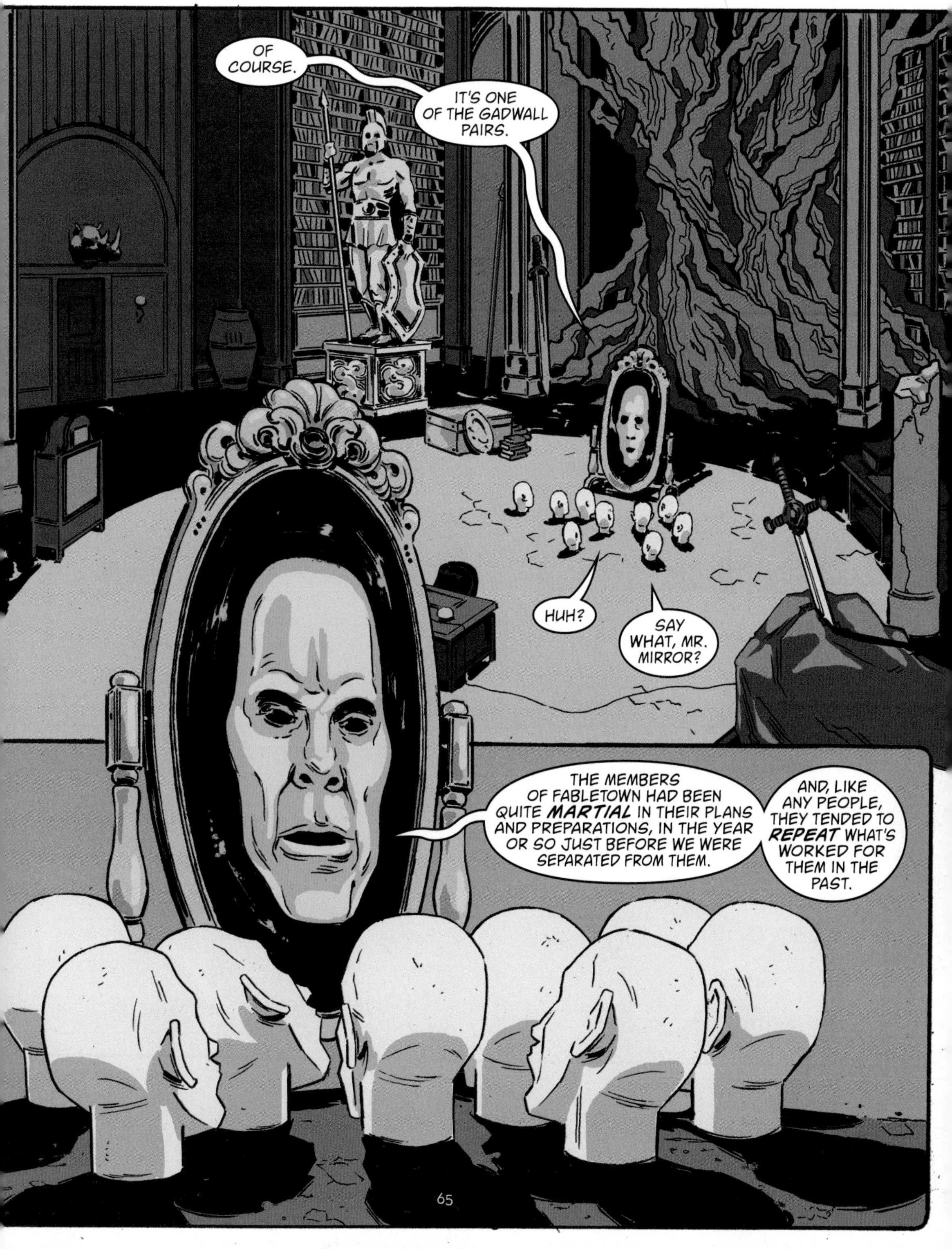
OF COURSE.
IT'S ONE OF THE GADWALL PAIRS.
HUH?
SAY WHAT, MR. MIRROR?
THE MEMBERS OF FABLETOWN HAD BEEN QUITE MARTIAL IN THEIR PLANS AND PREPARATIONS, IN THE YEAR OR SO JUST BEFORE WE WERE SEPARATED FROM THEM.
AND, LIKE ANY PEOPLE, THEY TENDED TO REPEAT WHAT'S WORKED FOR THEM IN THE PAST.

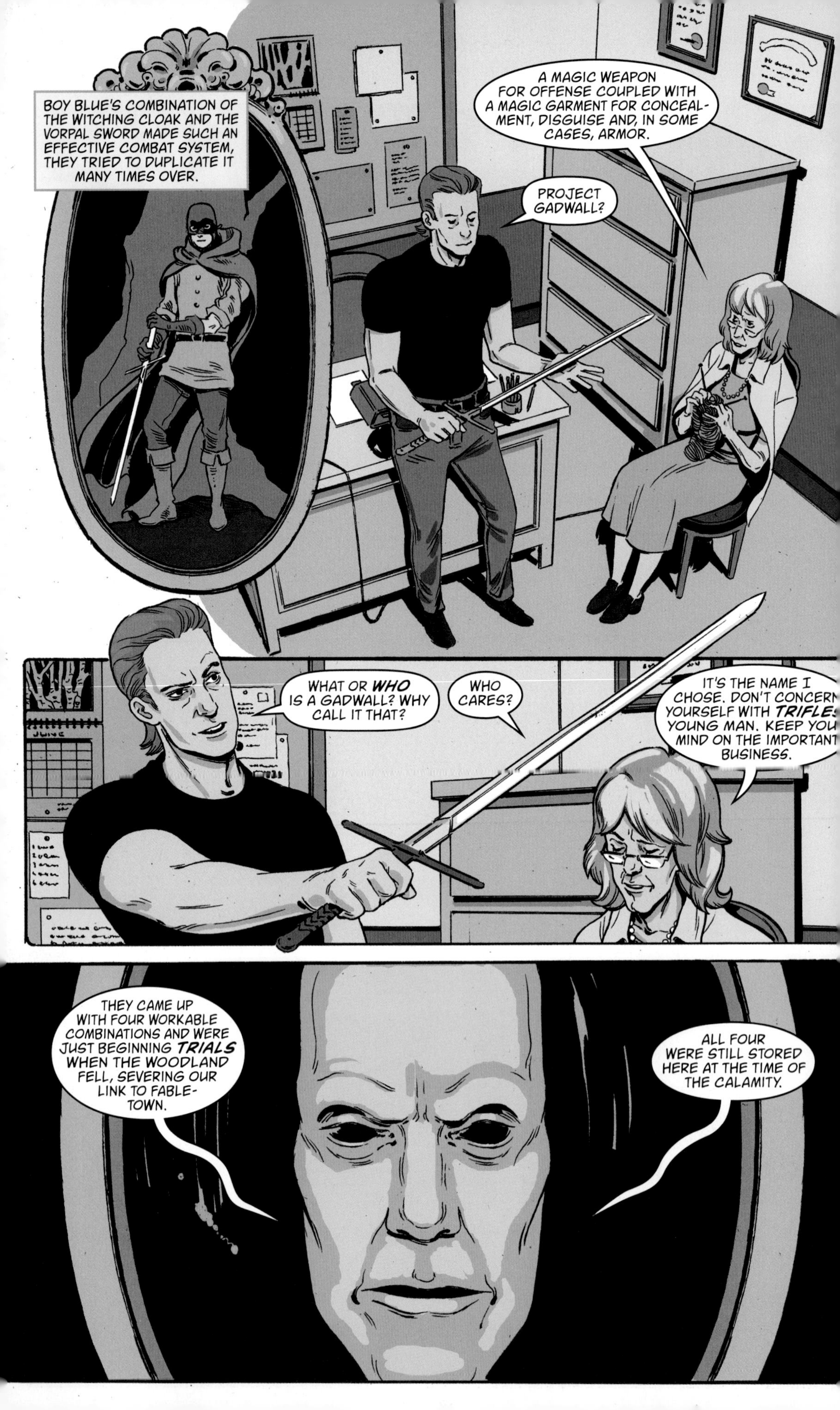

BOY BLUE'S COMBINATION OF THE WITCHING CLOAK AND THE VORPAL SWORD MADE SUCH AN EFFECTIVE COMBAT SYSTEM, THEY TRIED TO DUPLICATE IT MANY TIMES OVER.
A MAGIC WEAPON FOR OFFENSE COUPLED WITH A MAGIC GARMENT FOR CONCEAL-MENT, DISGUISE AND, IN SOME CASES, ARMOR.
PROJECT GADWALL?
WHAT OR **WHO** IS A GADWALL? WHY CALL IT THAT?
WHO CARES?
IT'S THE NAME I CHOSE. DON'T CONCERN YOURSELF WITH **TRIFLES**, YOUNG MAN. KEEP YOUR MIND ON THE IMPORTANT BUSINESS.
THEY CAME UP WITH FOUR WORKABLE COMBINATIONS AND WERE JUST BEGINNING **TRIALS** WHEN THE WOODLAND FELL, SEVERING OUR LINK TO FABLE-TOWN.
ALL FOUR WERE STILL STORED HERE AT THE TIME OF THE CALAMITY.

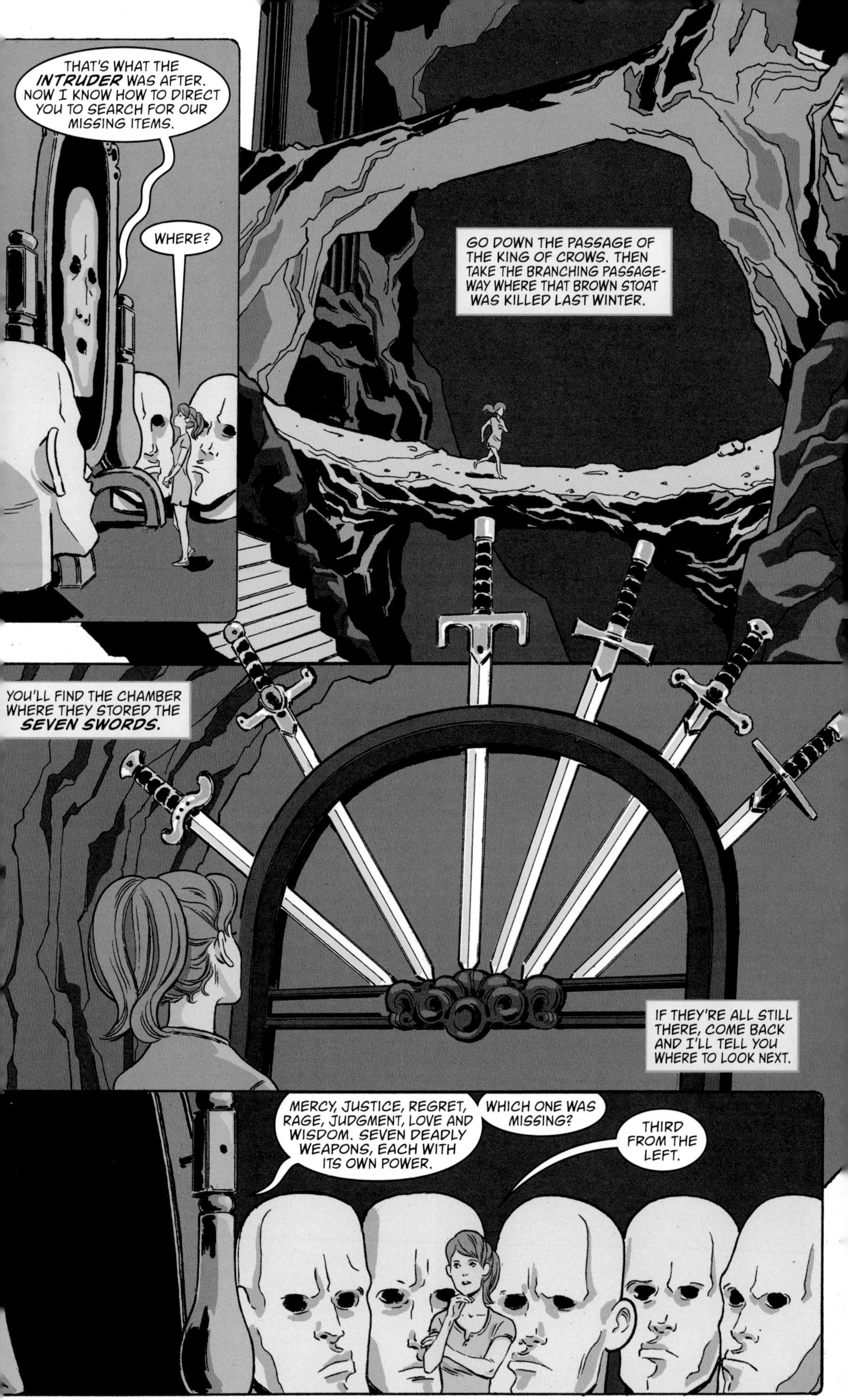

THAT'S WHAT THE INTRUDER WAS AFTER. NOW I KNOW HOW TO DIRECT YOU TO SEARCH FOR OUR MISSING ITEMS.
WHERE?
GO DOWN THE PASSAGE OF THE KING OF CROWS. THEN TAKE THE BRANCHING PASSAGEWAY WHERE THAT BROWN STOAT WAS KILLED LAST WINTER.
YOU'LL FIND THE CHAMBER WHERE THEY STORED THE SEVEN SWORDS.
IF THEY'RE ALL STILL THERE, COME BACK AND I'LL TELL YOU WHERE TO LOOK NEXT.
MERCY, JUSTICE, REGRET, RAGE, JUDGMENT, LOVE AND WISDOM. SEVEN DEADLY WEAPONS, EACH WITH ITS OWN POWER.
WHICH ONE WAS MISSING?
THIRD FROM THE LEFT.

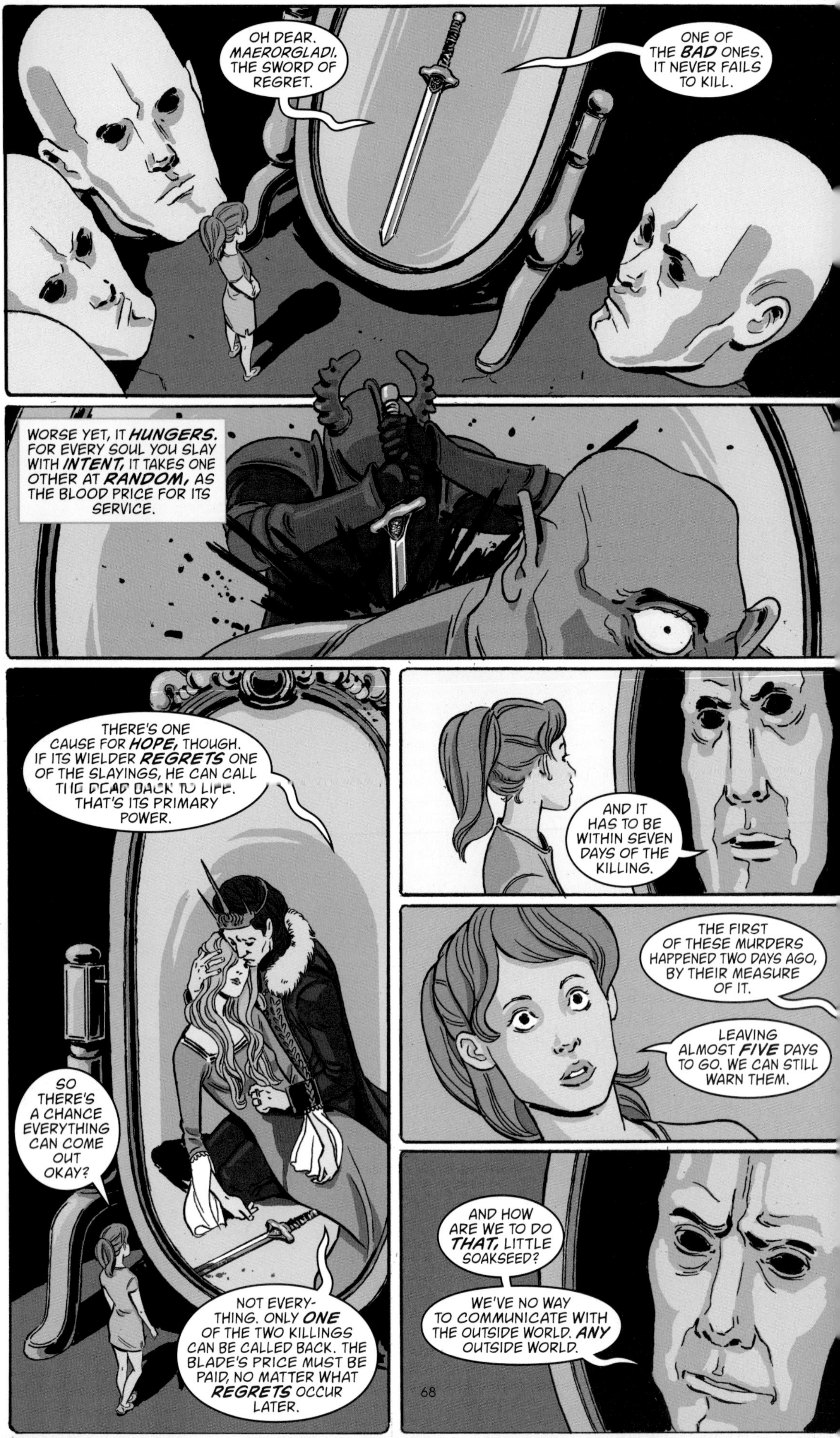
OH DEAR. MAERORGLADI. THE SWORD OF REGRET.
ONE OF THE BAD ONES. IT NEVER FAILS TO KILL.
WORSE YET, IT HUNGERS. FOR EVERY SOUL YOU SLAY WITH INTENT, IT TAKES ONE OTHER AT RANDOM, AS THE BLOOD PRICE FOR ITS SERVICE.
THERE'S ONE CAUSE FOR HOPE, THOUGH. IF ITS WIELDER REGRETS ONE OF THE SLAYINGS, HE CAN CALL THE DEAD BACK TO LIFE. THAT'S ITS PRIMARY POWER.
AND IT HAS TO BE WITHIN SEVEN DAYS OF THE KILLING.
THE FIRST OF THESE MURDERS HAPPENED TWO DAYS AGO, BY THEIR MEASURE OF IT.
LEAVING ALMOST FIVE DAYS TO GO. WE CAN STILL WARN THEM.
SO THERE'S A CHANCE EVERYTHING CAN COME OUT OKAY?
NOT EVERY-THING. ONLY ONE OF THE TWO KILLINGS CAN BE CALLED BACK. THE BLADE'S PRICE MUST BE PAID, NO MATTER WHAT REGRETS OCCUR LATER.
AND HOW ARE WE TO DO THAT, LITTLE SOAKSEED?
WE'VE NO WAY TO COMMUNICATE WITH THE OUTSIDE WORLD. ANY OUTSIDE WORLD.

TWO BY TWO

Russ Braun: artist • Andrew Dalhouse: colorist

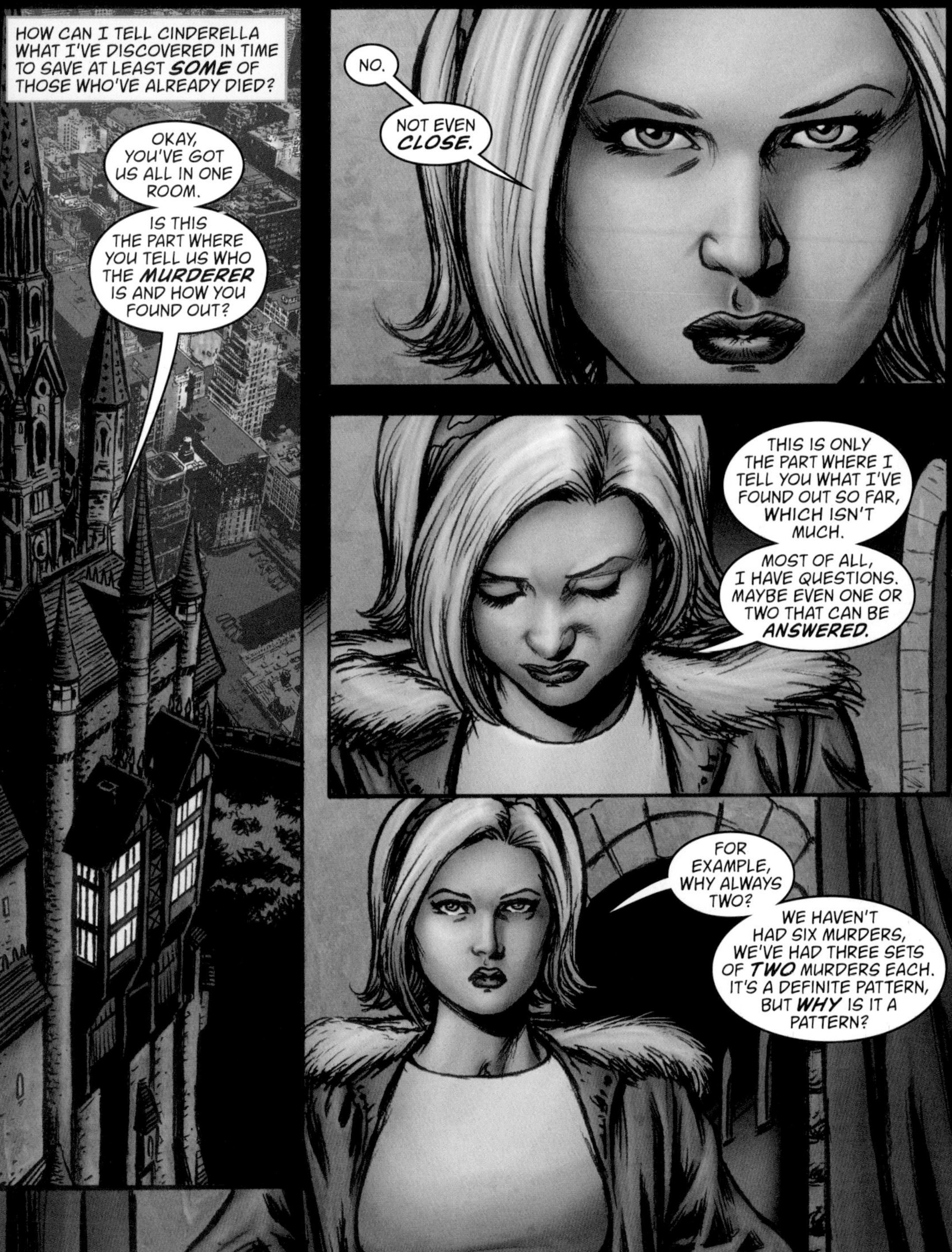
HOW CAN I TELL CINDERELLA WHAT I'VE DISCOVERED IN TIME TO SAVE AT LEAST *SOME* OF THOSE WHO'VE ALREADY DIED?
OKAY, YOU'VE GOT US ALL IN ONE ROOM.
IS THIS THE PART WHERE YOU TELL US WHO THE *MURDERER* IS AND HOW YOU FOUND OUT?
NO.
NOT EVEN *CLOSE.*
THIS IS ONLY THE PART WHERE I TELL YOU WHAT I'VE FOUND OUT SO FAR, **WHICH** ISN'T MUCH.
MOST OF ALL, I HAVE QUESTIONS. MAYBE EVEN ONE OR TWO THAT CAN BE *ANSWERED.*
FOR EXAMPLE, WHY ALWAYS TWO?
WE HAVEN'T HAD SIX MURDERS, WE'VE HAD THREE SETS OF *TWO* MURDERS EACH. IT'S A DEFINITE PATTERN, BUT *WHY* IS IT A PATTERN?

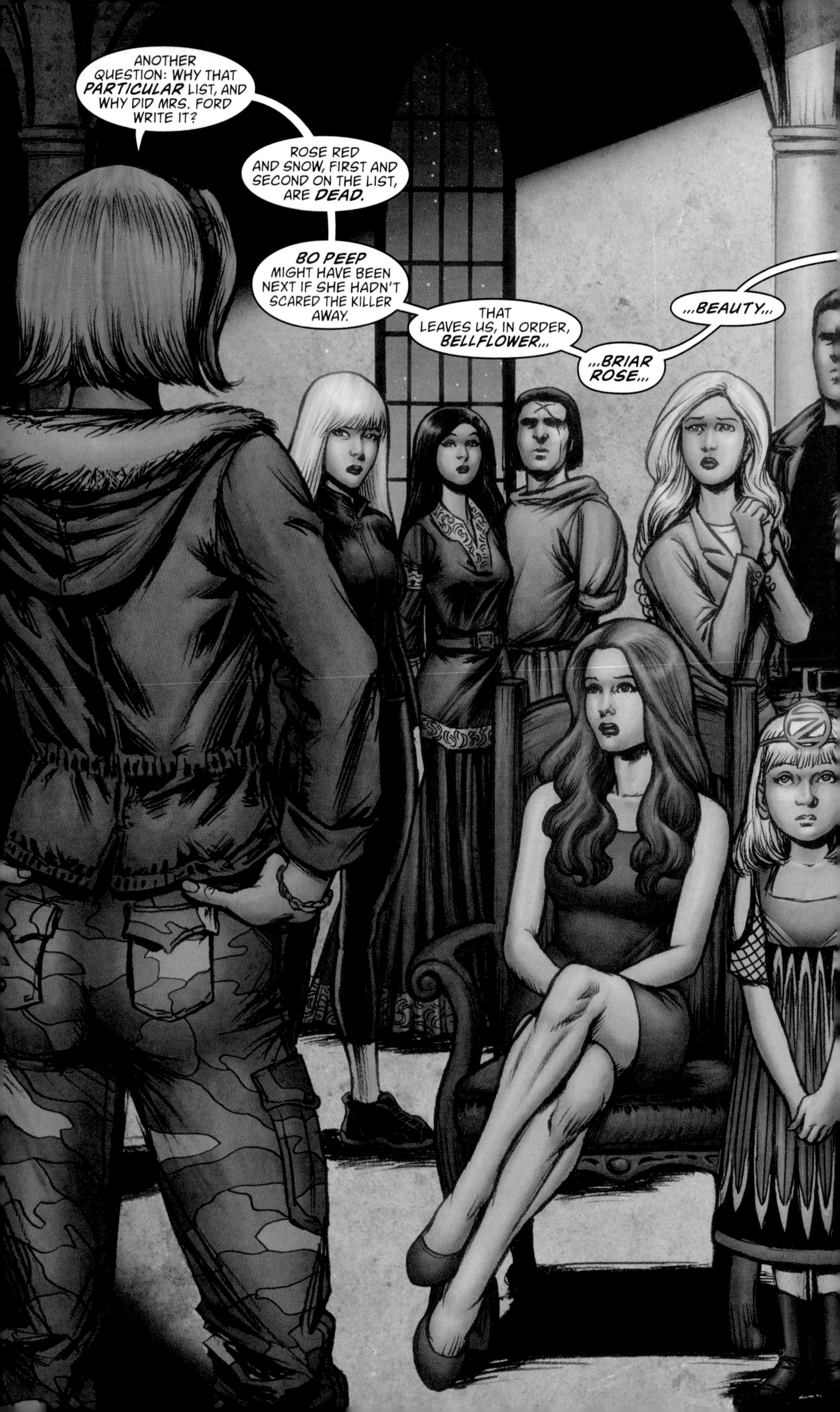
ANOTHER QUESTION: WHY THAT PARTICULAR LIST, AND WHY DID MRS. FORD WRITE IT?
ROSE RED AND SNOW, FIRST AND SECOND ON THE LIST, ARE DEAD.
BO PEEP MIGHT HAVE BEEN NEXT IF SHE HADN'T SCARED THE KILLER AWAY.
THAT LEAVES US, IN ORDER, BELLFLOWER...
...BRIAR ROSE...
...BEAUTY...

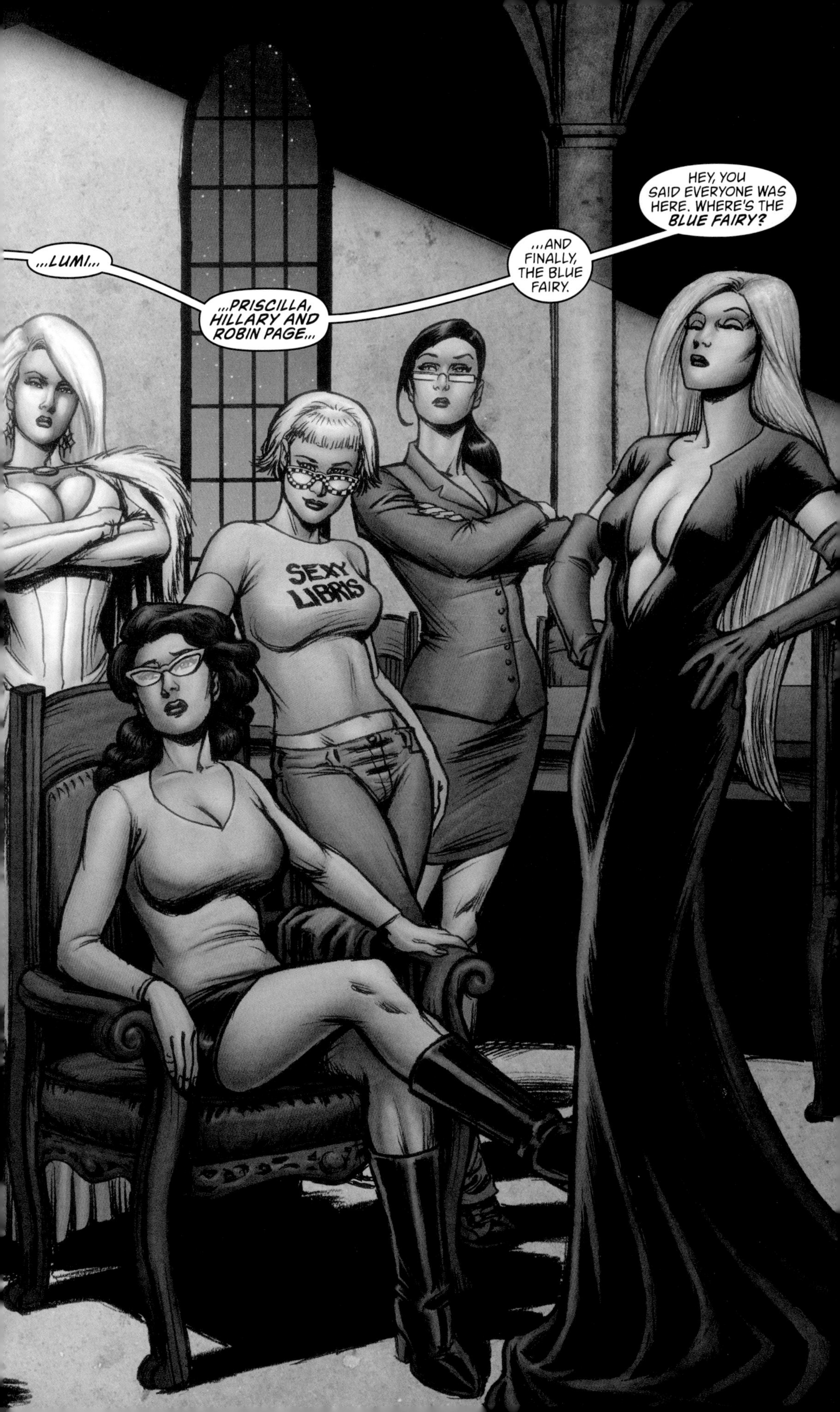
...LUMI...
...PRISCILLA, HILLARY AND ROBIN PAGE...
...AND FINALLY, THE BLUE FAIRY.
HEY, YOU SAID EVERYONE WAS HERE. WHERE'S THE BLUE FAIRY?
SEXY LIBRIS

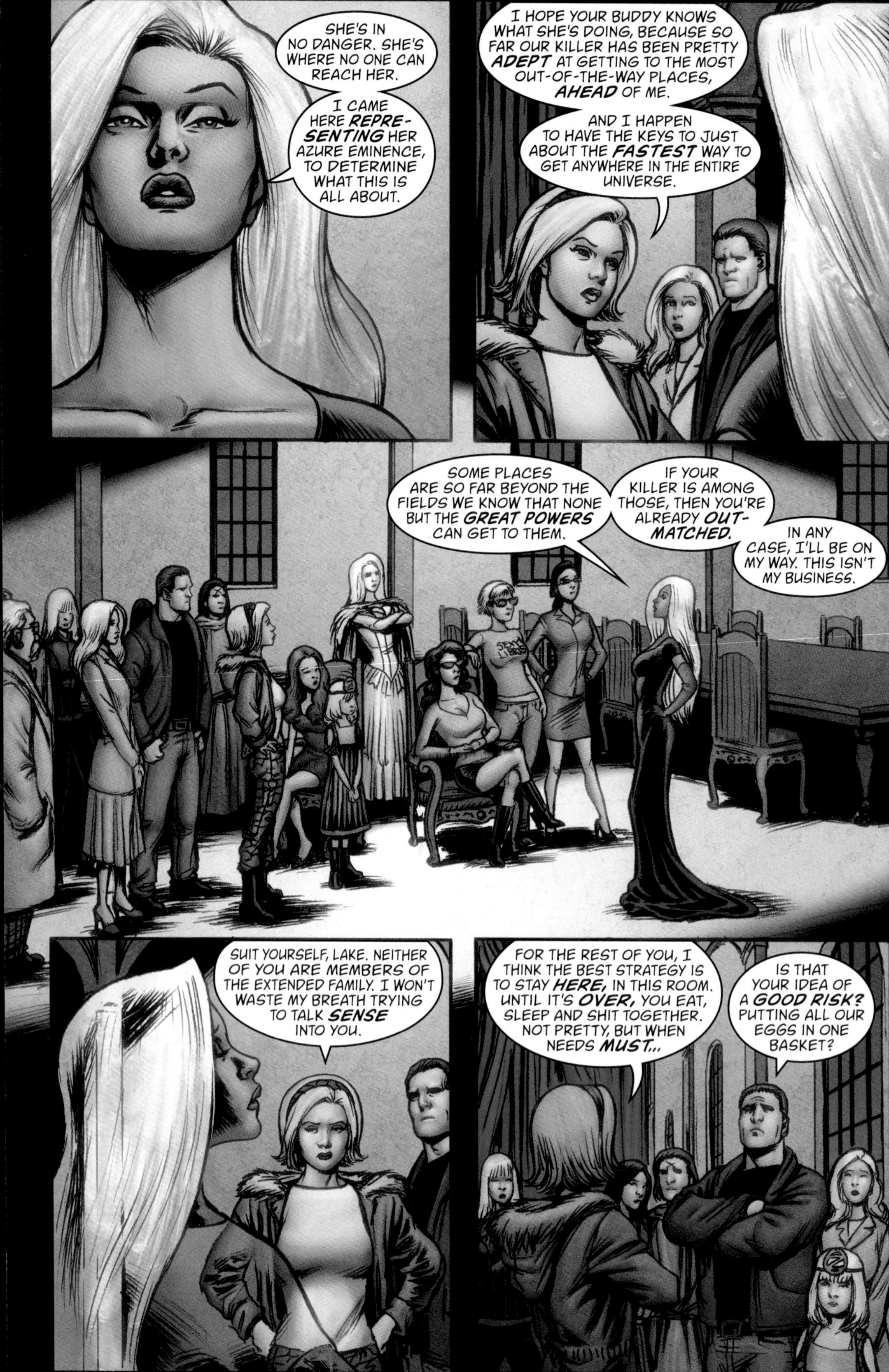
SHE'S IN NO DANGER. SHE'S WHERE NO ONE CAN REACH HER.
I CAME HERE REPRESENTING HER AZURE EMINENCE, TO DETERMINE WHAT THIS IS ALL ABOUT.
I HOPE YOUR BUDDY KNOWS WHAT SHE'S DOING, BECAUSE SO FAR OUR KILLER HAS BEEN PRETTY ADEPT AT GETTING TO THE MOST OUT-OF-THE-WAY PLACES, AHEAD OF ME.
AND I HAPPEN TO HAVE THE KEYS TO JUST ABOUT THE FASTEST WAY TO GET ANYWHERE IN THE ENTIRE UNIVERSE.
SOME PLACES ARE SO FAR BEYOND THE FIELDS WE KNOW THAT NONE BUT THE GREAT POWERS CAN GET TO THEM.
IF YOUR KILLER IS AMONG THOSE, THEN YOU'RE ALREADY OUT-MATCHED.
IN ANY CASE, I'LL BE ON MY WAY. THIS ISN'T MY BUSINESS.
SUIT YOURSELF, LAKE. NEITHER OF YOU ARE MEMBERS OF THE EXTENDED FAMILY. I WON'T WASTE MY BREATH TRYING TO TALK SENSE INTO YOU.
FOR THE REST OF YOU, I THINK THE BEST STRATEGY IS TO STAY HERE, IN THIS ROOM. UNTIL IT'S OVER, YOU EAT, SLEEP AND SHIT TOGETHER. NOT PRETTY, BUT WHEN NEEDS MUST...
IS THAT YOUR IDEA OF A GOOD RISK? PUTTING ALL OUR EGGS IN ONE BASKET?

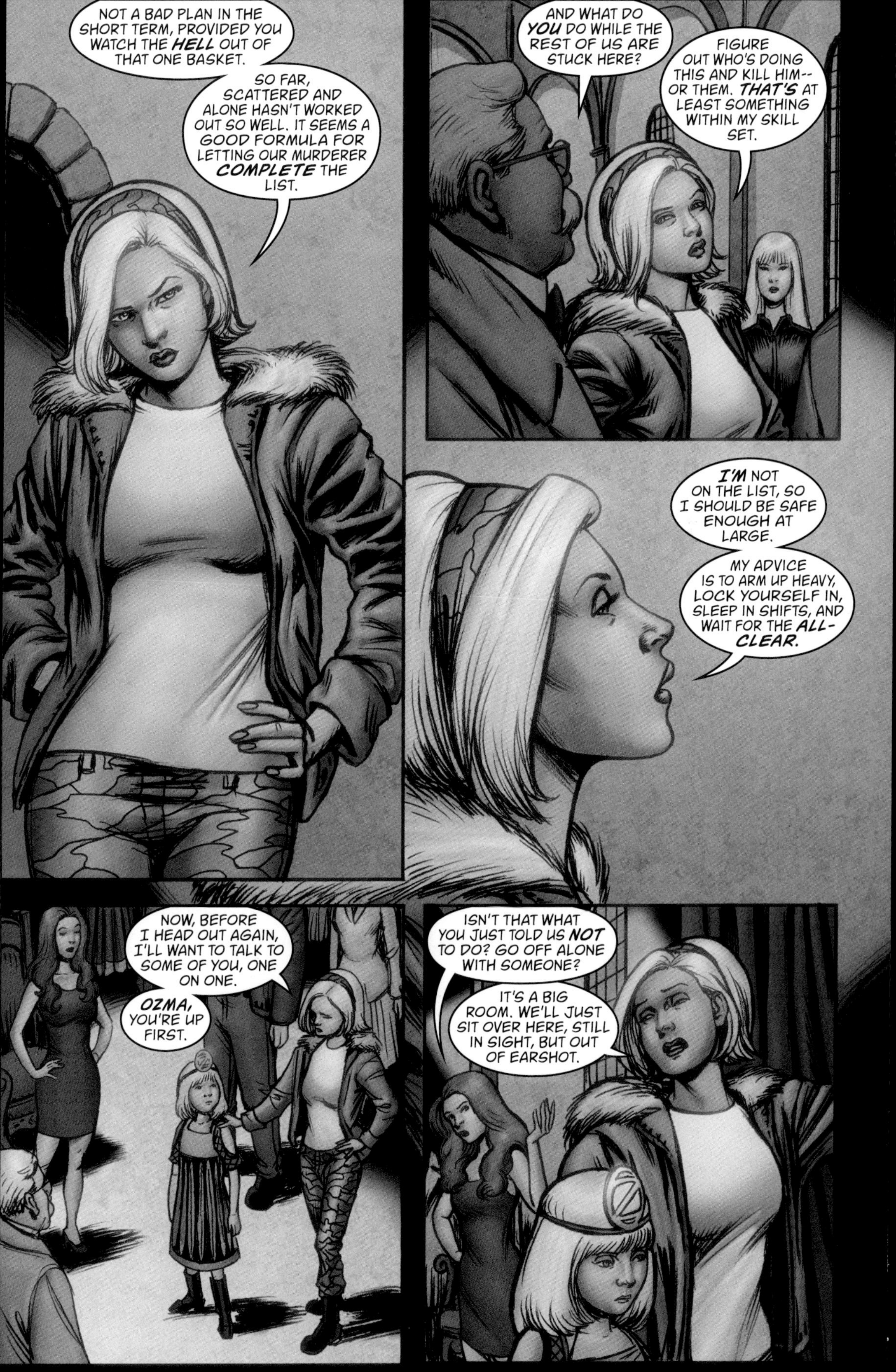
NOT A BAD PLAN IN THE SHORT TERM, PROVIDED YOU WATCH THE **HELL** OUT OF THAT ONE BASKET.
SO FAR, SCATTERED AND ALONE HASN'T WORKED OUT SO WELL. IT SEEMS A GOOD FORMULA FOR LETTING OUR MURDERER **COMPLETE** THE LIST.
AND WHAT DO **YOU** DO WHILE THE REST OF US ARE STUCK HERE?
FIGURE OUT WHO'S DOING THIS AND KILL HIM-- OR THEM. **THAT'S** AT LEAST SOMETHING WITHIN MY SKILL SET.
I'M NOT ON THE LIST, SO I SHOULD BE SAFE ENOUGH AT LARGE.
MY ADVICE IS TO ARM UP HEAVY, LOCK YOURSELF IN, SLEEP IN SHIFTS, AND WAIT FOR THE **ALL-CLEAR.**
NOW, BEFORE I HEAD OUT AGAIN, I'LL WANT TO TALK TO SOME OF YOU, ONE ON ONE.
OZMA, YOU'RE UP FIRST.
ISN'T THAT WHAT YOU JUST TOLD US **NOT** TO DO? GO OFF ALONE WITH SOMEONE?
IT'S A BIG ROOM. WE'LL JUST SIT OVER HERE, STILL IN SIGHT, BUT OUT OF EARSHOT.

THE TESTIMONY OF THE GOOD WITCH OZMA

Ming Doyle: artist

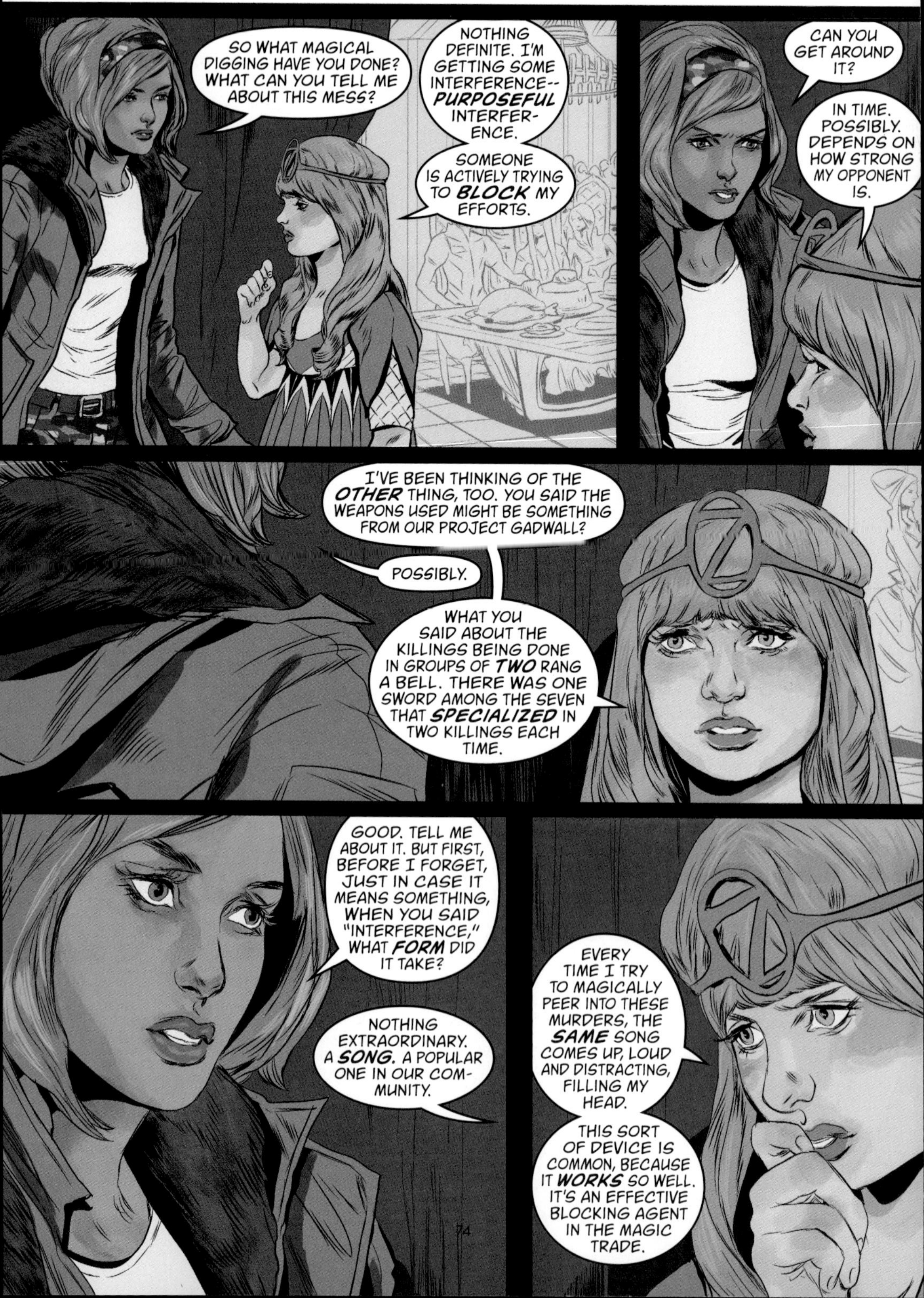
SO WHAT MAGICAL DIGGING HAVE YOU DONE? WHAT CAN YOU TELL ME ABOUT THIS MESS?
NOTHING DEFINITE. I'M GETTING SOME INTERFERENCE-- PURPOSEFUL INTERFERENCE.
SOMEONE IS ACTIVELY TRYING TO BLOCK MY EFFORTS.
CAN YOU GET AROUND IT?
IN TIME. POSSIBLY. DEPENDS ON HOW STRONG MY OPPONENT IS.
I'VE BEEN THINKING OF THE OTHER THING, TOO. YOU SAID THE WEAPONS USED MIGHT BE SOMETHING FROM OUR PROJECT GADWALL?
POSSIBLY.
WHAT YOU SAID ABOUT THE KILLINGS BEING DONE IN GROUPS OF TWO RANG A BELL. THERE WAS ONE SWORD AMONG THE SEVEN THAT SPECIALIZED IN TWO KILLINGS EACH TIME.
GOOD. TELL ME ABOUT IT. BUT FIRST, BEFORE I FORGET, JUST IN CASE IT MEANS SOMETHING, WHEN YOU SAID "INTERFERENCE," WHAT FORM DID IT TAKE?
NOTHING EXTRAORDINARY. A SONG. A POPULAR ONE IN OUR COMMUNITY.
EVERY TIME I TRY TO MAGICALLY PEER INTO THESE MURDERS, THE SAME SONG COMES UP, LOUD AND DISTRACTING, FILLING MY HEAD.
THIS SORT OF DEVICE IS COMMON, BECAUSE IT WORKS SO WELL. IT'S AN EFFECTIVE BLOCKING AGENT IN THE MAGIC TRADE.

NUMBER TWELVE, WITH A BULLET

Chris Sprouse: penciller • Karl Story: inker
Jordie Bellaire: colorist

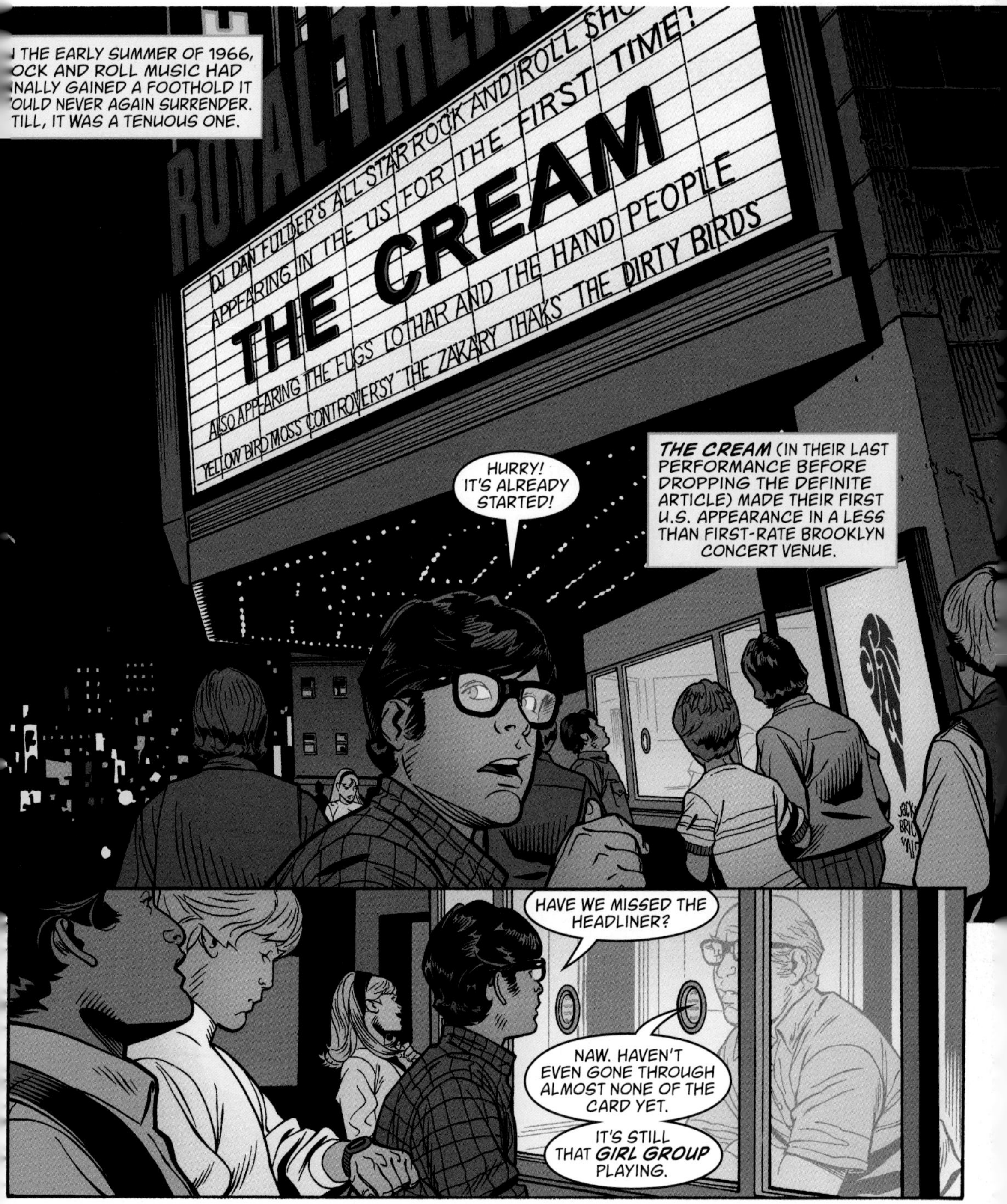
N THE EARLY SUMMER OF 1966, OCK AND ROLL MUSIC HAD NALLY GAINED A FOOTHOLD IT OULD NEVER AGAIN SURRENDER. TILL, IT WAS A TENUOUS ONE.
DJ DAN FULDER'S ALL STAR ROCK AND ROLL SHO
APPEARING IN THE US FOR THE FIRST TIME!
THE CREAM
ALSO APPEARING THE FUGS LOTHAR AND THE HAND PEOPLE
YELLOW BIRD MOSS CONTROVERSY THE ZAKARY THAKS THE DIRTY BIRDS
HURRY! IT'S ALREADY STARTED!
THE CREAM (IN THEIR LAST PERFORMANCE BEFORE DROPPING THE DEFINITE ARTICLE) MADE THEIR FIRST U.S. APPEARANCE IN A LESS THAN FIRST-RATE BROOKLYN CONCERT VENUE.
HAVE WE MISSED THE HEADLINER?
NAW. HAVEN'T EVEN GONE THROUGH ALMOST NONE OF THE CARD YET.
IT'S STILL THAT GIRL GROUP PLAYING.

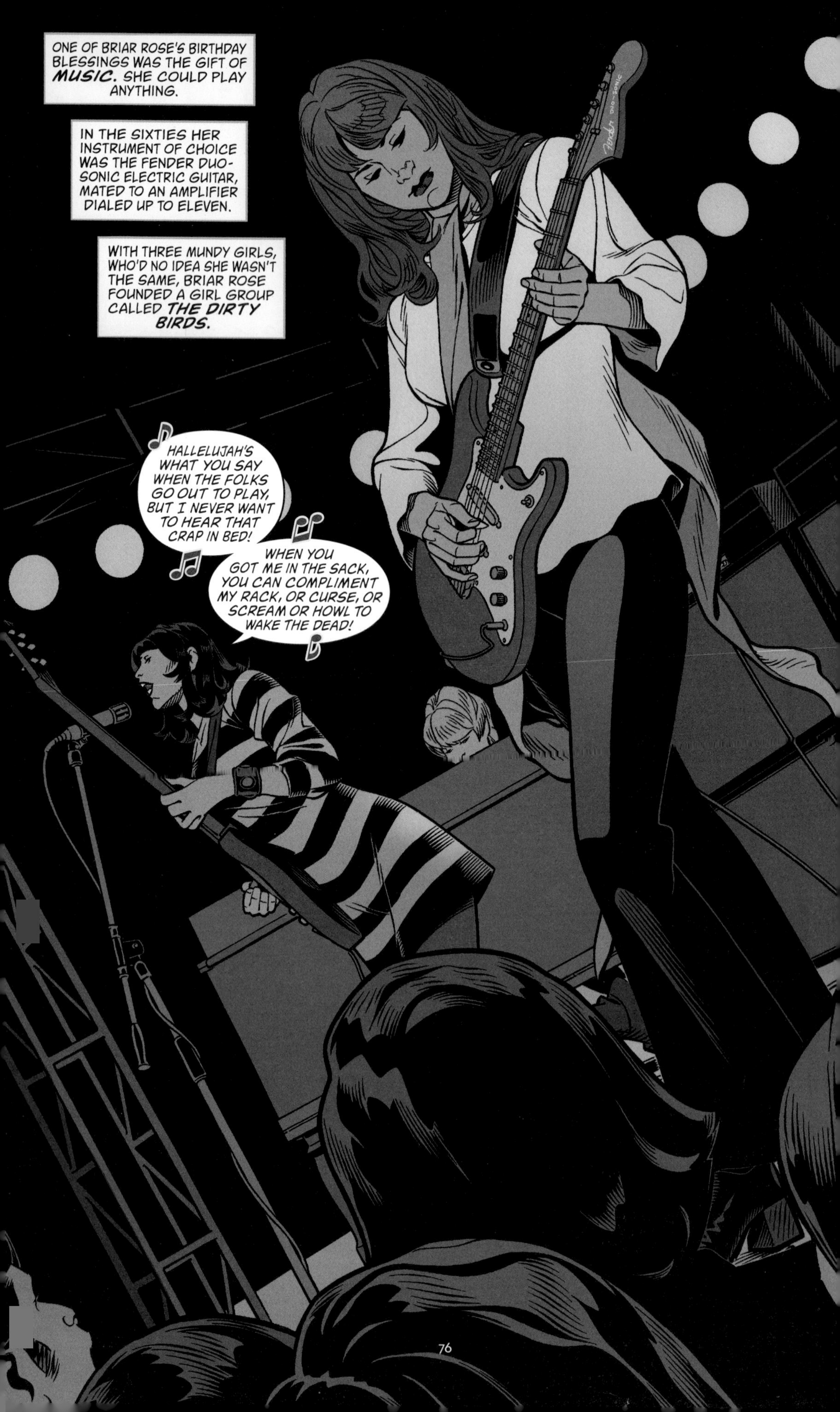
ONE OF BRIAR ROSE'S BIRTHDAY BLESSINGS WAS THE GIFT OF MUSIC. SHE COULD PLAY ANYTHING.
IN THE SIXTIES HER INSTRUMENT OF CHOICE WAS THE FENDER DUO-SONIC ELECTRIC GUITAR, MATED TO AN AMPLIFIER DIALED UP TO ELEVEN.
WITH THREE MUNDY GIRLS, WHO'D NO IDEA SHE WASN'T THE SAME, BRIAR ROSE FOUNDED A GIRL GROUP CALLED THE DIRTY BIRDS.
HALLELUJAH'S WHAT YOU SAY WHEN THE FOLKS GO OUT TO PLAY, BUT I NEVER WANT TO HEAR THAT CRAP IN BED!
WHEN YOU GOT ME IN THE SACK, YOU CAN COMPLIMENT MY RACK, OR CURSE, OR SCREAM OR HOWL TO WAKE THE DEAD!

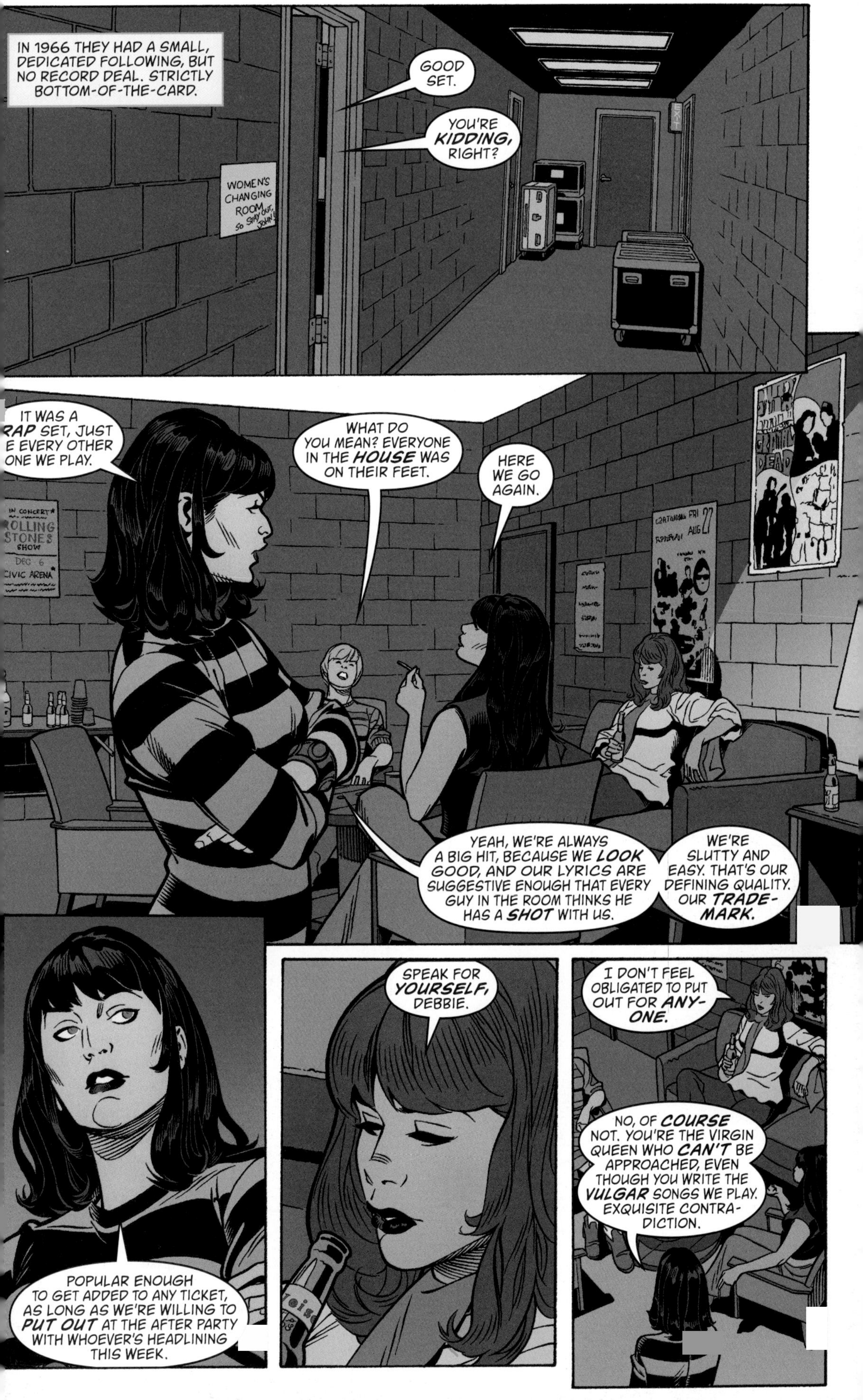

IN 1966 THEY HAD A SMALL, DEDICATED FOLLOWING, BUT NO RECORD DEAL. STRICTLY BOTTOM-OF-THE-CARD.
GOOD SET.
YOU'RE KIDDING, RIGHT?
WOMEN'S CHANGING ROOM so STAY OUT, JOHN!!
EXIT
IT WAS A RAP SET, JUST E EVERY OTHER ONE WE PLAY.
WHAT DO YOU MEAN? EVERYONE IN THE HOUSE WAS ON THEIR FEET.
HERE WE GO AGAIN.
IN CONCERT OLLING STONES SHOW DEC. 6 CIVIC ARENA
YEAH, WE'RE ALWAYS A BIG HIT, BECAUSE WE LOOK GOOD, AND OUR LYRICS ARE SUGGESTIVE ENOUGH THAT EVERY GUY IN THE ROOM THINKS HE HAS A SHOT WITH US.
WE'RE SLUTTY AND EASY. THAT'S OUR DEFINING QUALITY. OUR TRADE-MARK.
POPULAR ENOUGH TO GET ADDED TO ANY TICKET, AS LONG AS WE'RE WILLING TO PUT OUT AT THE AFTER PARTY WITH WHOEVER'S HEADLINING THIS WEEK.
SPEAK FOR YOURSELF, DEBBIE.
I DON'T FEEL OBLIGATED TO PUT OUT FOR ANY-ONE.
NO, OF COURSE NOT. YOU'RE THE VIRGIN QUEEN WHO CAN'T BE APPROACHED, EVEN THOUGH YOU WRITE THE VULGAR SONGS WE PLAY. EXQUISITE CONTRA-DICTION.

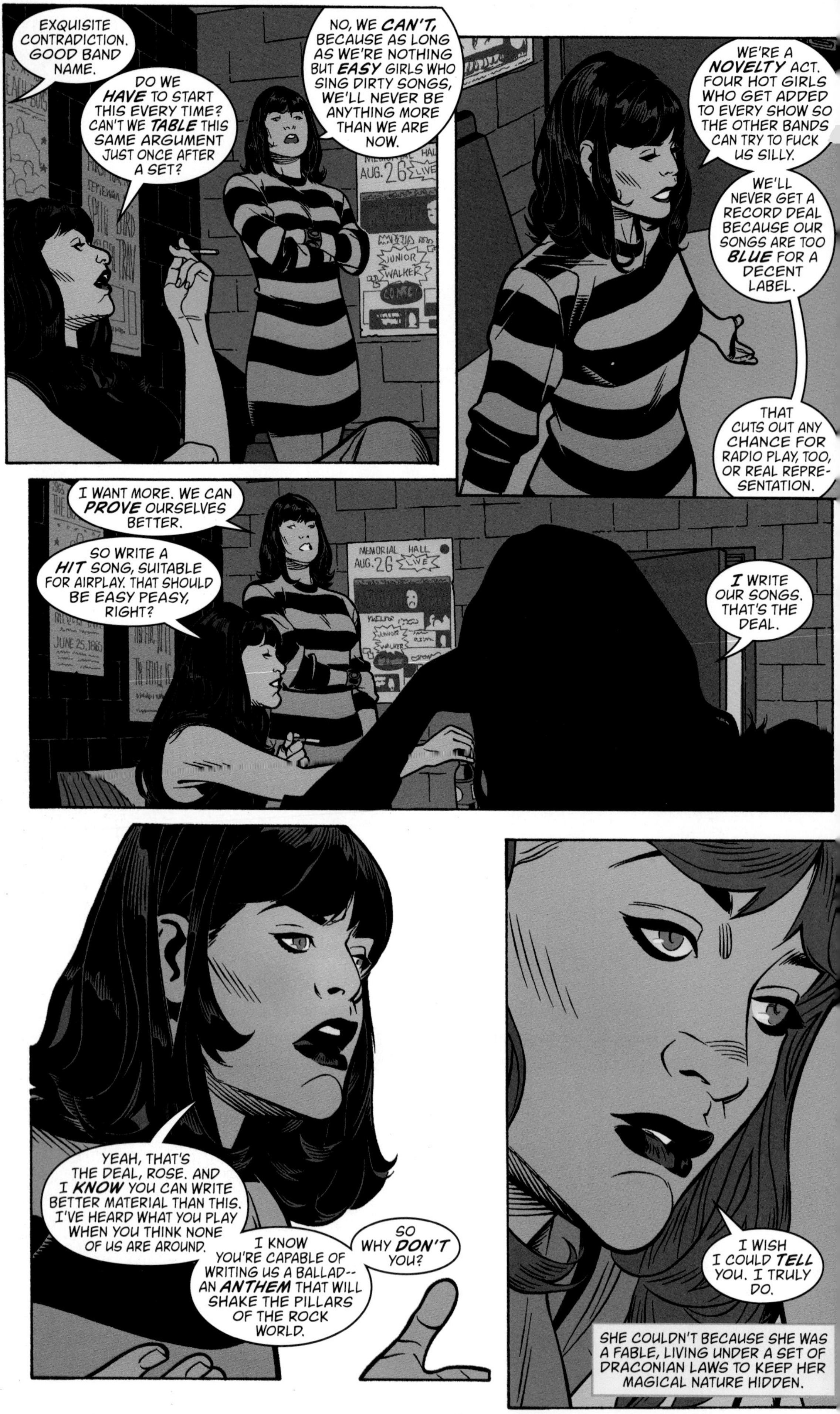

EXQUISITE CONTRADICTION. GOOD BAND NAME.
DO WE HAVE TO START THIS EVERY TIME? CAN'T WE TABLE THIS SAME ARGUMENT JUST ONCE AFTER A SET?
NO, WE CAN'T, BECAUSE AS LONG AS WE'RE NOTHING BUT EASY GIRLS WHO SING DIRTY SONGS, WE'LL NEVER BE ANYTHING MORE THAN WE ARE NOW.
WE'RE A NOVELTY ACT. FOUR HOT GIRLS WHO GET ADDED TO EVERY SHOW SO THE OTHER BANDS CAN TRY TO FUCK US SILLY.
WE'LL NEVER GET A RECORD DEAL BECAUSE OUR SONGS ARE TOO BLUE FOR A DECENT LABEL.
THAT CUTS OUT ANY CHANCE FOR RADIO PLAY, TOO, OR REAL REPRESENTATION.
I WANT MORE. WE CAN PROVE OURSELVES BETTER.
SO WRITE A HIT SONG, SUITABLE FOR AIRPLAY. THAT SHOULD BE EASY PEASY, RIGHT?
I WRITE OUR SONGS. THAT'S THE DEAL.
YEAH, THAT'S THE DEAL, ROSE. AND I KNOW YOU CAN WRITE BETTER MATERIAL THAN THIS. I'VE HEARD WHAT YOU PLAY WHEN YOU THINK NONE OF US ARE AROUND.
I KNOW YOU'RE CAPABLE OF WRITING US A BALLAD-- AN ANTHEM THAT WILL SHAKE THE PILLARS OF THE ROCK WORLD.
SO WHY DON'T YOU?
I WISH I COULD TELL YOU. I TRULY DO.
SHE COULDN'T BECAUSE SHE WAS A FABLE, LIVING UNDER A SET OF DRACONIAN LAWS TO KEEP HER MAGICAL NATURE HIDDEN.

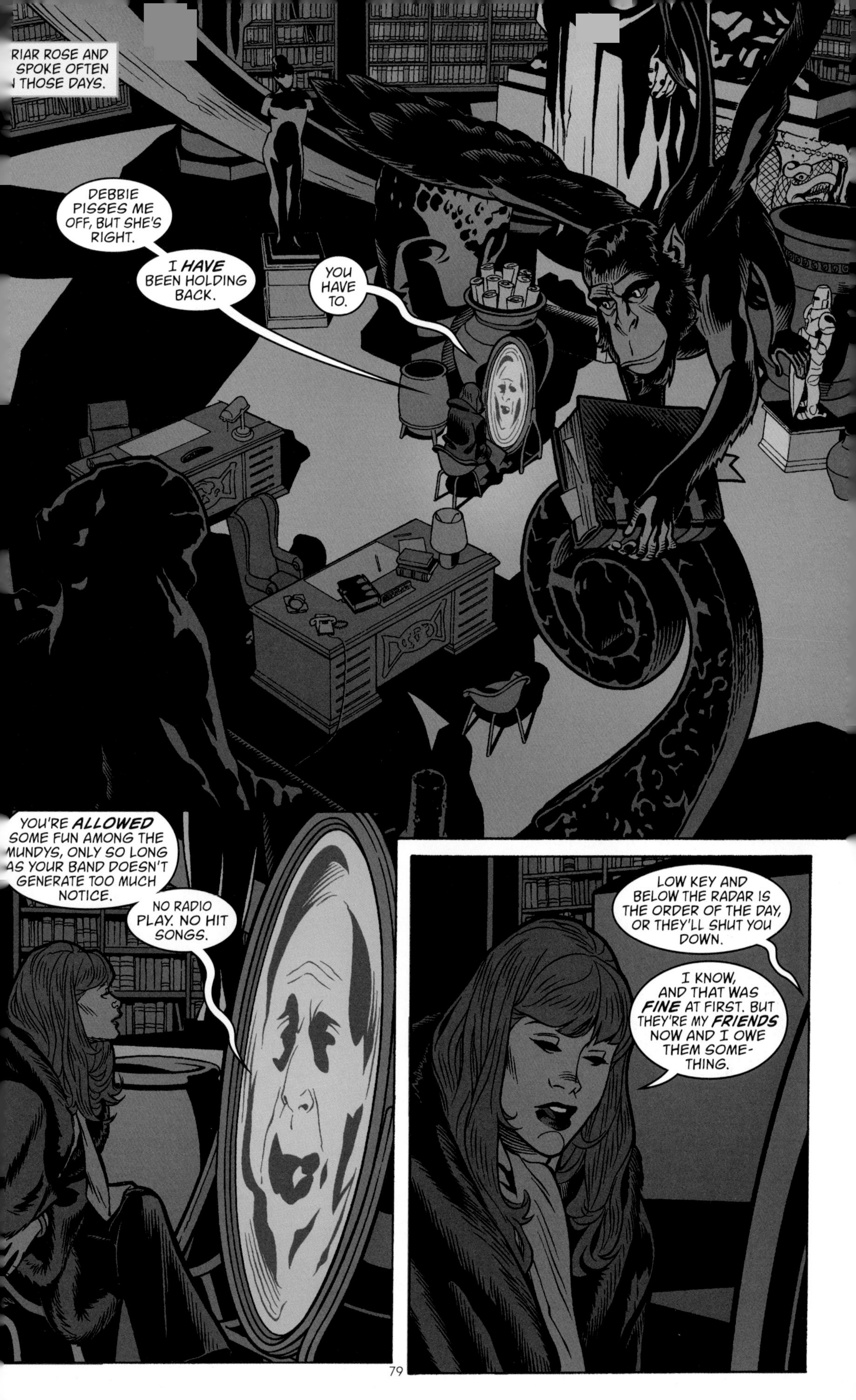

RIAR ROSE AND SPOKE OFTEN N THOSE DAYS.
DEBBIE PISSES ME OFF, BUT SHE'S RIGHT.
I *HAVE* BEEN HOLDING BACK.
YOU HAVE TO.
YOU'RE ***ALLOWED*** SOME FUN AMONG THE MUNDYS, ONLY SO LONG AS YOUR BAND DOESN'T GENERATE TOO MUCH NOTICE.
NO RADIO PLAY. NO HIT SONGS.
LOW KEY AND BELOW THE RADAR IS THE ORDER OF THE DAY, OR THEY'LL SHUT YOU DOWN.
I KNOW, AND THAT WAS ***FINE*** AT FIRST. BUT THEY'RE MY ***FRIENDS*** NOW AND I OWE THEM SOME-THING.

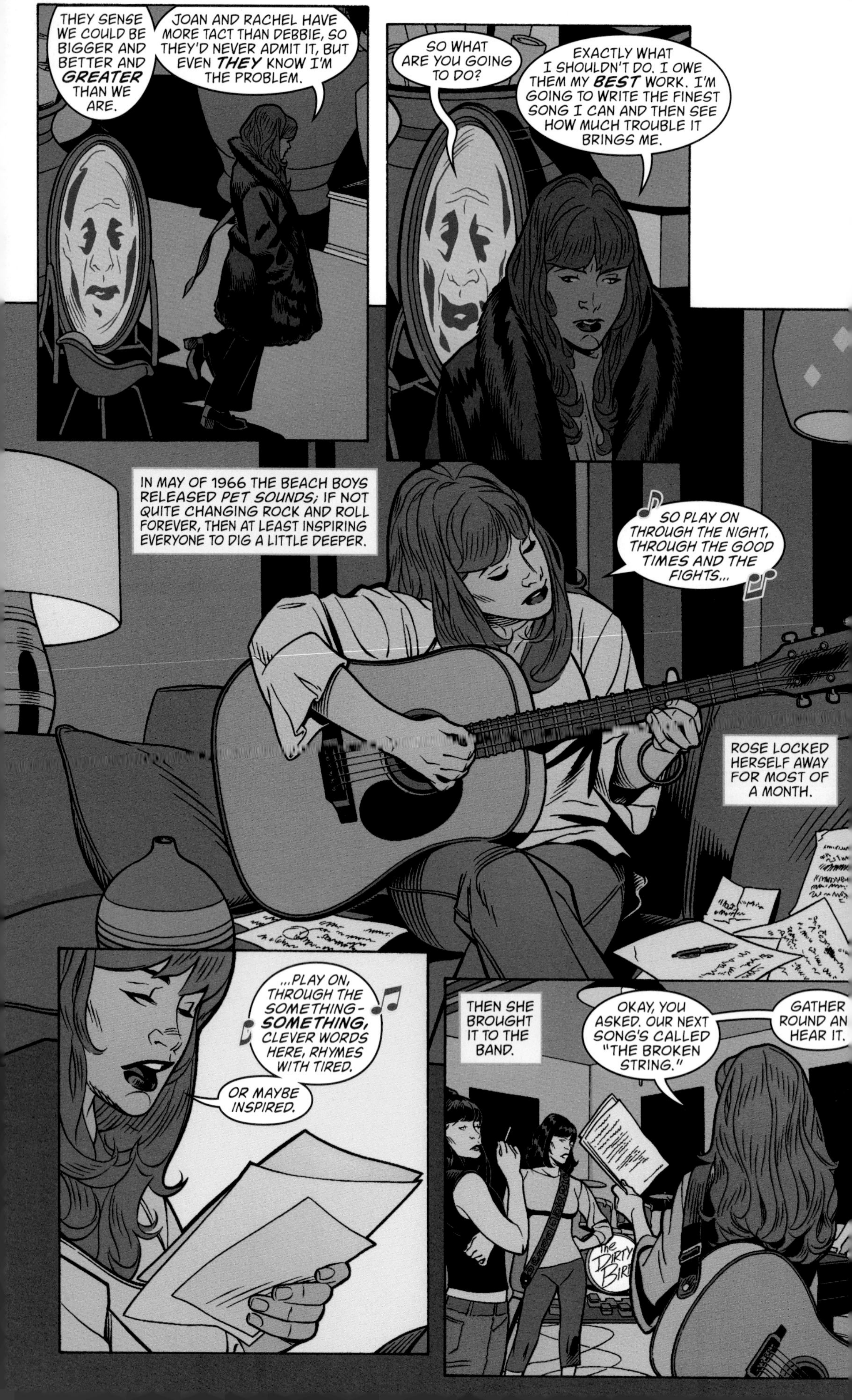
THEY SENSE WE COULD BE BIGGER AND BETTER AND GREATER THAN WE ARE.
JOAN AND RACHEL HAVE MORE TACT THAN DEBBIE, SO THEY'D NEVER ADMIT IT, BUT EVEN THEY KNOW I'M THE PROBLEM.
SO WHAT ARE YOU GOING TO DO?
EXACTLY WHAT I SHOULDN'T DO. I OWE THEM MY BEST WORK. I'M GOING TO WRITE THE FINEST SONG I CAN AND THEN SEE HOW MUCH TROUBLE IT BRINGS ME.
IN MAY OF 1966 THE BEACH BOYS RELEASED PET SOUNDS; IF NOT QUITE CHANGING ROCK AND ROLL FOREVER, THEN AT LEAST INSPIRING EVERYONE TO DIG A LITTLE DEEPER.
SO PLAY ON THROUGH THE NIGHT, THROUGH THE GOOD TIMES AND THE FIGHTS...
ROSE LOCKED HERSELF AWAY FOR MOST OF A MONTH.
...PLAY ON, THROUGH THE SOMETHING-SOMETHING, CLEVER WORDS HERE, RHYMES WITH TIRED.
OR MAYBE INSPIRED.
THEN SHE BROUGHT IT TO THE BAND.
OKAY, YOU ASKED. OUR NEXT SONG'S CALLED "THE BROKEN STRING."
GATHER ROUND AN' HEAR IT.
THE DIRTY BIRDS

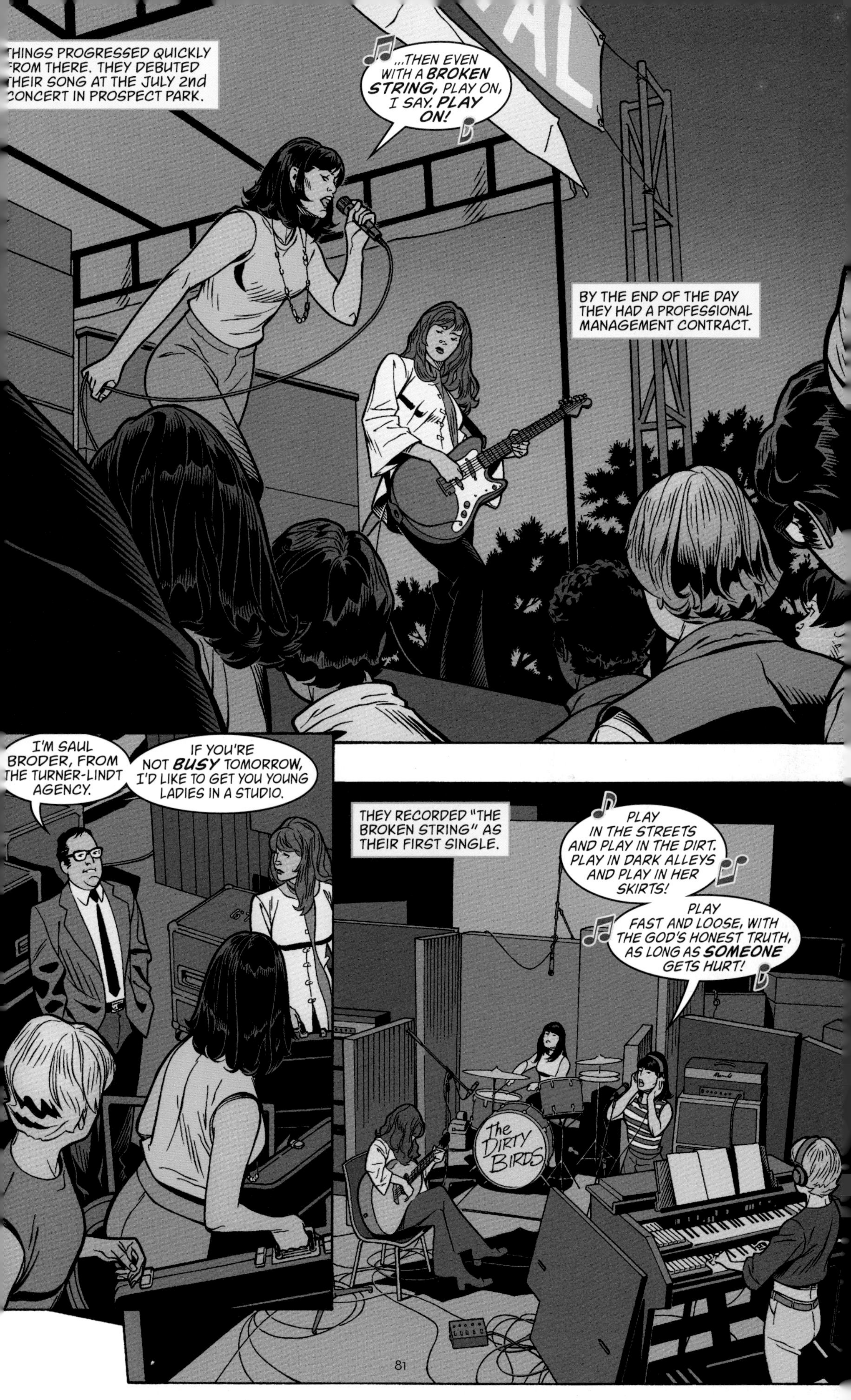
THINGS PROGRESSED QUICKLY FROM THERE. THEY DEBUTED THEIR SONG AT THE JULY 2nd CONCERT IN PROSPECT PARK.
...THEN EVEN WITH A BROKEN STRING, PLAY ON, I SAY. PLAY ON!
BY THE END OF THE DAY THEY HAD A PROFESSIONAL MANAGEMENT CONTRACT.
I'M SAUL BRODER, FROM THE TURNER-LINDT AGENCY.
IF YOU'RE NOT BUSY TOMORROW, I'D LIKE TO GET YOU YOUNG LADIES IN A STUDIO.
THEY RECORDED "THE BROKEN STRING" AS THEIR FIRST SINGLE.
PLAY IN THE STREETS AND PLAY IN THE DIRT. PLAY IN DARK ALLEYS AND PLAY IN HER SKIRTS!
PLAY FAST AND LOOSE, WITH THE GOD'S HONEST TRUTH, AS LONG AS SOMEONE GETS HURT!
The DIRTY BIRDS

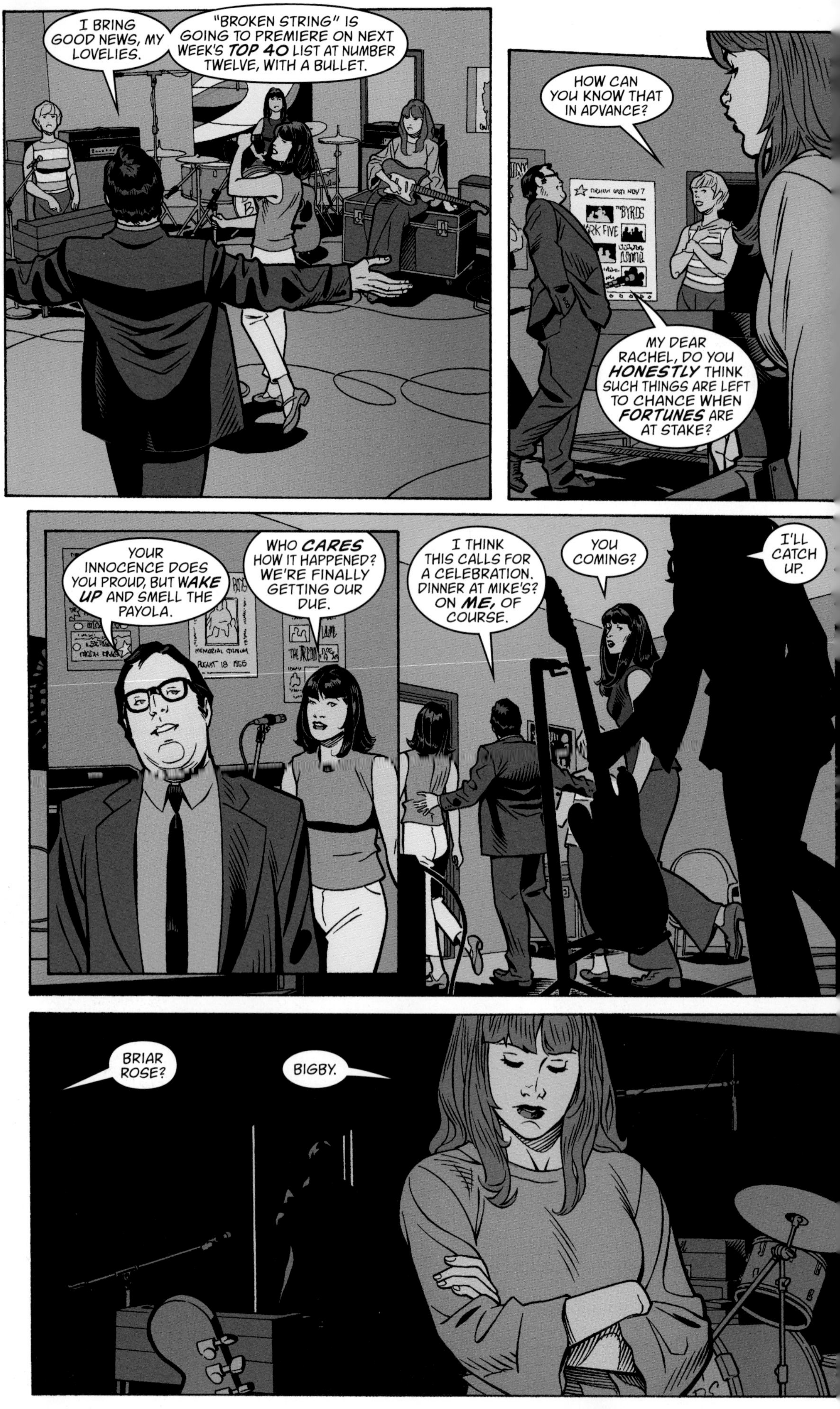

I BRING GOOD NEWS, MY LOVELIES.
"BROKEN STRING" IS GOING TO PREMIERE ON NEXT WEEK'S TOP 40 LIST AT NUMBER TWELVE, WITH A BULLET.
HOW CAN YOU KNOW THAT IN ADVANCE?
THE BYRDS
YARK FIVE
MY DEAR RACHEL, DO YOU HONESTLY THINK SUCH THINGS ARE LEFT TO CHANCE WHEN FORTUNES ARE AT STAKE?
YOUR INNOCENCE DOES YOU PROUD, BUT WAKE UP AND SMELL THE PAYOLA.
WHO CARES HOW IT HAPPENED? WE'RE FINALLY GETTING OUR DUE.
MEMORIAL GILLIUM
AUGUST 18 1955
I THINK THIS CALLS FOR A CELEBRATION. DINNER AT MIKE'S? ON ME, OF COURSE.
YOU COMING?
I'LL CATCH UP.
BRIAR ROSE?
BIGBY.

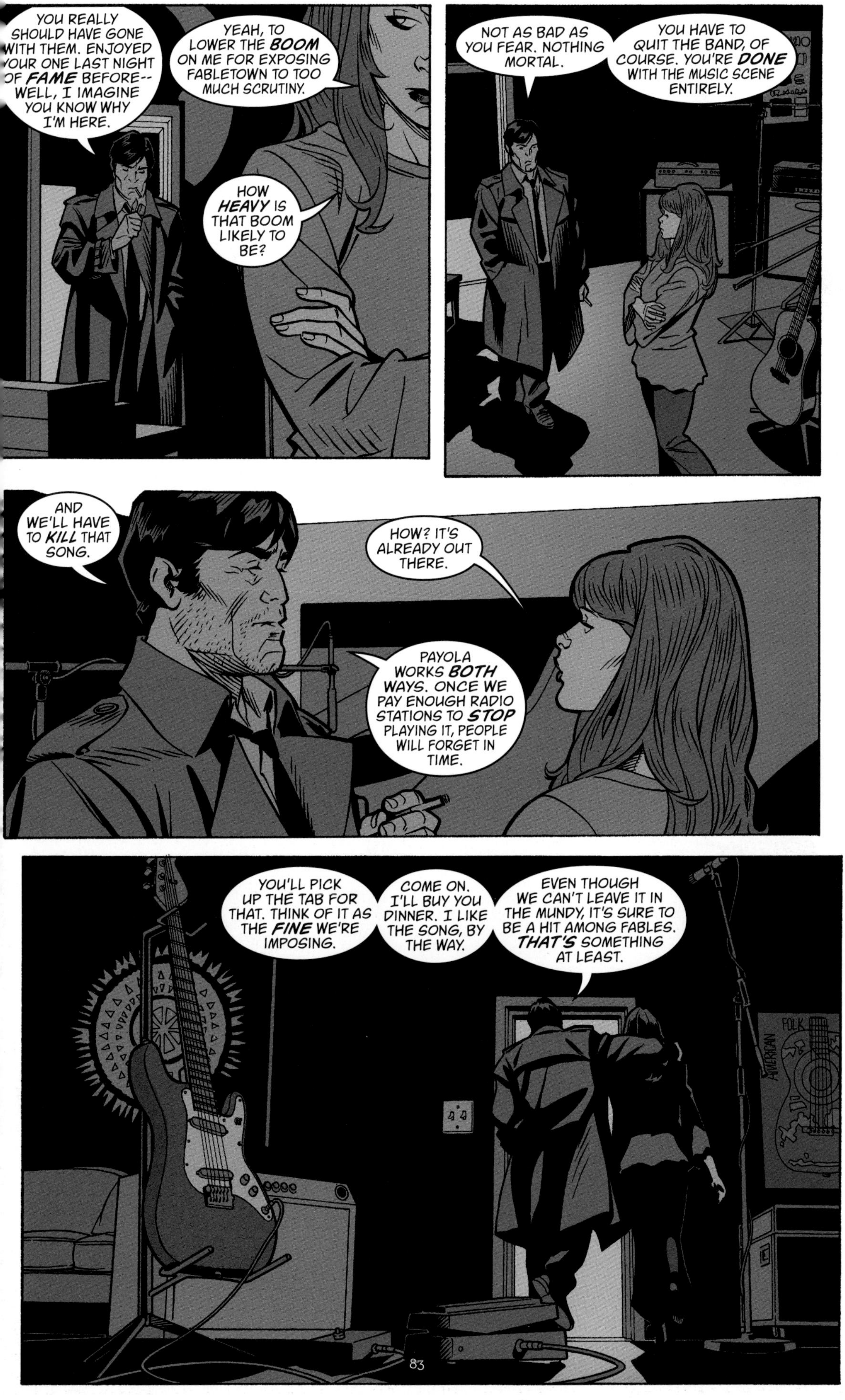
YOU REALLY SHOULD HAVE GONE WITH THEM. ENJOYED YOUR ONE LAST NIGHT OF FAME BEFORE-- WELL, I IMAGINE YOU KNOW WHY I'M HERE.
YEAH, TO LOWER THE BOOM ON ME FOR EXPOSING FABLETOWN TO TOO MUCH SCRUTINY.
HOW HEAVY IS THAT BOOM LIKELY TO BE?
NOT AS BAD AS YOU FEAR. NOTHING MORTAL.
YOU HAVE TO QUIT THE BAND, OF COURSE. YOU'RE DONE WITH THE MUSIC SCENE ENTIRELY.
AND WE'LL HAVE TO KILL THAT SONG.
HOW? IT'S ALREADY OUT THERE.
PAYOLA WORKS BOTH WAYS. ONCE WE PAY ENOUGH RADIO STATIONS TO STOP PLAYING IT, PEOPLE WILL FORGET IN TIME.
YOU'LL PICK UP THE TAB FOR THAT. THINK OF IT AS THE FINE WE'RE IMPOSING.
COME ON. I'LL BUY YOU DINNER. I LIKE THE SONG, BY THE WAY.
EVEN THOUGH WE CAN'T LEAVE IT IN THE MUNDY, IT'S SURE TO BE A HIT AMONG FABLES. THAT'S SOMETHING AT LEAST.
AMERICAN FOLK

THURSDAY

Oh, Cindy, quit focusing on the song. That's just a distraction, which is exactly what it was designed to be. Whoever's behind this is playing you, young missy.

It's the sword you need to look at. You were so close to figuring it out, before you let yourself be misdirected. You complain about being a bad detective. Fine. Then be a good spy. You've encountered diversions before. Your case history shows a hundred missions where you didn't fall for the opposition's attempted diversions.

Work the real problem.

THE TESTIMONY OF BRIAR ROSE

Nimit Malavia: artist

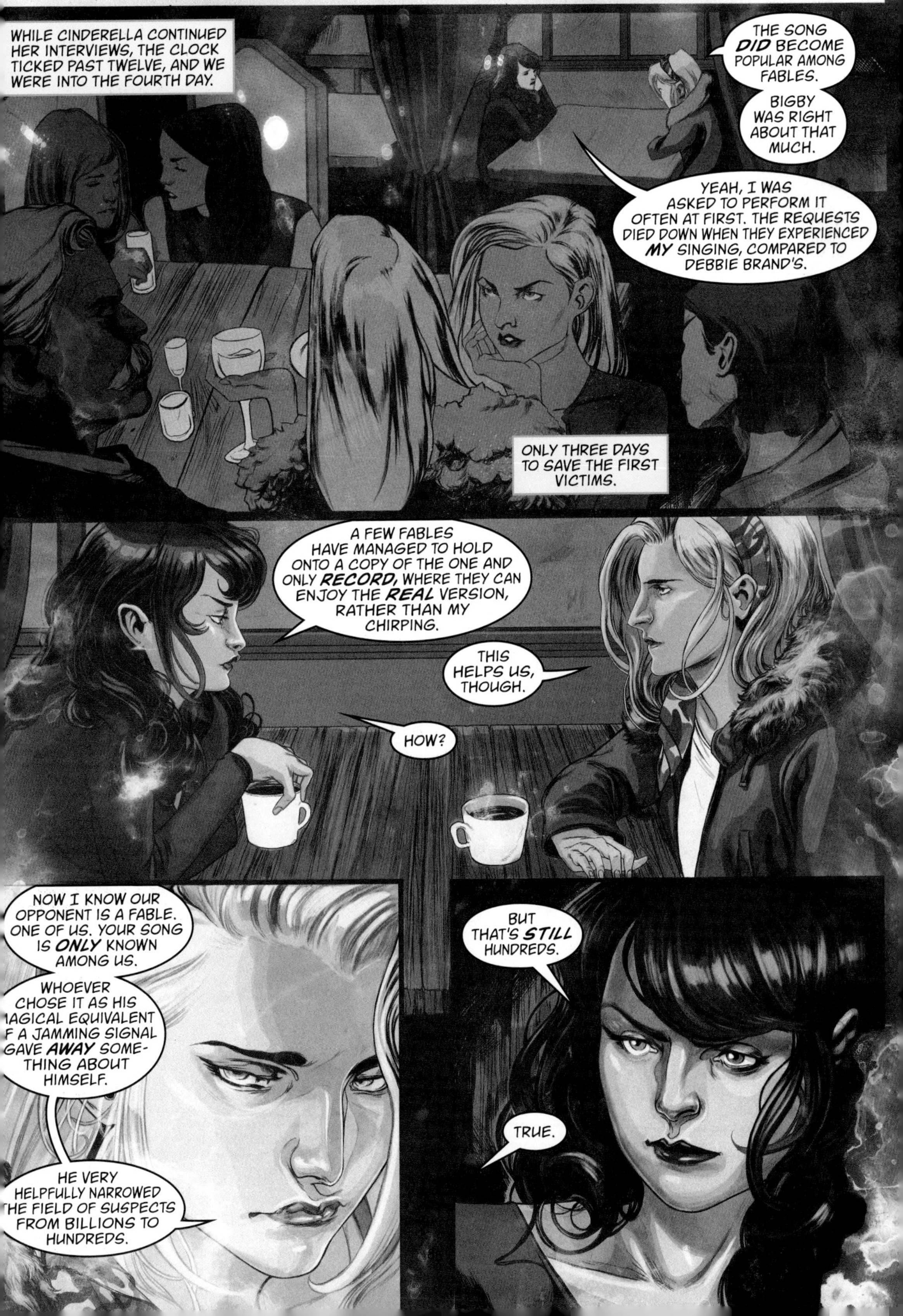

WHILE CINDERELLA CONTINUED HER INTERVIEWS, THE CLOCK TICKED PAST TWELVE, AND WE WERE INTO THE FOURTH DAY.
THE SONG DID BECOME POPULAR AMONG FABLES.
BIGBY WAS RIGHT ABOUT THAT MUCH.
YEAH, I WAS ASKED TO PERFORM IT OFTEN AT FIRST. THE REQUESTS DIED DOWN WHEN THEY EXPERIENCED MY SINGING, COMPARED TO DEBBIE BRAND'S.
ONLY THREE DAYS TO SAVE THE FIRST VICTIMS.
A FEW FABLES HAVE MANAGED TO HOLD ONTO A COPY OF THE ONE AND ONLY RECORD, WHERE THEY CAN ENJOY THE REAL VERSION, RATHER THAN MY CHIRPING.
THIS HELPS US, THOUGH.
HOW?
NOW I KNOW OUR OPPONENT IS A FABLE. ONE OF US. YOUR SONG IS ONLY KNOWN AMONG US.
WHOEVER CHOSE IT AS HIS AGICAL EQUIVALENT F A JAMMING SIGNAL GAVE AWAY SOME-THING ABOUT HIMSELF.
HE VERY HELPFULLY NARROWED THE FIELD OF SUSPECTS FROM BILLIONS TO HUNDREDS.
BUT THAT'S STILL HUNDREDS.
TRUE.

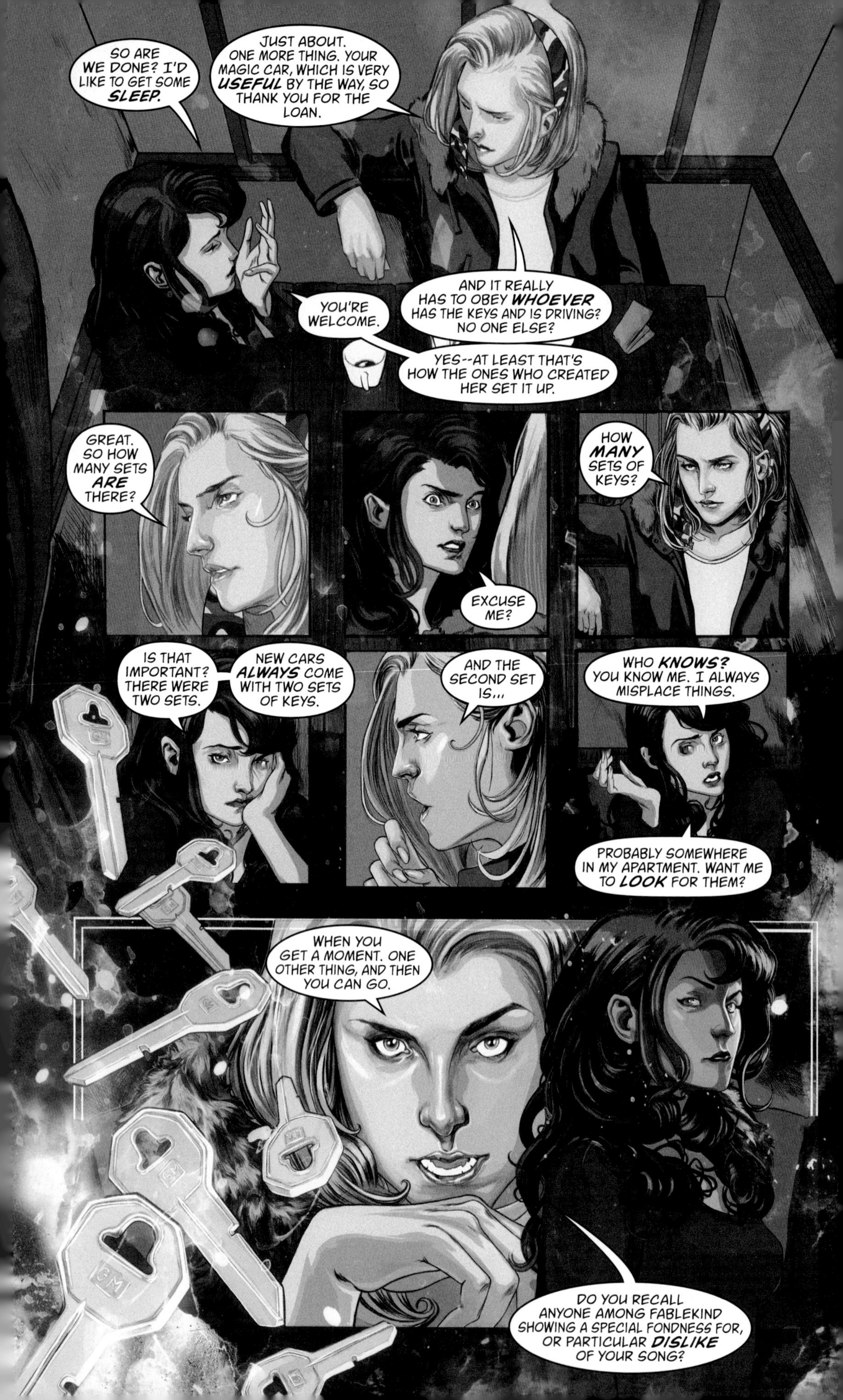

SO ARE WE DONE? I'D LIKE TO GET SOME SLEEP.
JUST ABOUT. ONE MORE THING. YOUR MAGIC CAR, WHICH IS VERY USEFUL BY THE WAY, SO THANK YOU FOR THE LOAN.
YOU'RE WELCOME.
AND IT REALLY HAS TO OBEY WHOEVER HAS THE KEYS AND IS DRIVING? NO ONE ELSE?
YES--AT LEAST THAT'S HOW THE ONES WHO CREATED HER SET IT UP.
GREAT. SO HOW MANY SETS ARE THERE?
EXCUSE ME?
HOW MANY SETS OF KEYS?
IS THAT IMPORTANT? THERE WERE TWO SETS.
NEW CARS ALWAYS COME WITH TWO SETS OF KEYS.
AND THE SECOND SET IS...
WHO KNOWS? YOU KNOW ME. I ALWAYS MISPLACE THINGS.
PROBABLY SOMEWHERE IN MY APARTMENT. WANT ME TO LOOK FOR THEM?
WHEN YOU GET A MOMENT. ONE OTHER THING, AND THEN YOU CAN GO.
DO YOU RECALL ANYONE AMONG FABLEKIND SHOWING A SPECIAL FONDNESS FOR, OR PARTICULAR DISLIKE OF YOUR SONG?

1972

Tony Akins: artist • Lee Loughridge: colorist

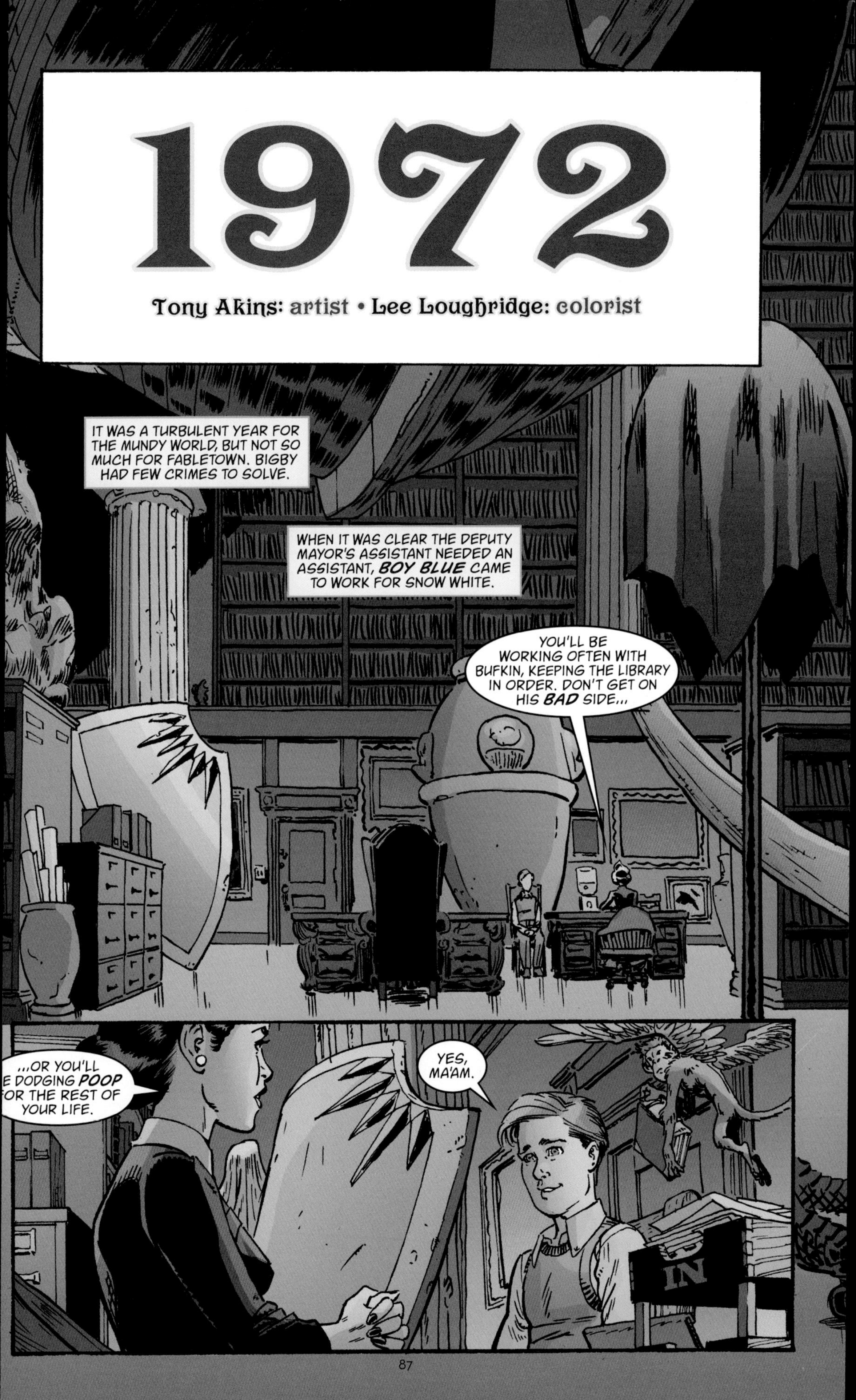

IT WAS A TURBULENT YEAR FOR THE MUNDY WORLD, BUT NOT SO MUCH FOR FABLETOWN. BIGBY HAD FEW CRIMES TO SOLVE.
WHEN IT WAS CLEAR THE DEPUTY MAYOR'S ASSISTANT NEEDED AN ASSISTANT, BOY BLUE CAME TO WORK FOR SNOW WHITE.
YOU'LL BE WORKING OFTEN WITH BUFKIN, KEEPING THE LIBRARY IN ORDER. DON'T GET ON HIS BAD SIDE...
...OR YOU'LL E DODGING POOP OR THE REST OF YOUR LIFE.
YES, MA'AM.
IN

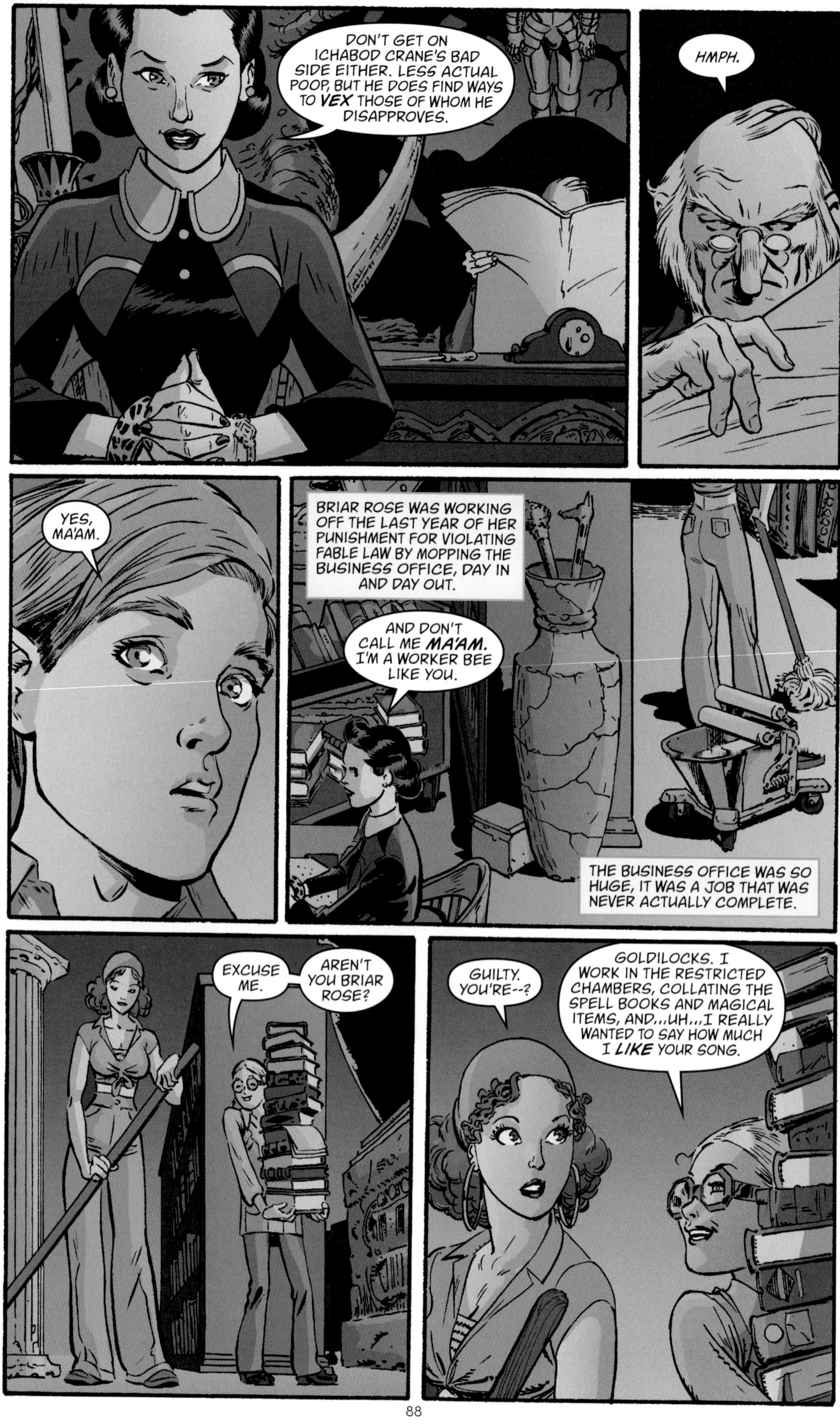

DON'T GET ON ICHABOD CRANE'S BAD SIDE EITHER. LESS ACTUAL POOP, BUT HE DOES FIND WAYS TO VEX THOSE OF WHOM HE DISAPPROVES.
HMPH.
YES, MA'AM.
BRIAR ROSE WAS WORKING OFF THE LAST YEAR OF HER PUNISHMENT FOR VIOLATING FABLE LAW BY MOPPING THE BUSINESS OFFICE, DAY IN AND DAY OUT.
AND DON'T CALL ME MA'AM. I'M A WORKER BEE LIKE YOU.
THE BUSINESS OFFICE WAS SO HUGE, IT WAS A JOB THAT WAS NEVER ACTUALLY COMPLETE.
EXCUSE ME.
AREN'T YOU BRIAR ROSE?
GUILTY. YOU'RE--?
GOLDILOCKS. I WORK IN THE RESTRICTED CHAMBERS, COLLATING THE SPELL BOOKS AND MAGICAL ITEMS, AND...UH...I REALLY WANTED TO SAY HOW MUCH I LIKE YOUR SONG.

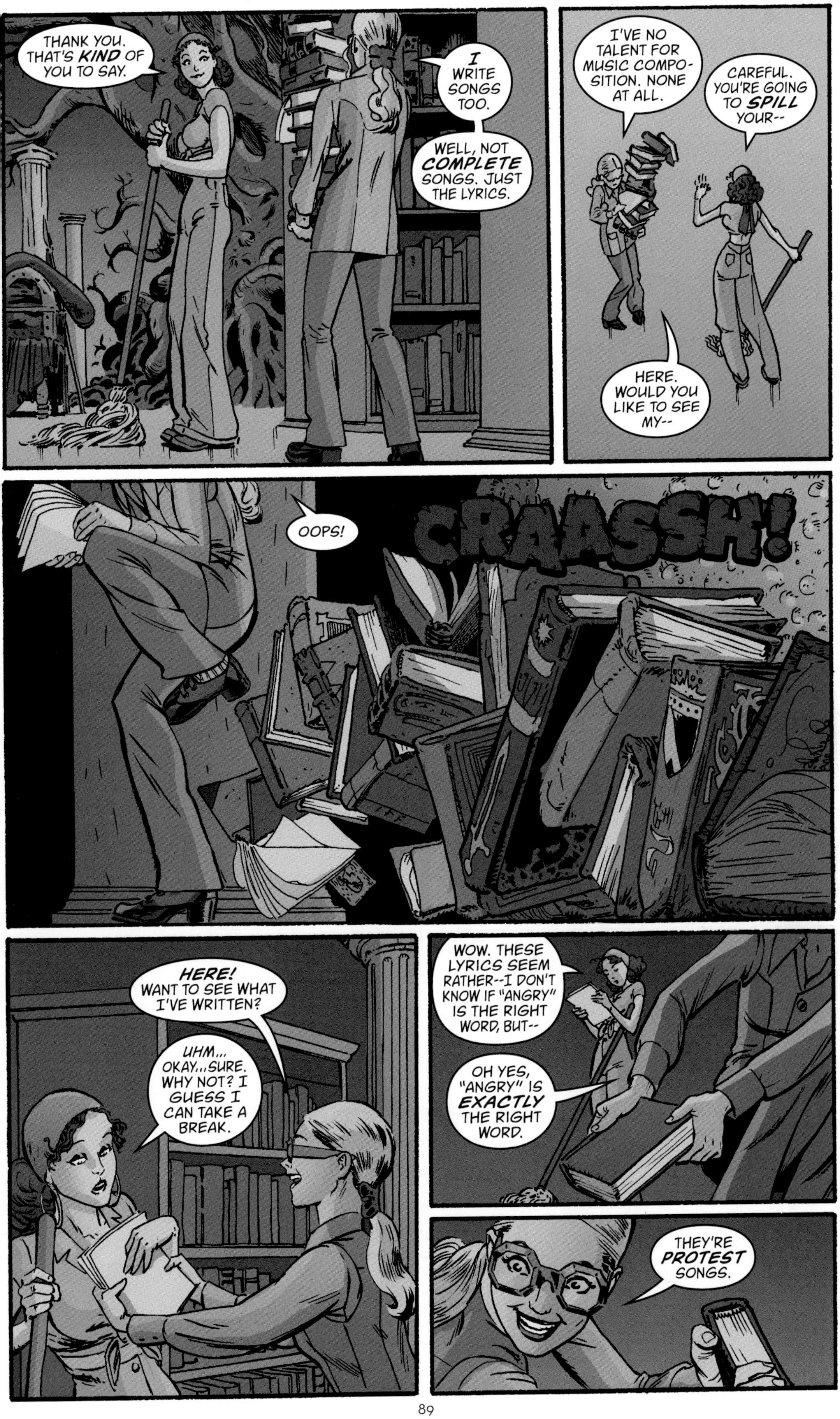
THANK YOU. THAT'S KIND OF YOU TO SAY.
I WRITE SONGS TOO.
WELL, NOT COMPLETE SONGS. JUST THE LYRICS.
I'VE NO TALENT FOR MUSIC COMPO-SITION. NONE AT ALL.
CAREFUL. YOU'RE GOING TO SPILL YOUR--
HERE. WOULD YOU LIKE TO SEE MY--
OOPS!
CRAASSH!
HERE! WANT TO SEE WHAT I'VE WRITTEN?
UHM... OKAY...SURE. WHY NOT? I GUESS I CAN TAKE A BREAK.
WOW. THESE LYRICS SEEM RATHER--I DON'T KNOW IF "ANGRY" IS THE RIGHT WORD, BUT--
OH YES, "ANGRY" IS EXACTLY THE RIGHT WORD.
THEY'RE PROTEST SONGS.

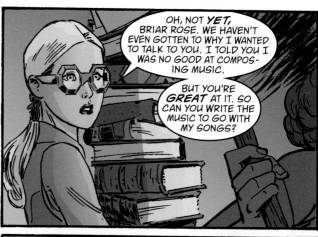

I'M INSPIRED BY WOODY GUTHRIE, JOE HILL, AUNT MOLLY JACKSON, AND--WELL, *ALL* THE GREATS.

OKAY, SO...UH... GOOD LUCK WITH THESE. IT WAS GREAT MEETING YOU, GOLDILOCKS, BUT I REALLY SHOULD GET BACK *TO* IT.

OH, NOT *YET,* BRIAR ROSE. WE HAVEN'T EVEN GOTTEN TO WHY I WANTED TO TALK TO YOU. I TOLD YOU I WAS NO GOOD AT COMPOS- ING MUSIC.

BUT YOU'RE *GREAT* AT IT. SO CAN YOU WRITE THE MUSIC TO GO WITH MY SONGS?

THAT'S QUITE A TALL ORDER.

MAYBE I'D HAVE TIME TO THINK ABOUT IT *SOMEDAY,* BUT I'M KEPT PRETTY BUSY JUST NOW.

OH *NO,* THAT WON'T DO. IT JUST WON'T DO. I'M *LEAVING* SOON.

I'M BEING TRANSFERRED UP TO THE *FARM* IN A MONTH AND I WANT ALL OF THESE SONGS READY TO GO *WITH* ME.

WHILE I MAY APPRECIATE THAT, IT'S NOT *MY* RESPONSIBILITY NOW, IS IT?

OH? WHAT DO YOU MEAN?

YOU'RE FORCING ME TO BE *BLUNT.*

I'M *NOT* GOING TO SET THOSE INCENDIARY WORDS TO MUSIC. I WOULDN'T DO SO HAD I ALL THE TIME IN THE WORLD. YOUR CAUSES AREN'T *MY* CAUSES.

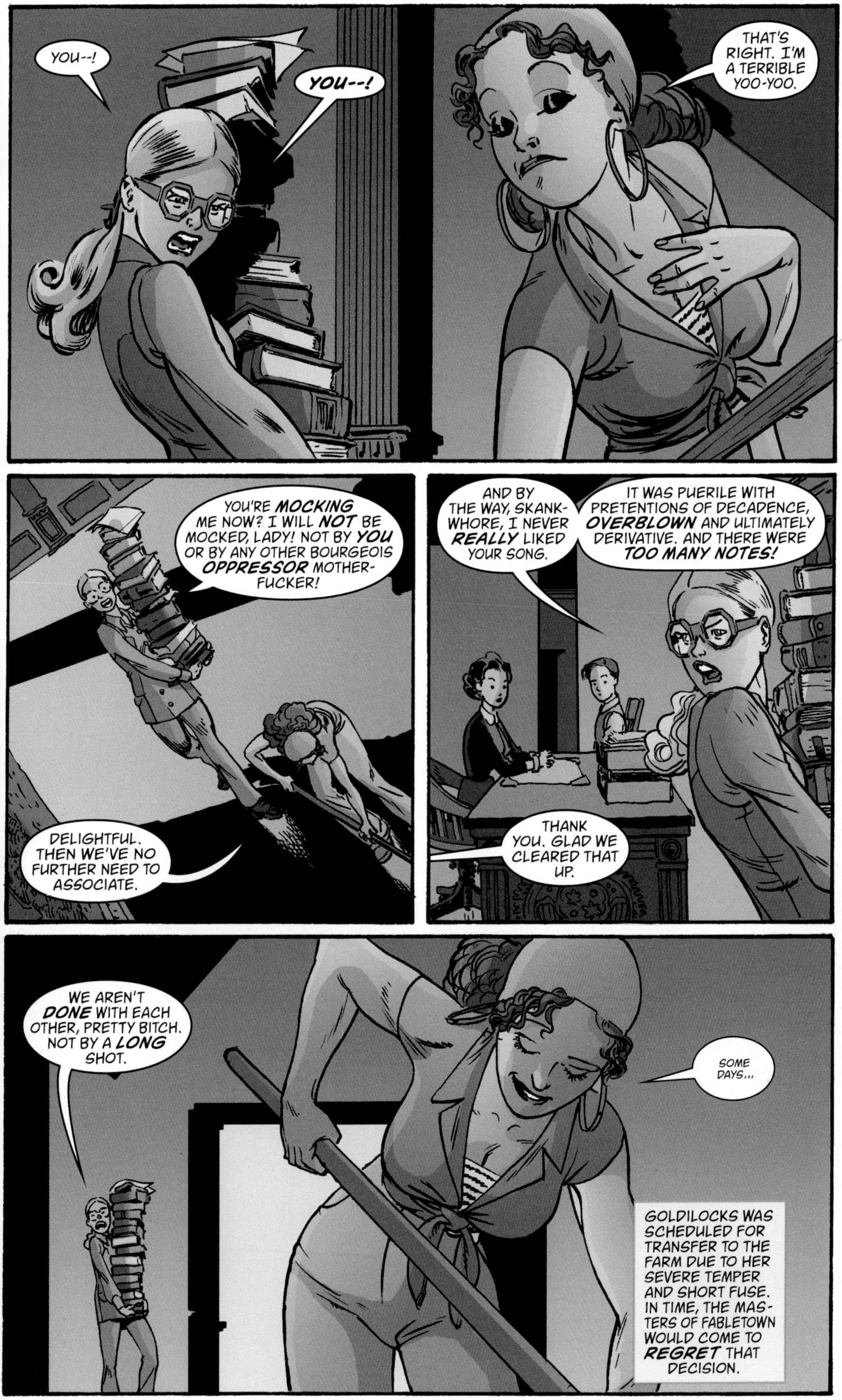
YOU--!
YOU--!
THAT'S RIGHT. I'M A TERRIBLE YOO-YOO.
YOU'RE MOCKING ME NOW? I WILL NOT BE MOCKED, LADY! NOT BY YOU OR BY ANY OTHER BOURGEOIS OPPRESSOR MOTHER-FUCKER!
DELIGHTFUL. THEN WE'VE NO FURTHER NEED TO ASSOCIATE.
AND BY THE WAY, SKANK-WHORE, I NEVER REALLY LIKED YOUR SONG.
IT WAS PUERILE WITH PRETENTIONS OF DECADENCE, OVERBLOWN AND ULTIMATELY DERIVATIVE. AND THERE WERE TOO MANY NOTES!
THANK YOU. GLAD WE CLEARED THAT UP.
WE AREN'T DONE WITH EACH OTHER, PRETTY BITCH. NOT BY A LONG SHOT.
SOME DAYS...
GOLDILOCKS WAS SCHEDULED FOR TRANSFER TO THE FARM DUE TO HER SEVERE TEMPER AND SHORT FUSE. IN TIME, THE MAS-TERS OF FABLETOWN WOULD COME TO REGRET THAT DECISION.

THE TESTIMONY OF BROCK BLUEHEART

Dean Ormston: artist • Lee Loughridge: colorist

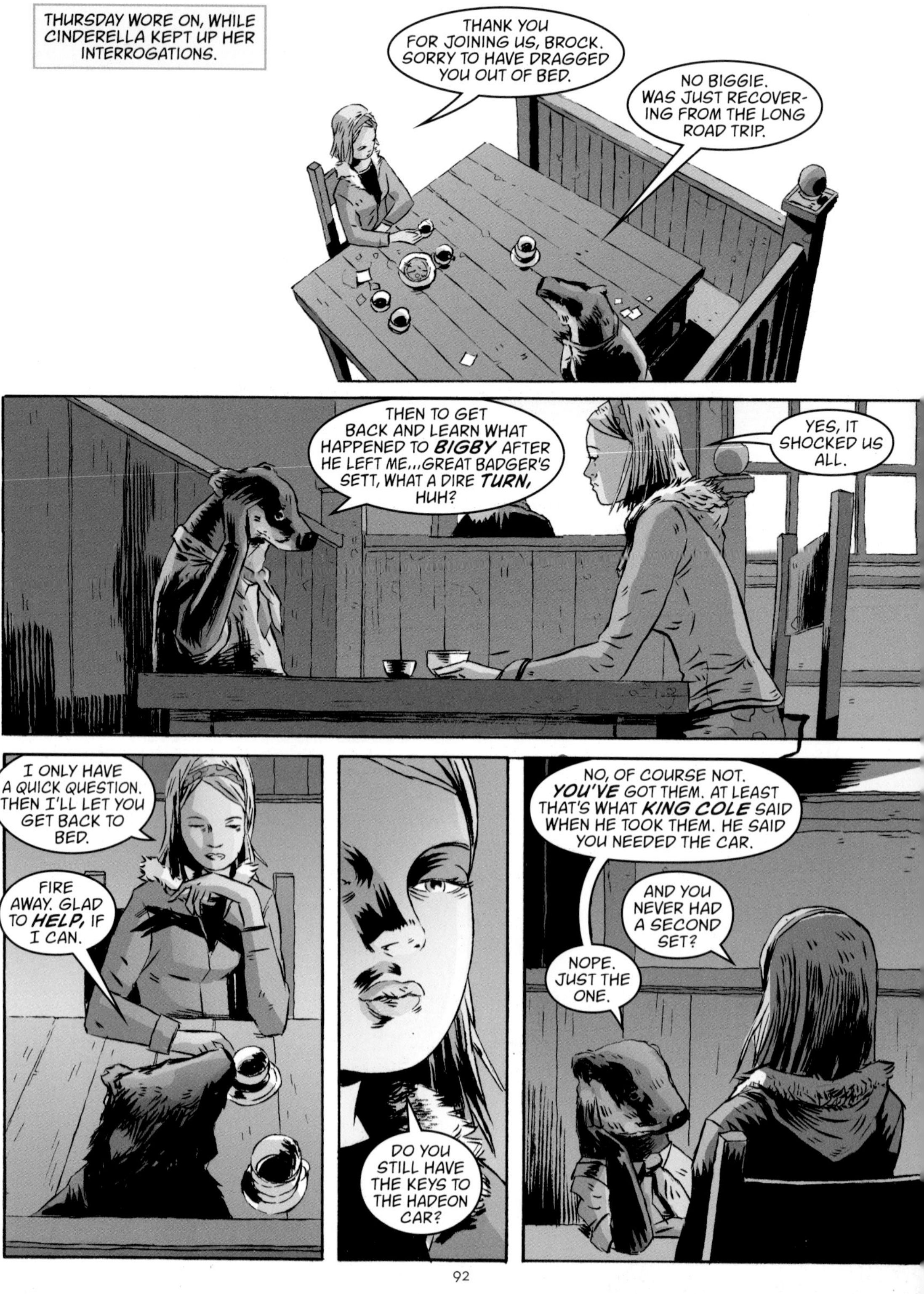
THURSDAY WORE ON, WHILE CINDERELLA KEPT UP HER INTERROGATIONS.
THANK YOU FOR JOINING US, BROCK. SORRY TO HAVE DRAGGED YOU OUT OF BED.
NO BIGGIE. WAS JUST RECOVERING FROM THE LONG ROAD TRIP.
THEN TO GET BACK AND LEARN WHAT HAPPENED TO *BIGBY* AFTER HE LEFT ME...GREAT BADGER'S SETT, WHAT A DIRE *TURN,* HUH?
YES, IT SHOCKED US ALL.
I ONLY HAVE A QUICK QUESTION. THEN I'LL LET YOU GET BACK TO BED.
FIRE AWAY. GLAD TO *HELP,* IF I CAN.
DO YOU STILL HAVE THE KEYS TO THE HADEON CAR?
NO, OF COURSE NOT. *YOU'VE* GOT THEM. AT LEAST THAT'S WHAT *KING COLE* SAID WHEN HE TOOK THEM. HE SAID YOU NEEDED THE CAR.
AND YOU NEVER HAD A SECOND SET?
NOPE. JUST THE ONE.

MOSTLY WE JUST LEFT THEM IN THE IGNITION, FOR WHEN WE SWITCHED DRIVERS.

WHEN YOU AND BIGBY SWITCHED?

YEAH, AND THEN ME AND THE GIRL, AFTER BIGS LEFT.

GIRL? *WHAT* GIRL?

HEY, YOU CAN'T BLAME ME. A ROAD TRIP LIKE THAT IS A *MINIMUM* TWO-MAN OPERATION. DRIVERS NEED TO SWITCH OFF, RIGHT?

WHEN BIGBY CUT OUT ON ME--FOR DAMN *GOOD* REASONS, MIND YOU, SO I'M NOT BLAMING ANYONE--WHEN HE LEFT, I WORE MYSELF *OUT* TRYING TO DO IT ALL ON MY OWN.

SO I PICKED UP A GIRL. BUT DON'T WORRY. SHE WAS A *FABLE*. I DON'T SPILL SECRETS TO OUTSIDERS.

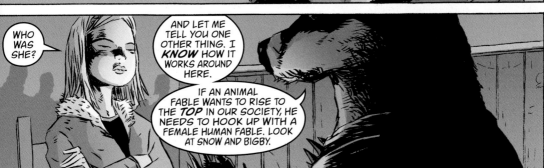

WHO WAS SHE?

AND LET ME TELL YOU ONE OTHER THING. I *KNOW* HOW IT WORKS AROUND HERE.

IF AN ANIMAL FABLE WANTS TO RISE TO THE *TOP* IN OUR SOCIETY, HE NEEDS TO HOOK UP WITH A FEMALE HUMAN FABLE. LOOK AT SNOW AND BIGBY.

SO OF COURSE I WAS GOING TO TRY IT OUT. AND I *DID.* AND LET ME TELL YOU: IT *SUCKED.* CROSS SPECIES HANKY-PANKY JUST ISN'T FOR ME.

EVEN THOUGH SHE WAS INTO ALL SORTS OF FREAKY STUFF. AND I *DO* MEAN *FREAK!*

STINKY! *WHO WAS SHE?*

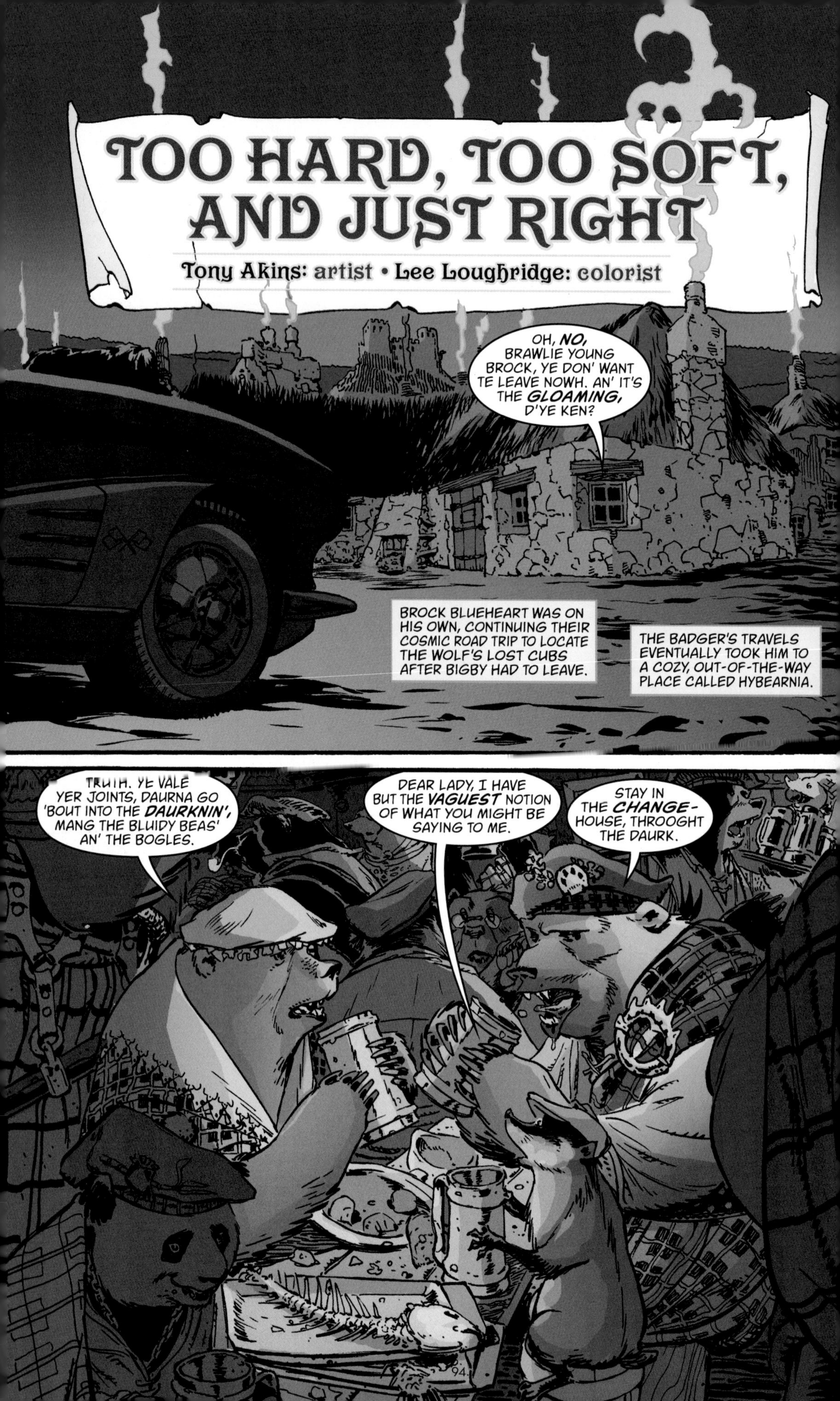
TOO HARD, TOO SOFT, AND JUST RIGHT
Tony Akins: artist • Lee Loughridge: colorist
OH, NO, BRAWLIE YOUNG BROCK, YE DON' WANT TE LEAVE NOWH. AN' IT'S THE GLOAMING, D'YE KEN?
BROCK BLUEHEART WAS ON HIS OWN, CONTINUING THEIR COSMIC ROAD TRIP TO LOCATE THE WOLF'S LOST CUBS AFTER BIGBY HAD TO LEAVE.
THE BADGER'S TRAVELS EVENTUALLY TOOK HIM TO A COZY, OUT-OF-THE-WAY PLACE CALLED HYBEARNIA.
TRUTH. YE VALE YER JOINTS, DAURNA GO 'BOUT INTO THE DAURKNIN', MANG THE BLUIDY BEAS' AN' THE BOGLES.
DEAR LADY, I HAVE BUT THE VAGUEST NOTION OF WHAT YOU MIGHT BE SAYING TO ME.
STAY IN THE CHANGE-HOUSE, THROOGHT THE DAURK.

YES, THAT'S QUITE INTERESTING.

NOW, BACK TO WHAT I WAS SAYING ABOUT THE MISSING CHILDREN...

AYE, YER BLETHERSKATE ABOOT LOST BAIRNS IN BLAE, WA COME TE *SAUF* US ALL SOMEDAWIN' HYNE?

NO, NO NO! YOU'RE MIXING UP TWO CONVERSATIONS.

ON THE *ONE* HAND I'M LOOKING FOR A FRIEND'S TWO LOST CHILDREN.

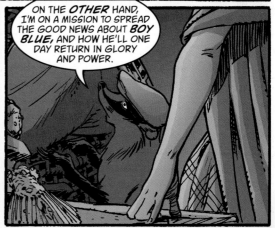

ON THE *OTHER* HAND, I'M ON A MISSION TO SPREAD THE GOOD NEWS ABOUT *BOY BLUE*, AND HOW HE'LL ONE DAY RETURN IN GLORY AND POWER.

TWO SEPARATE THINGS. UNDERSTAND?

HEY, *I* KNOW YOU.

GOLDILOCKS?

WHAT ARE *YOU* DOING WAY OUT HERE IN THE MIDDLE OF NOWHERE?

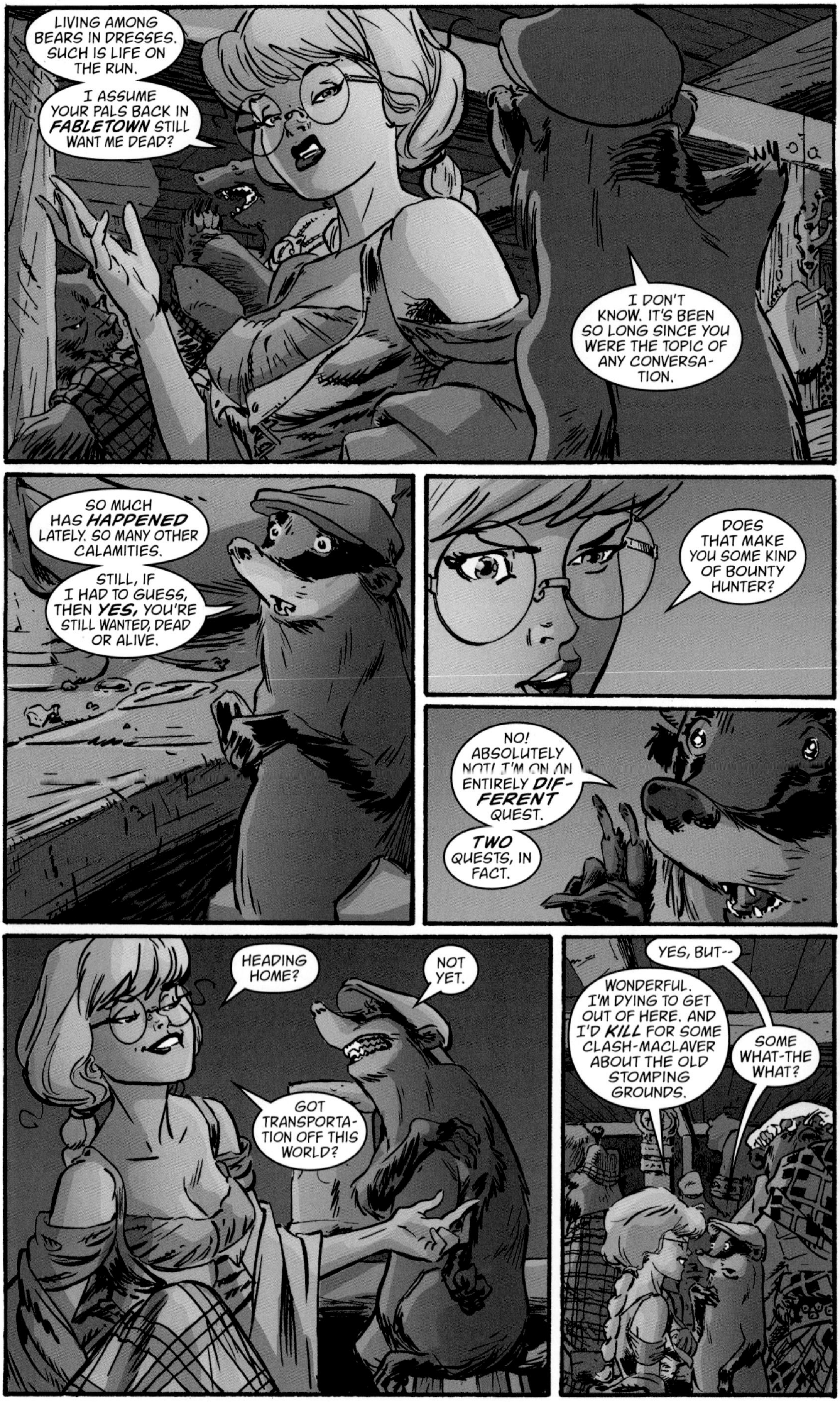

LIVING AMONG BEARS IN DRESSES. SUCH IS LIFE ON THE RUN.
I ASSUME YOUR PALS BACK IN FABLETOWN STILL WANT ME DEAD?
I DON'T KNOW. IT'S BEEN SO LONG SINCE YOU WERE THE TOPIC OF ANY CONVERSATION.
SO MUCH HAS HAPPENED LATELY. SO MANY OTHER CALAMITIES.
STILL, IF I HAD TO GUESS, THEN YES, YOU'RE STILL WANTED, DEAD OR ALIVE.
DOES THAT MAKE YOU SOME KIND OF BOUNTY HUNTER?
NO! ABSOLUTELY NOT! I'M ON AN ENTIRELY DIFFERENT QUEST.
TWO QUESTS, IN FACT.
HEADING HOME?
NOT YET.
GOT TRANSPORTATION OFF THIS WORLD?
YES, BUT--
WONDERFUL. I'M DYING TO GET OUT OF HERE. AND I'D KILL FOR SOME CLASH-MACLAVER ABOUT THE OLD STOMPING GROUNDS.
SOME WHAT-THE WHAT?

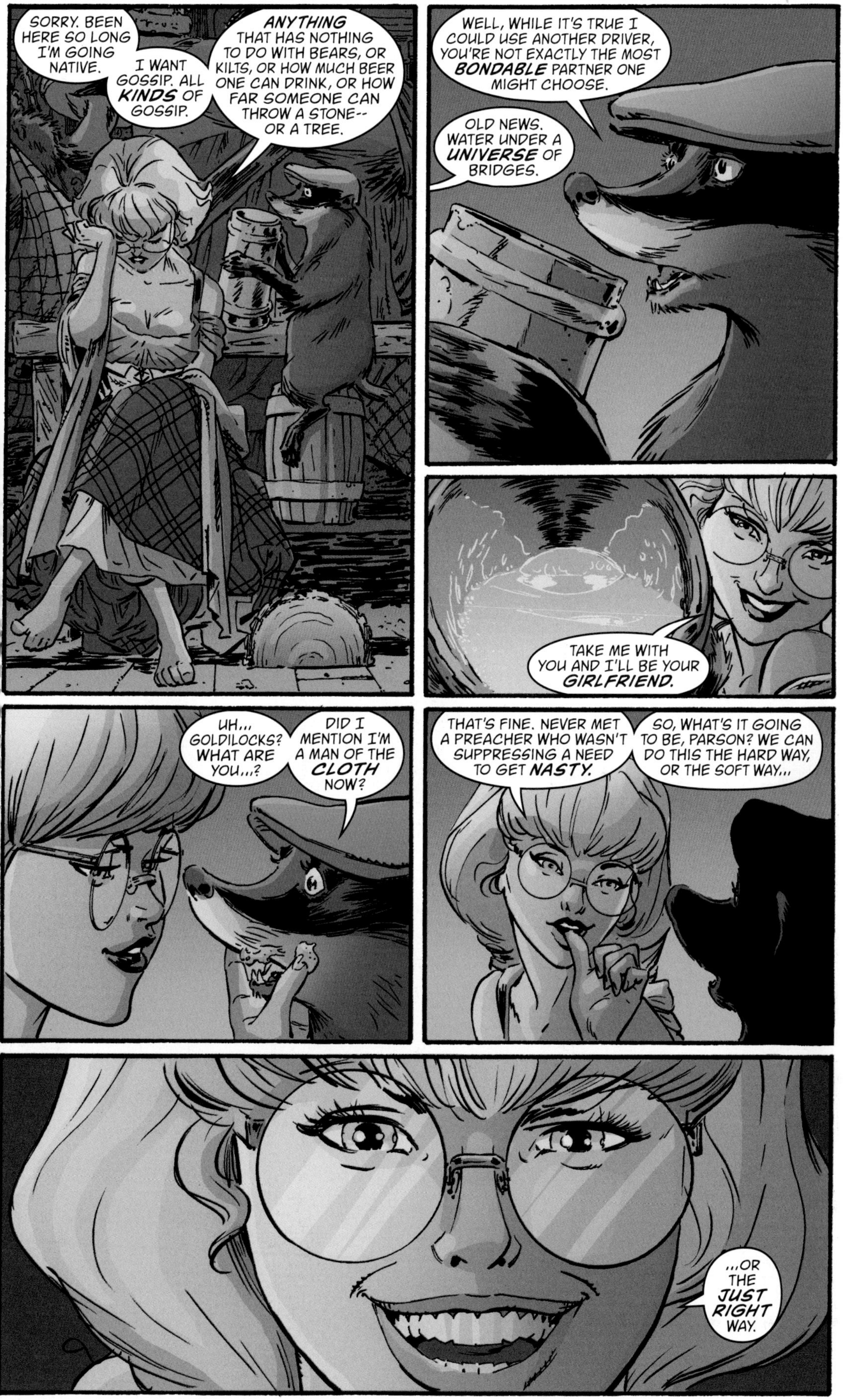
SORRY. BEEN HERE SO LONG I'M GOING NATIVE.
I WANT GOSSIP. ALL KINDS OF GOSSIP.
ANYTHING THAT HAS NOTHING TO DO WITH BEARS, OR KILTS, OR HOW MUCH BEER ONE CAN DRINK, OR HOW FAR SOMEONE CAN THROW A STONE-- OR A TREE.
WELL, WHILE IT'S TRUE I COULD USE ANOTHER DRIVER, YOU'RE NOT EXACTLY THE MOST BONDABLE PARTNER ONE MIGHT CHOOSE.
OLD NEWS. WATER UNDER A UNIVERSE OF BRIDGES.
TAKE ME WITH YOU AND I'LL BE YOUR GIRLFRIEND.
UH... GOLDILOCKS? WHAT ARE YOU...?
DID I MENTION I'M A MAN OF THE CLOTH NOW?
THAT'S FINE. NEVER MET A PREACHER WHO WASN'T SUPPRESSING A NEED TO GET NASTY.
SO, WHAT'S IT GOING TO BE, PARSON? WE CAN DO THIS THE HARD WAY, OR THE SOFT WAY...
...OR THE JUST RIGHT WAY.

THE TESTIMONY OF BO PEEP

Ming Doyle: artist

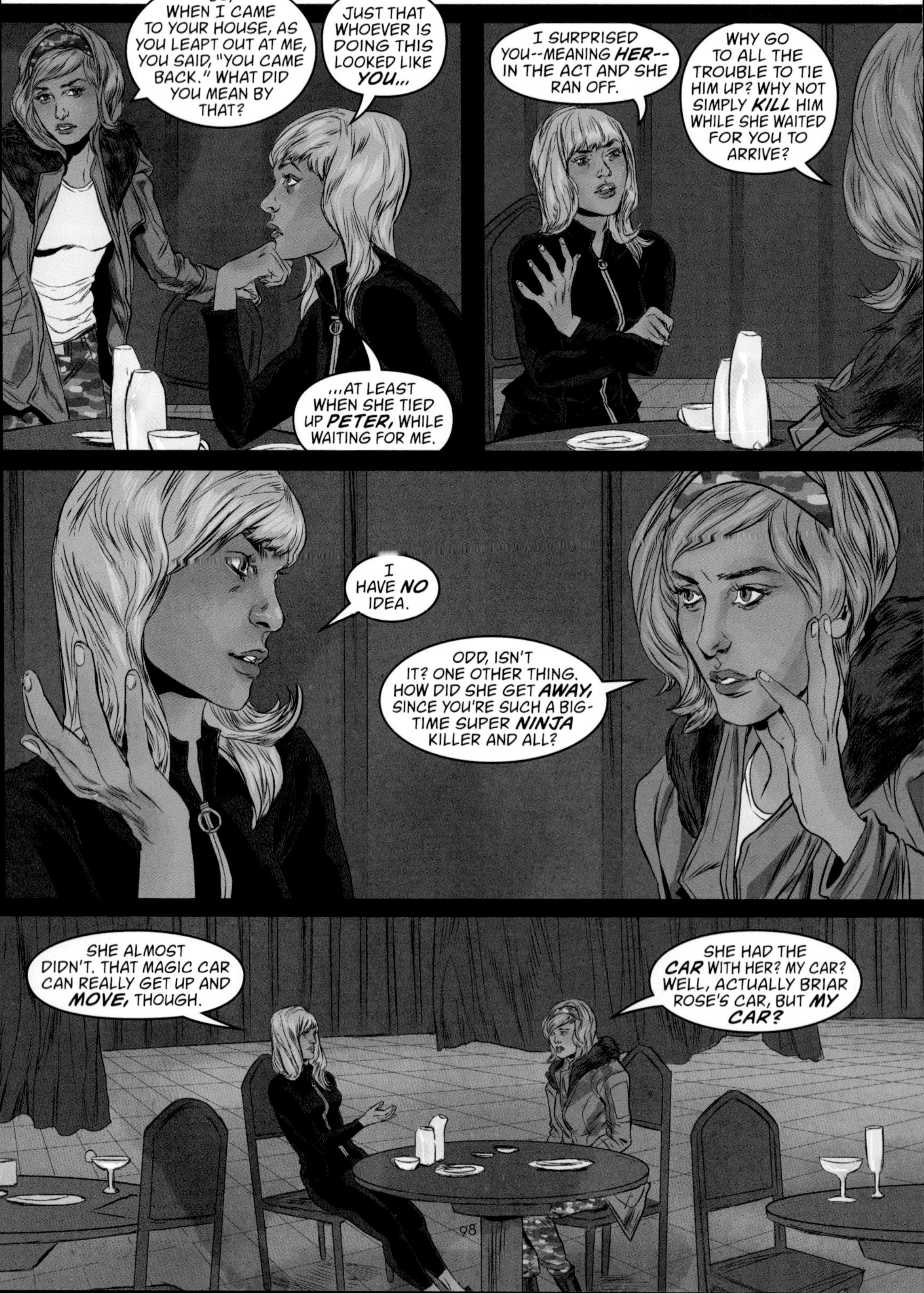
BO, WHEN I CAME TO YOUR HOUSE, AS YOU LEAPT OUT AT ME, YOU SAID, "YOU CAME BACK." WHAT DID YOU MEAN BY THAT?
JUST THAT WHOEVER IS DOING THIS LOOKED LIKE *YOU*...
...AT LEAST WHEN SHE TIED UP *PETER,* WHILE WAITING FOR ME.
I SURPRISED YOU--MEANING *HER*-- IN THE ACT AND SHE RAN OFF.
WHY GO TO ALL THE TROUBLE TO TIE HIM UP? WHY NOT SIMPLY *KILL* HIM WHILE SHE WAITED FOR YOU TO ARRIVE?
I HAVE *NO* IDEA.
ODD, ISN'T IT? ONE OTHER THING. HOW DID SHE GET *AWAY,* SINCE YOU'RE SUCH A BIG-TIME SUPER *NINJA* KILLER AND ALL?
SHE ALMOST DIDN'T. THAT MAGIC CAR CAN REALLY GET UP AND *MOVE,* THOUGH.
SHE HAD THE *CAR* WITH HER? MY CAR? WELL, ACTUALLY BRIAR ROSE'S CAR, BUT *MY CAR?*

FRIDAY

In the wee hours of Friday morning, feeling the pressure of the clock slipping away from us, and determined to find some way to help, I gathered all of the Barleycorn Women together, along with my permanently captive audience of heads.

"None of us have specific powers of communication across great distances," I said. "But we're all highly magical beings, and we're surrounded by a host of magic things. We're going to try to draw on this accumulation of energies for a single act of raw, amateur, improvisational spell-making."

"To what end?" Heathclamp, one of the woodenheads, said.

"Ozma in Fabletown is our target," I said. "Now, all at once, everyone concentrating together, we're going to tell her about the Sword of Regret and its power to undo its own mortal work within seven days. All together now, think of nothing else, for the next thirty minutes.

"Ready? Set? Go!"

Who knows? It could work.

A MISCALCULATION OF THE WIZARD CENDRÉE

Renae de Liz: penciller • Ray Dillon: inker & colorist

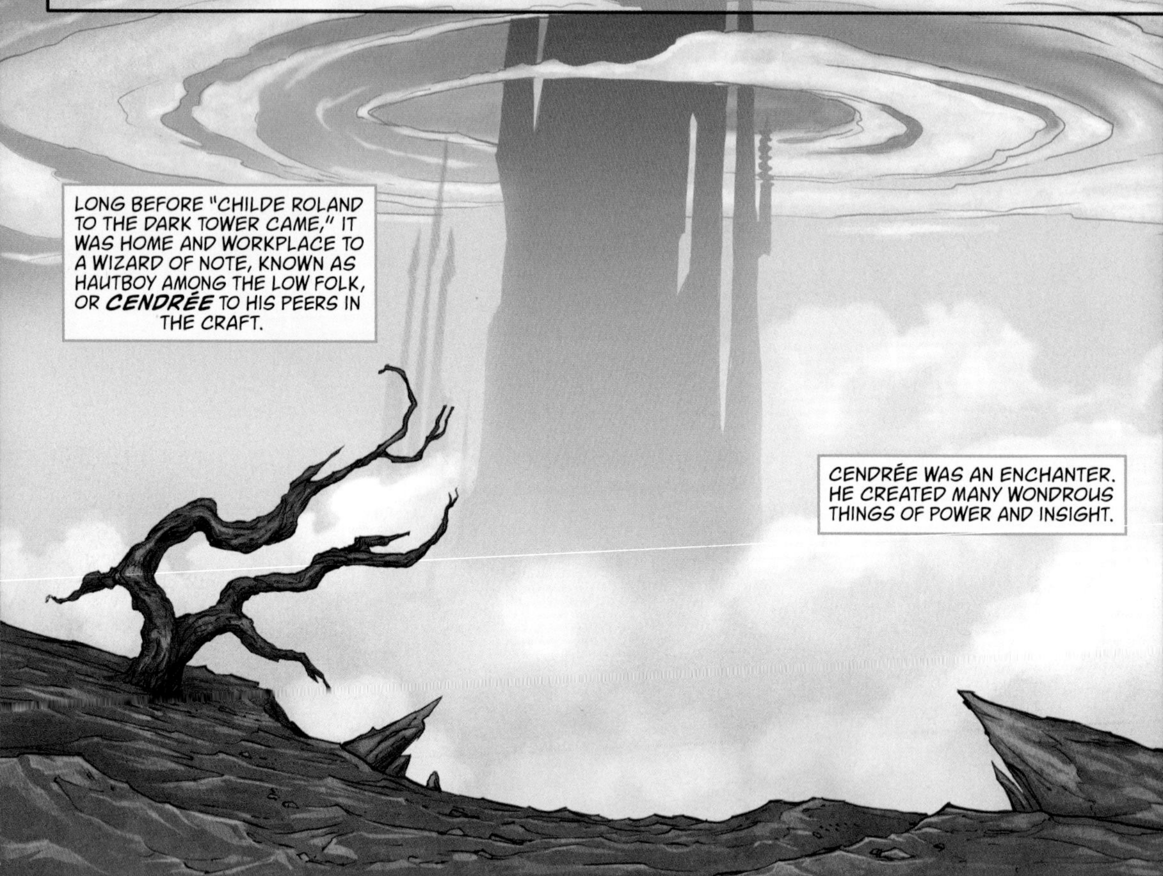
LONG BEFORE "CHILDE ROLAND TO THE DARK TOWER CAME," IT WAS HOME AND WORKPLACE TO A WIZARD OF NOTE, KNOWN AS HAUTBOY AMONG THE LOW FOLK, OR CENDRÉE TO HIS PEERS IN THE CRAFT.
CENDRÉE WAS AN ENCHANTER. HE CREATED MANY WONDROUS THINGS OF POWER AND INSIGHT.

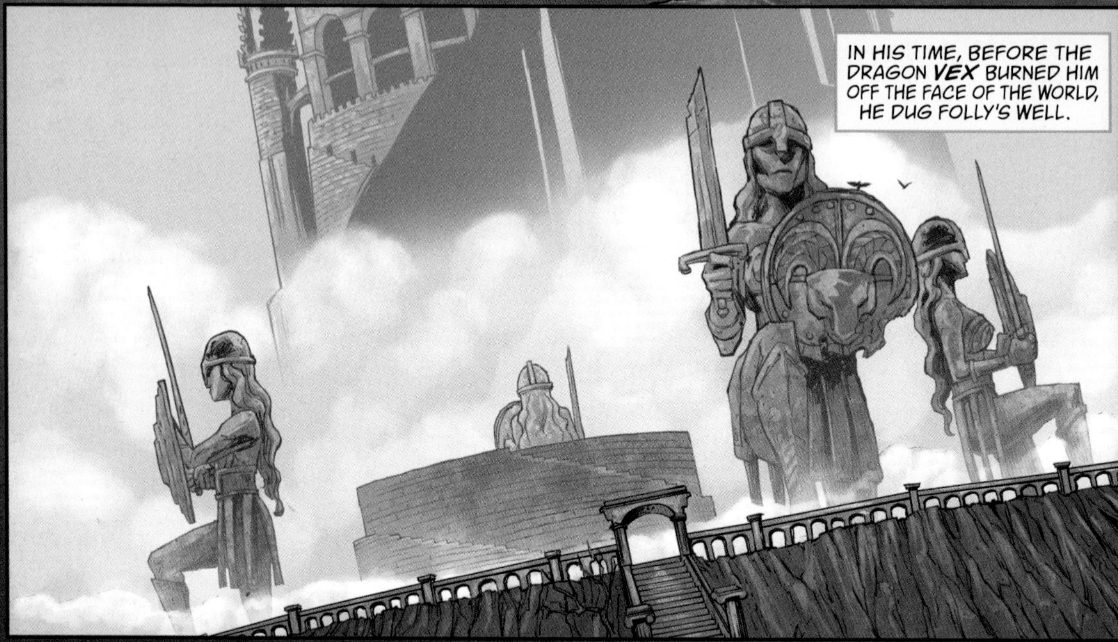
IN HIS TIME, BEFORE THE DRAGON VEX BURNED HIM OFF THE FACE OF THE WORLD, HE DUG FOLLY'S WELL.

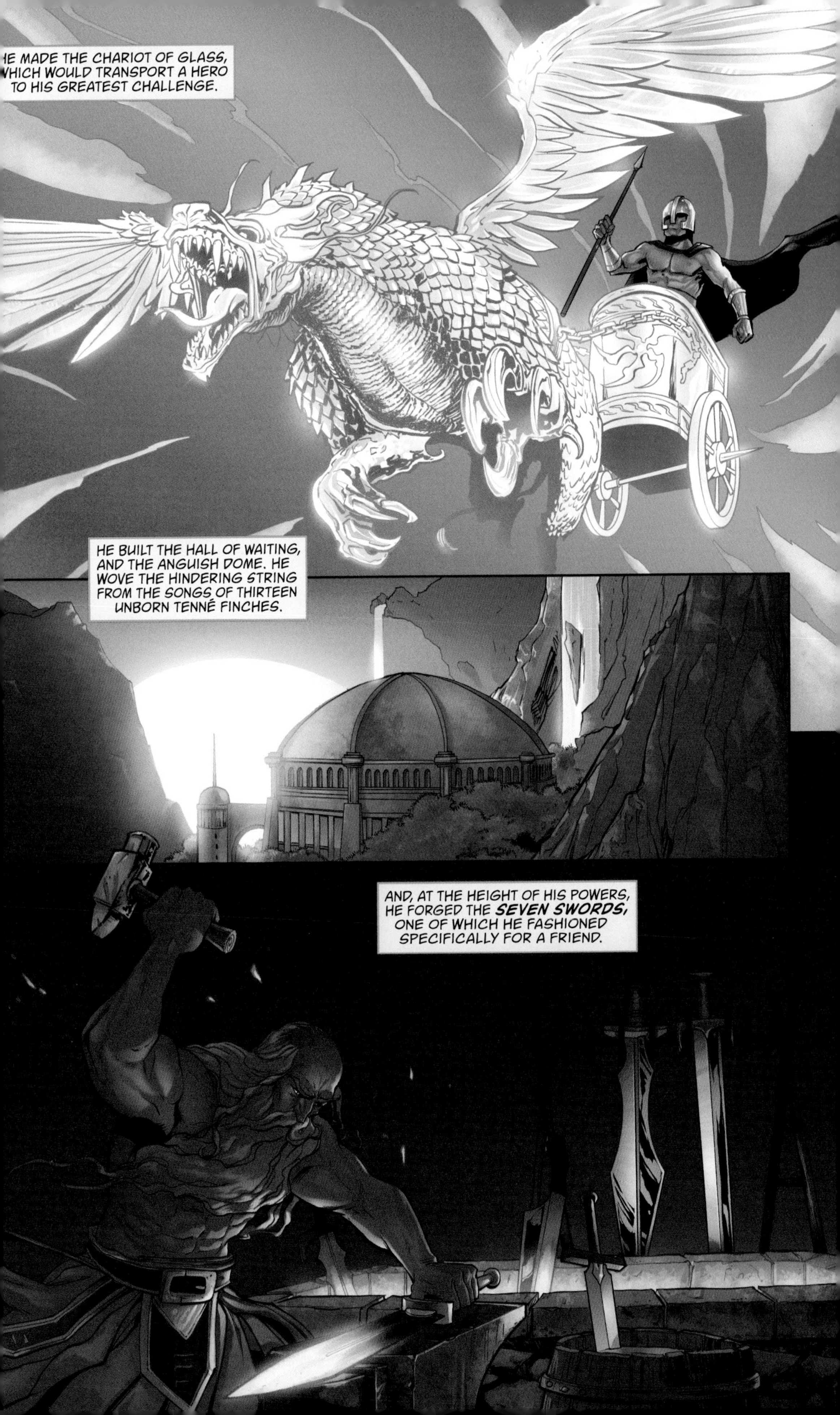
HE MADE THE CHARIOT OF GLASS, WHICH WOULD TRANSPORT A HERO TO HIS GREATEST CHALLENGE.
HE BUILT THE HALL OF WAITING, AND THE ANGUISH DOME. HE WOVE THE HINDERING STRING FROM THE SONGS OF THIRTEEN UNBORN TENNÉ FINCHES.
AND, AT THE HEIGHT OF HIS POWERS, HE FORGED THE ***SEVEN SWORDS,*** ONE OF WHICH HE FASHIONED SPECIFICALLY FOR A FRIEND.

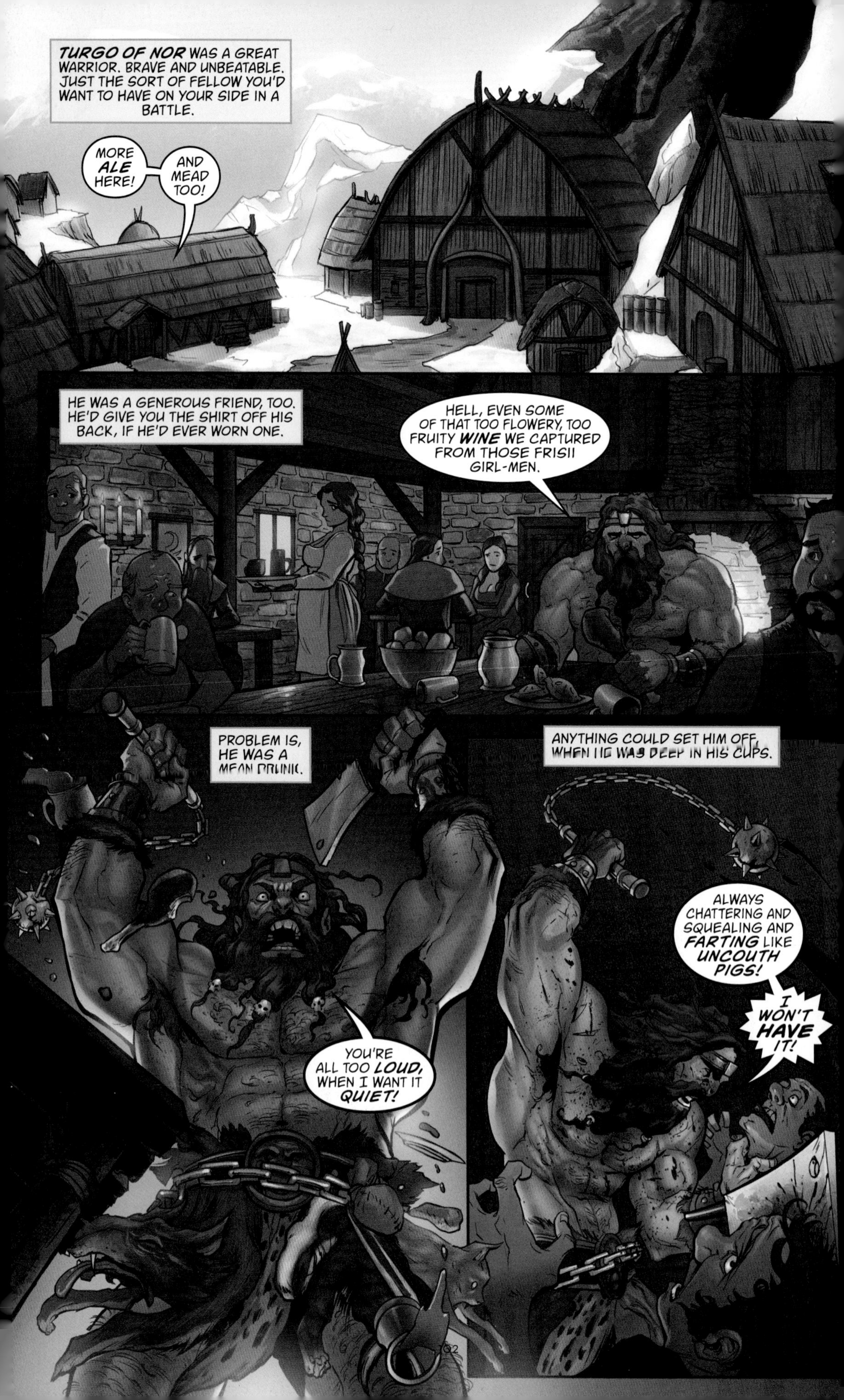

TURGO OF NOR WAS A GREAT WARRIOR. BRAVE AND UNBEATABLE. JUST THE SORT OF FELLOW YOU'D WANT TO HAVE ON YOUR SIDE IN A BATTLE.
MORE ALE HERE!
AND MEAD TOO!
HE WAS A GENEROUS FRIEND, TOO. HE'D GIVE YOU THE SHIRT OFF HIS BACK, IF HE'D EVER WORN ONE.
HELL, EVEN SOME OF THAT TOO FLOWERY, TOO FRUITY WINE WE CAPTURED FROM THOSE FRISII GIRL-MEN.
PROBLEM IS, HE WAS A MEAN DRUNK.
YOU'RE ALL TOO LOUD, WHEN I WANT IT QUIET!
ANYTHING COULD SET HIM OFF, WHEN HE WAS DEEP IN HIS CUPS.
ALWAYS CHATTERING AND SQUEALING AND FARTING LIKE UNCOUTH PIGS!
I WON'T HAVE IT!

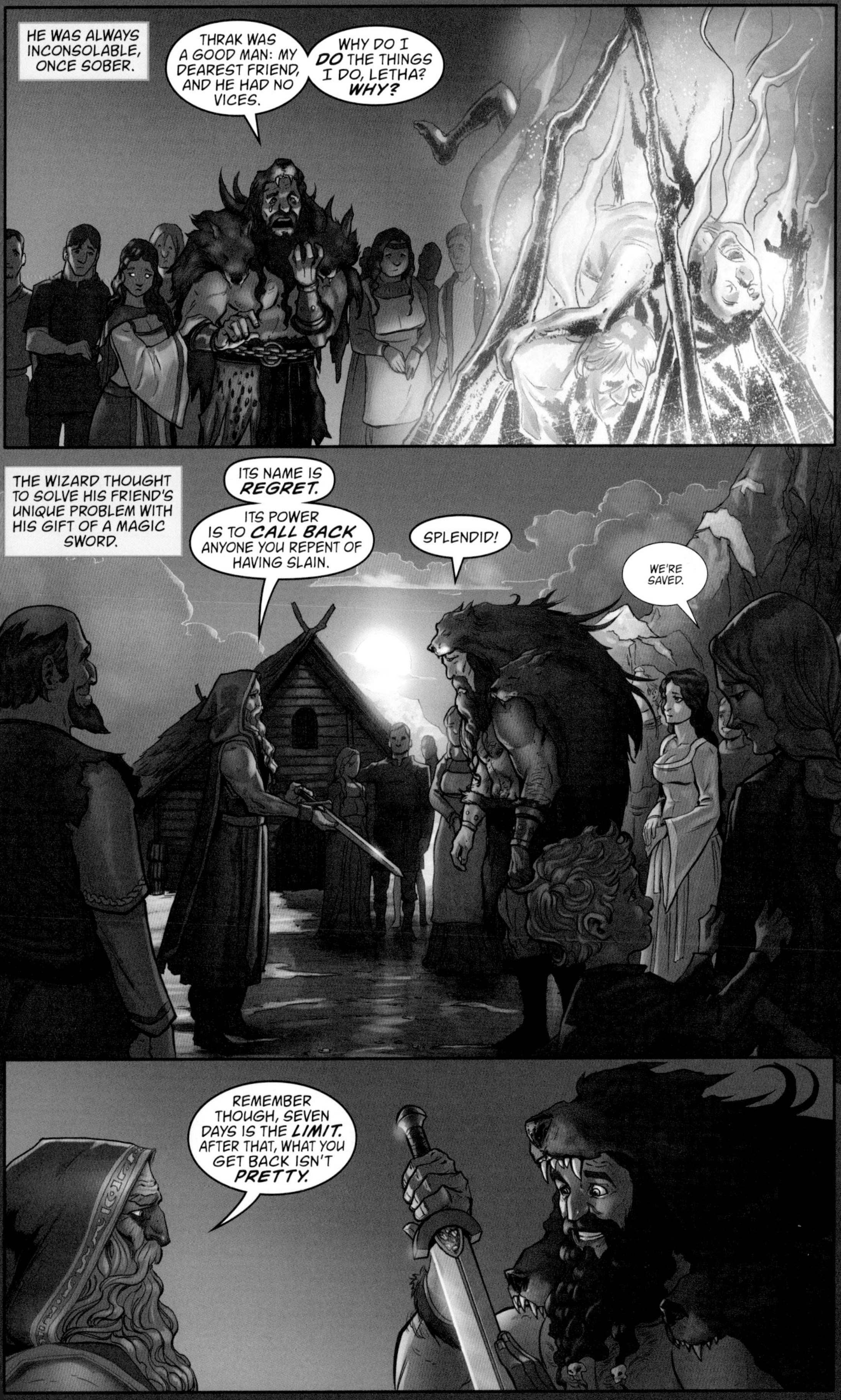
HE WAS ALWAYS INCONSOLABLE, ONCE SOBER.
THRAK WAS A GOOD MAN: MY DEAREST FRIEND, AND HE HAD NO VICES.
WHY DO I DO THE THINGS I DO, LETHA? WHY?
THE WIZARD THOUGHT TO SOLVE HIS FRIEND'S UNIQUE PROBLEM WITH HIS GIFT OF A MAGIC SWORD.
ITS NAME IS REGRET.
ITS POWER IS TO CALL BACK ANYONE YOU REPENT OF HAVING SLAIN.
SPLENDID!
WE'RE SAVED.
REMEMBER THOUGH, SEVEN DAYS IS THE LIMIT. AFTER THAT, WHAT YOU GET BACK ISN'T PRETTY.

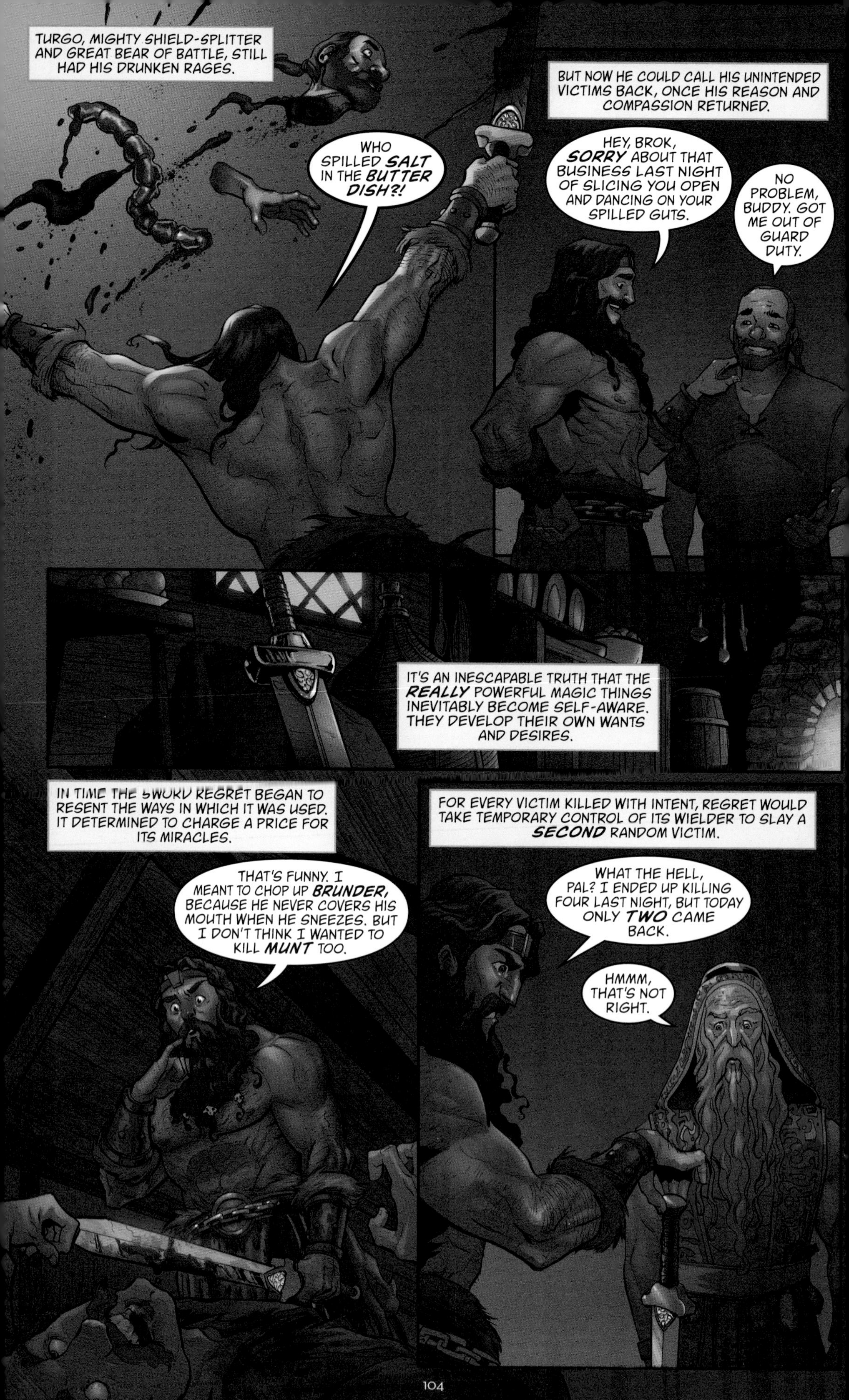
TURGO, MIGHTY SHIELD-SPLITTER AND GREAT BEAR OF BATTLE, STILL HAD HIS DRUNKEN RAGES.
WHO SPILLED SALT IN THE BUTTER DISH?!
BUT NOW HE COULD CALL HIS UNINTENDED VICTIMS BACK, ONCE HIS REASON AND COMPASSION RETURNED.
HEY, BROK, SORRY ABOUT THAT BUSINESS LAST NIGHT OF SLICING YOU OPEN AND DANCING ON YOUR SPILLED GUTS.
NO PROBLEM, BUDDY. GOT ME OUT OF GUARD DUTY.
IT'S AN INESCAPABLE TRUTH THAT THE REALLY POWERFUL MAGIC THINGS INEVITABLY BECOME SELF-AWARE. THEY DEVELOP THEIR OWN WANTS AND DESIRES.
IN TIME THE SWORD REGRET BEGAN TO RESENT THE WAYS IN WHICH IT WAS USED. IT DETERMINED TO CHARGE A PRICE FOR ITS MIRACLES.
THAT'S FUNNY. I MEANT TO CHOP UP BRUNDER, BECAUSE HE NEVER COVERS HIS MOUTH WHEN HE SNEEZES. BUT I DON'T THINK I WANTED TO KILL MUNT TOO.
FOR EVERY VICTIM KILLED WITH INTENT, REGRET WOULD TAKE TEMPORARY CONTROL OF ITS WIELDER TO SLAY A SECOND RANDOM VICTIM.
WHAT THE HELL, PAL? I ENDED UP KILLING FOUR LAST NIGHT, BUT TODAY ONLY TWO CAME BACK.
HMMM, THAT'S NOT RIGHT.

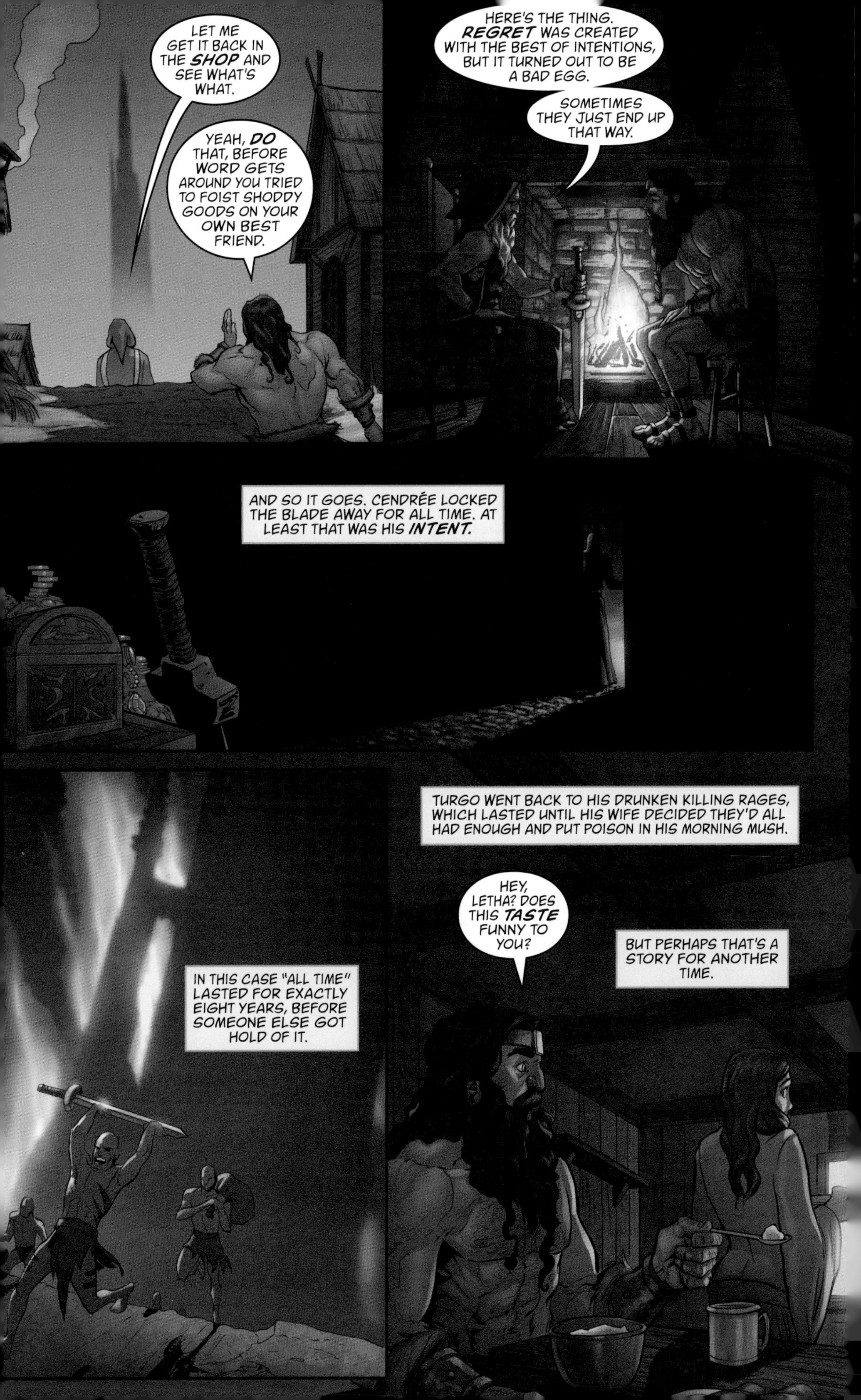
LET ME GET IT BACK IN THE *SHOP* AND SEE WHAT'S WHAT.
YEAH, *DO* THAT, BEFORE WORD GETS AROUND YOU TRIED TO FOIST SHODDY GOODS ON YOUR OWN BEST FRIEND.
HERE'S THE THING. *REGRET* WAS CREATED WITH THE BEST OF INTENTIONS, BUT IT TURNED OUT TO BE A BAD EGG.
SOMETIMES THEY JUST END UP THAT WAY.
AND SO IT GOES. CENDRÉE LOCKED THE BLADE AWAY FOR ALL TIME. AT LEAST THAT WAS HIS *INTENT.*
IN THIS CASE "ALL TIME" LASTED FOR EXACTLY EIGHT YEARS, BEFORE SOMEONE ELSE GOT HOLD OF IT.
TURGO WENT BACK TO HIS DRUNKEN KILLING RAGES, WHICH LASTED UNTIL HIS WIFE DECIDED THEY'D ALL HAD ENOUGH AND PUT POISON IN HIS MORNING MUSH.
HEY, LETHA? DOES THIS *TASTE* FUNNY TO YOU?
BUT PERHAPS THAT'S A STORY FOR ANOTHER TIME.

CERTAIN PREPARATIONS SEEMED EXPEDIENT

Meghan Hetrick: artist

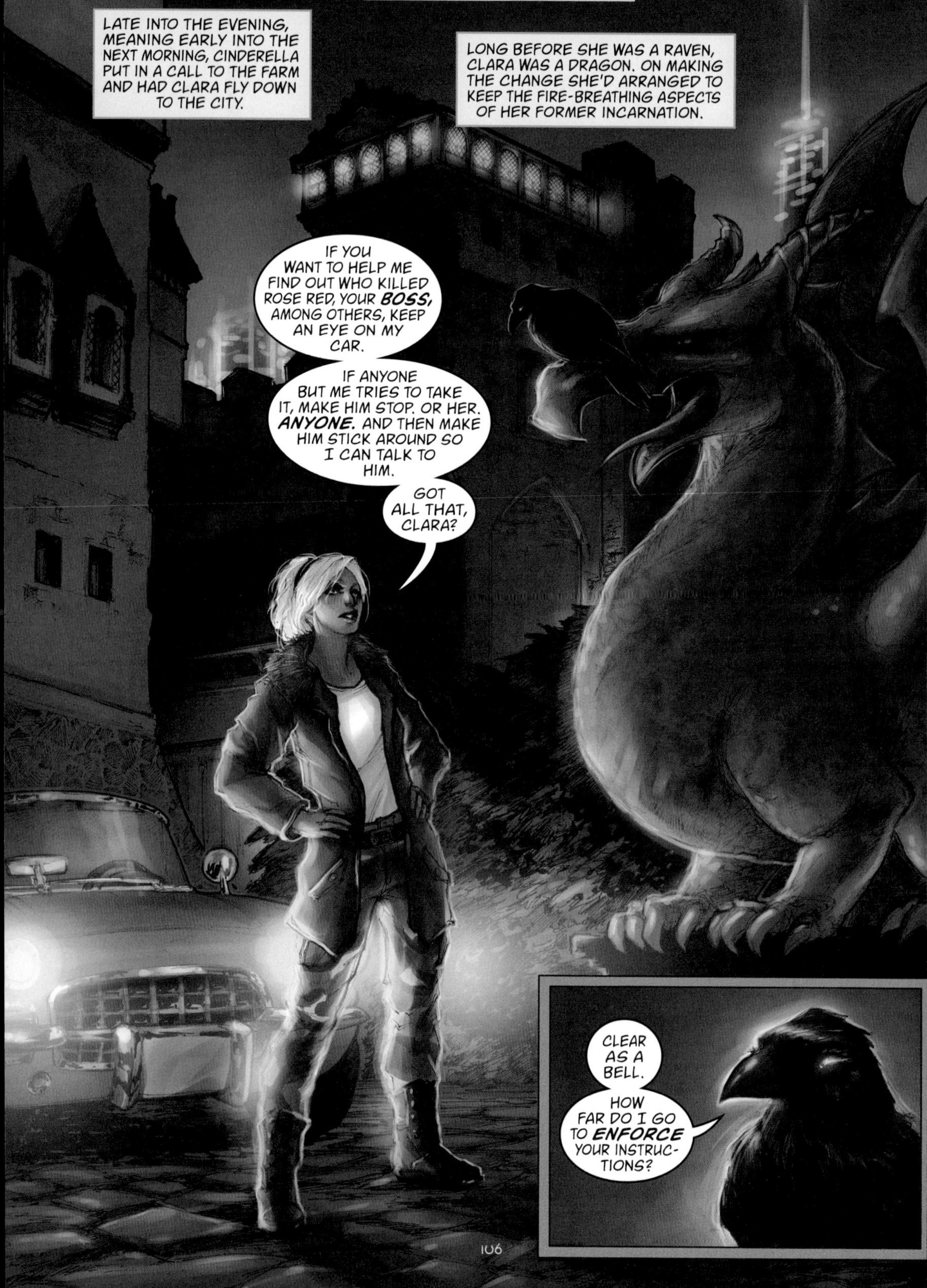
LATE INTO THE EVENING, MEANING EARLY INTO THE NEXT MORNING, CINDERELLA PUT IN A CALL TO THE FARM AND HAD CLARA FLY DOWN TO THE CITY.
LONG BEFORE SHE WAS A RAVEN, CLARA WAS A DRAGON. ON MAKING THE CHANGE SHE'D ARRANGED TO KEEP THE FIRE-BREATHING ASPECTS OF HER FORMER INCARNATION.
IF YOU WANT TO HELP ME FIND OUT WHO KILLED ROSE RED, YOUR ***BOSS,*** AMONG OTHERS, KEEP AN EYE ON MY CAR.
IF ANYONE BUT ME TRIES TO TAKE IT, MAKE HIM STOP. OR HER. ***ANYONE.*** AND THEN MAKE HIM STICK AROUND SO I CAN TALK TO HIM.
GOT ALL THAT, CLARA?
CLEAR AS A BELL.
HOW FAR DO I GO TO ***ENFORCE*** YOUR INSTRUC-TIONS?

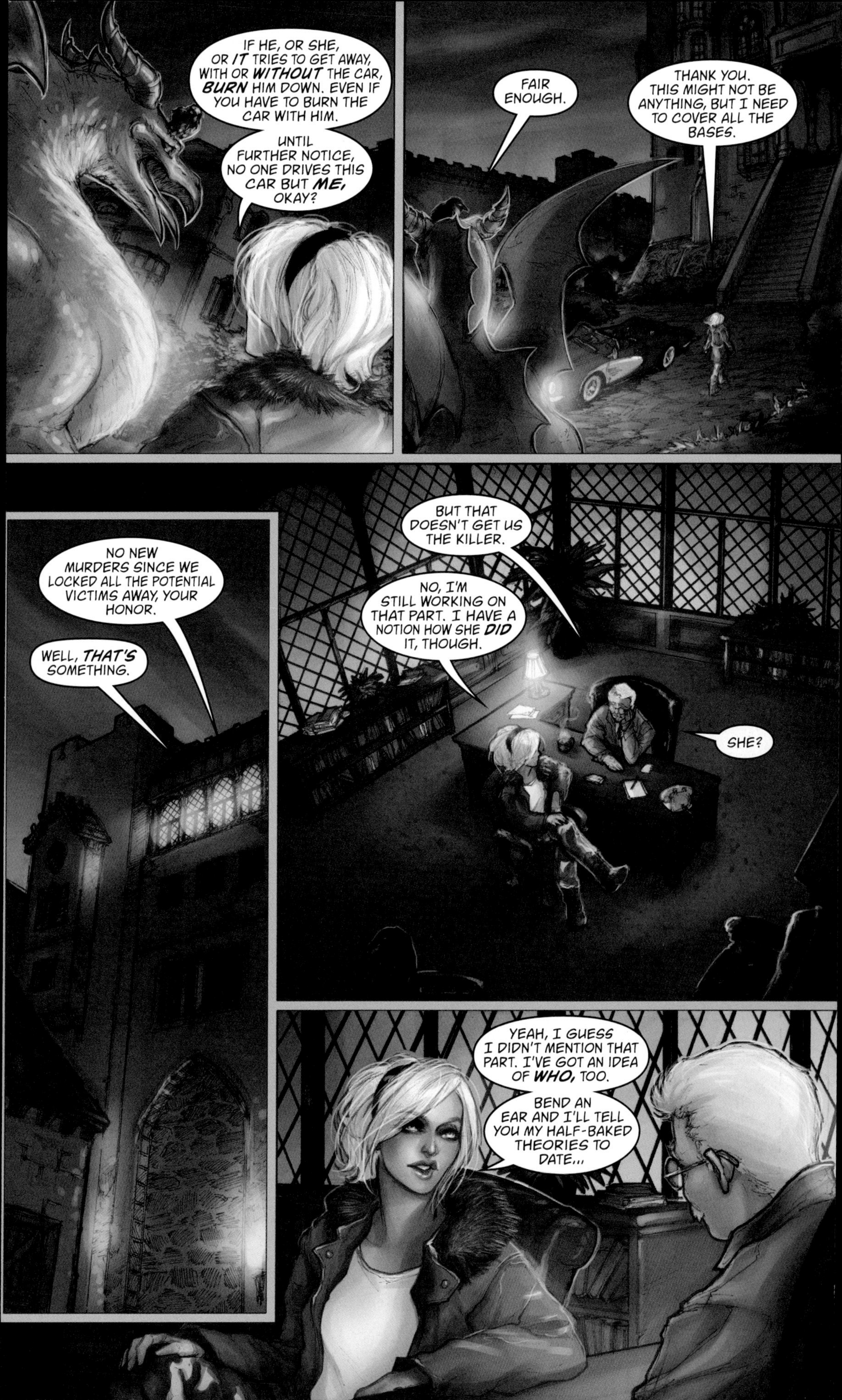
IF HE, OR SHE, OR *IT* TRIES TO GET AWAY, WITH OR ***WITHOUT*** THE CAR, ***BURN*** HIM DOWN. EVEN IF YOU HAVE TO BURN THE CAR WITH HIM.
UNTIL FURTHER NOTICE, NO ONE DRIVES THIS CAR BUT ***ME,*** OKAY?
FAIR ENOUGH.
THANK YOU. THIS MIGHT NOT BE ANYTHING, BUT I NEED TO COVER ALL THE BASES.
NO NEW MURDERS SINCE WE LOCKED ALL THE POTENTIAL VICTIMS AWAY, YOUR HONOR.
WELL, ***THAT'S*** SOMETHING.
BUT THAT DOESN'T GET US THE KILLER.
NO, I'M STILL WORKING ON THAT PART. I HAVE A NOTION HOW SHE ***DID*** IT, THOUGH.
SHE?
YEAH, I GUESS I DIDN'T MENTION THAT PART. I'VE GOT AN IDEA OF ***WHO,*** TOO.
BEND AN EAR AND I'LL TELL YOU MY HALF-BAKED THEORIES TO DATE...

THE LOUSY DETECTIVE DEDUCES SOME THINGS

Kurt Huggins: artist • Zelda Devon: colorist

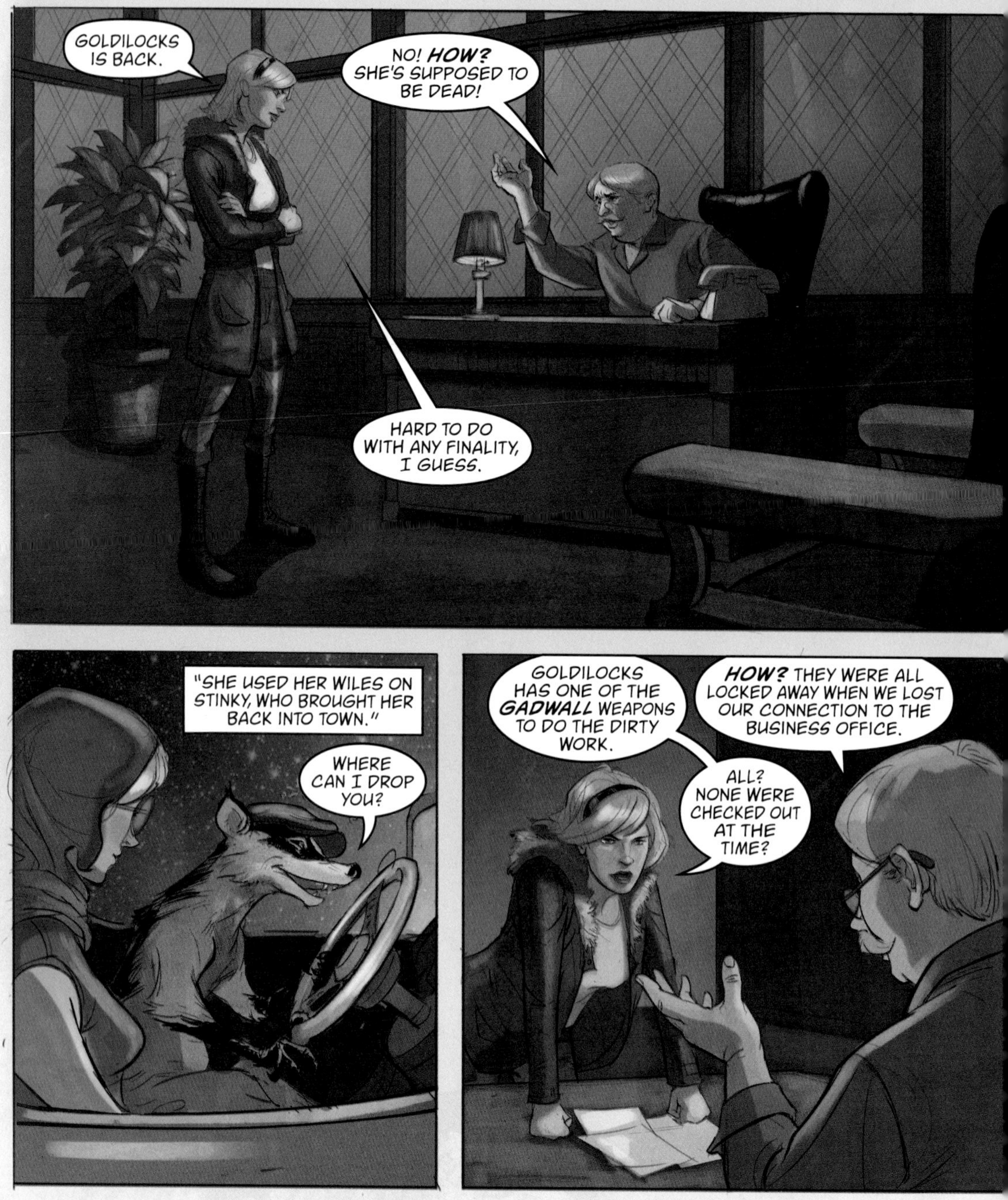
GOLDILOCKS IS BACK.
NO! *HOW?* SHE'S SUPPOSED TO BE DEAD!
HARD TO DO WITH ANY FINALITY, I GUESS.
"SHE USED HER WILES ON STINKY, WHO BROUGHT HER BACK INTO TOWN."
WHERE CAN I DROP YOU?
GOLDILOCKS HAS ONE OF THE *GADWALL* WEAPONS TO DO THE DIRTY WORK.
HOW? THEY WERE ALL LOCKED AWAY WHEN WE LOST OUR CONNECTION TO THE BUSINESS OFFICE.
ALL? NONE WERE CHECKED OUT AT THE TIME?

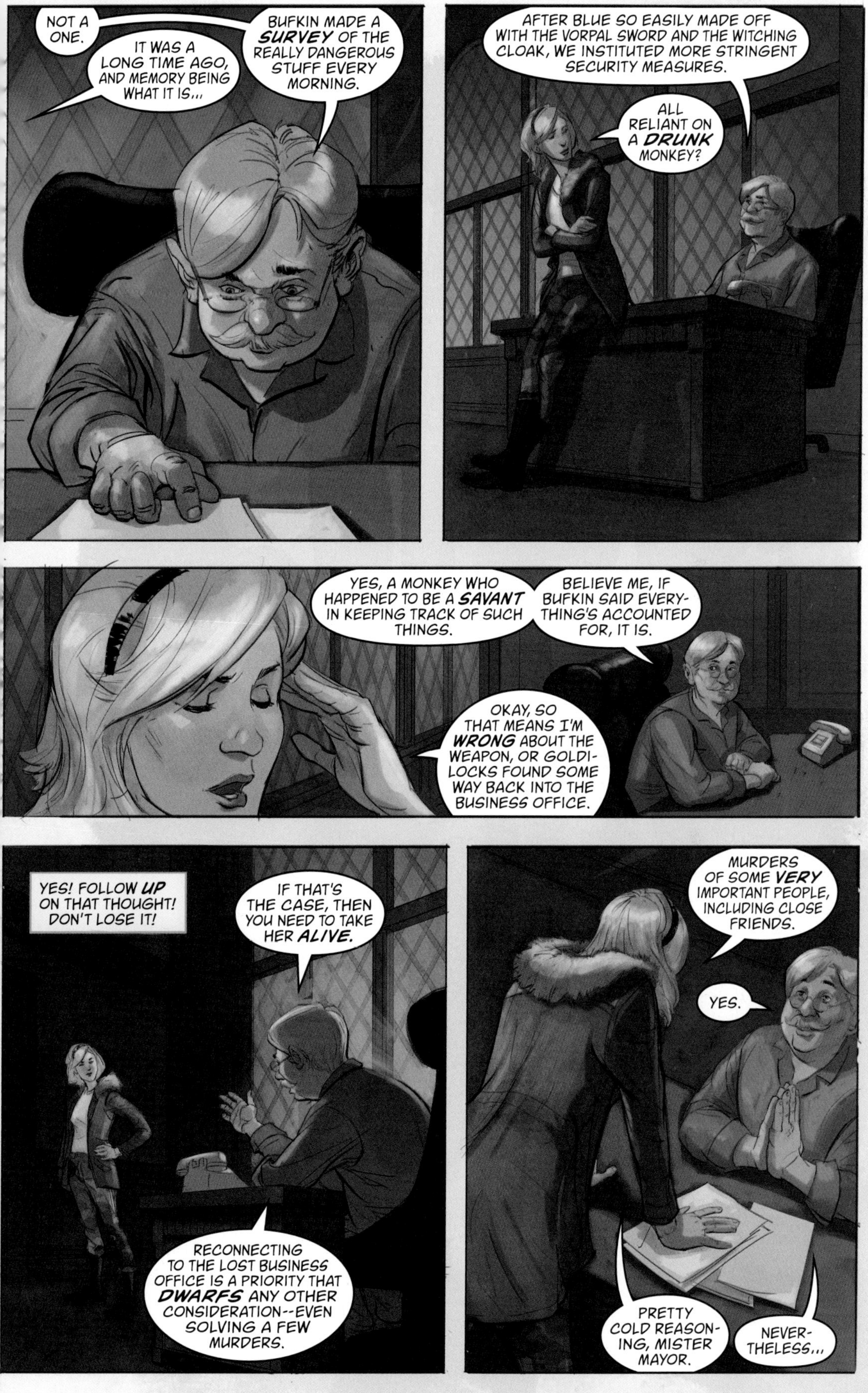
NOT A ONE.
IT WAS A LONG TIME AGO, AND MEMORY BEING WHAT IT IS...
BUFKIN MADE A SURVEY OF THE REALLY DANGEROUS STUFF EVERY MORNING.
AFTER BLUE SO EASILY MADE OFF WITH THE VORPAL SWORD AND THE WITCHING CLOAK, WE INSTITUTED MORE STRINGENT SECURITY MEASURES.
ALL RELIANT ON A DRUNK MONKEY?
YES, A MONKEY WHO HAPPENED TO BE A SAVANT IN KEEPING TRACK OF SUCH THINGS.
BELIEVE ME, IF BUFKIN SAID EVERYTHING'S ACCOUNTED FOR, IT IS.
OKAY, SO THAT MEANS I'M WRONG ABOUT THE WEAPON, OR GOLDILOCKS FOUND SOME WAY BACK INTO THE BUSINESS OFFICE.
YES! FOLLOW UP ON THAT THOUGHT! DON'T LOSE IT!
IF THAT'S THE CASE, THEN YOU NEED TO TAKE HER ALIVE.
RECONNECTING TO THE LOST BUSINESS OFFICE IS A PRIORITY THAT DWARFS ANY OTHER CONSIDERATION--EVEN SOLVING A FEW MURDERS.
MURDERS OF SOME VERY IMPORTANT PEOPLE, INCLUDING CLOSE FRIENDS.
YES.
PRETTY COLD REASONING, MISTER MAYOR.
NEVERTHELESS...

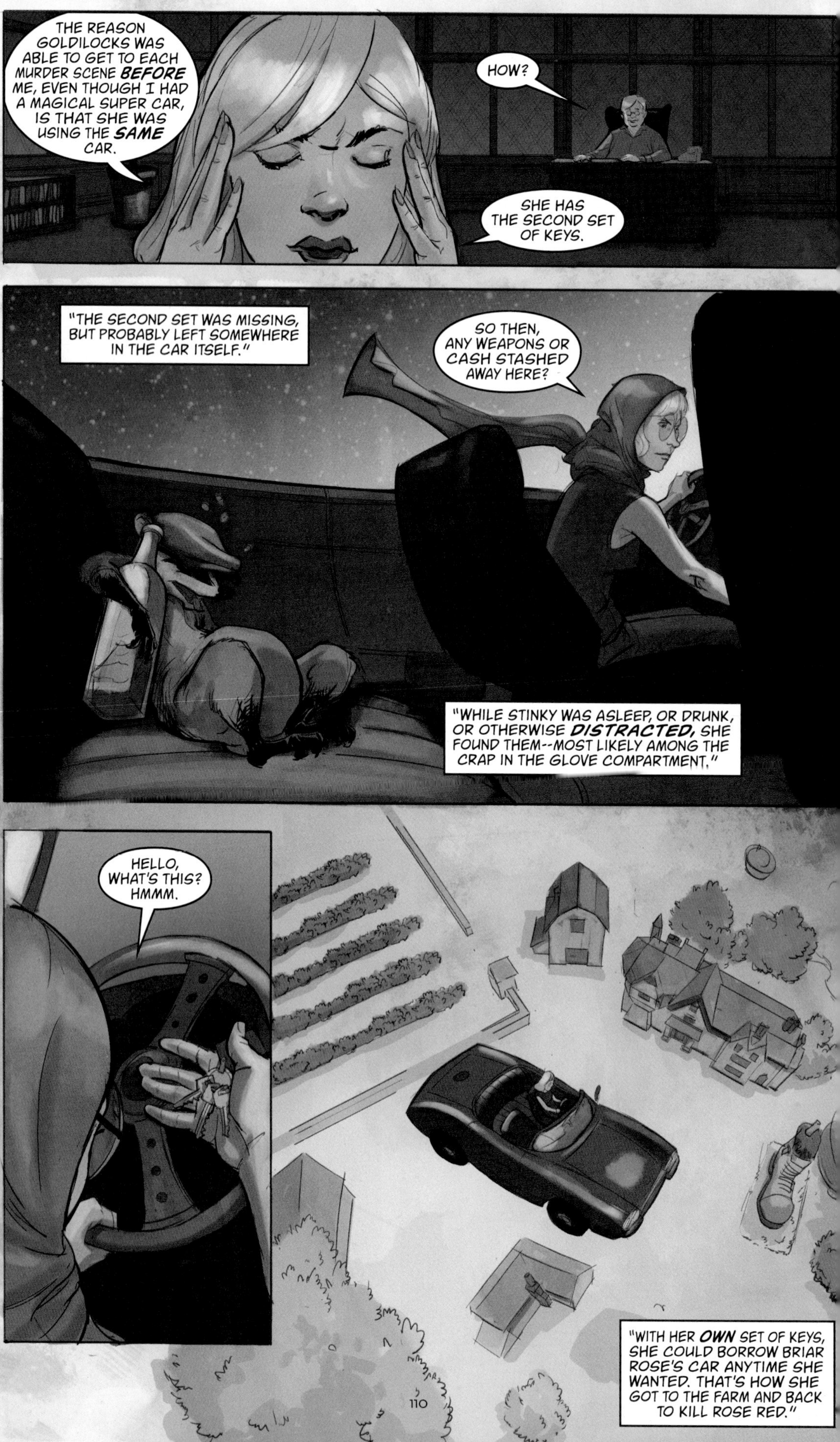

THE REASON GOLDILOCKS WAS ABLE TO GET TO EACH MURDER SCENE BEFORE ME, EVEN THOUGH I HAD A MAGICAL SUPER CAR, IS THAT SHE WAS USING THE SAME CAR.
HOW?
SHE HAS THE SECOND SET OF KEYS.
"THE SECOND SET WAS MISSING, BUT PROBABLY LEFT SOMEWHERE IN THE CAR ITSELF."
SO THEN, ANY WEAPONS OR CASH STASHED AWAY HERE?
"WHILE STINKY WAS ASLEEP, OR DRUNK, OR OTHERWISE DISTRACTED, SHE FOUND THEM--MOST LIKELY AMONG THE CRAP IN THE GLOVE COMPARTMENT."
HELLO, WHAT'S THIS? HMMM.
"WITH HER OWN SET OF KEYS, SHE COULD BORROW BRIAR ROSE'S CAR ANYTIME SHE WANTED. THAT'S HOW SHE GOT TO THE FARM AND BACK TO KILL ROSE RED."

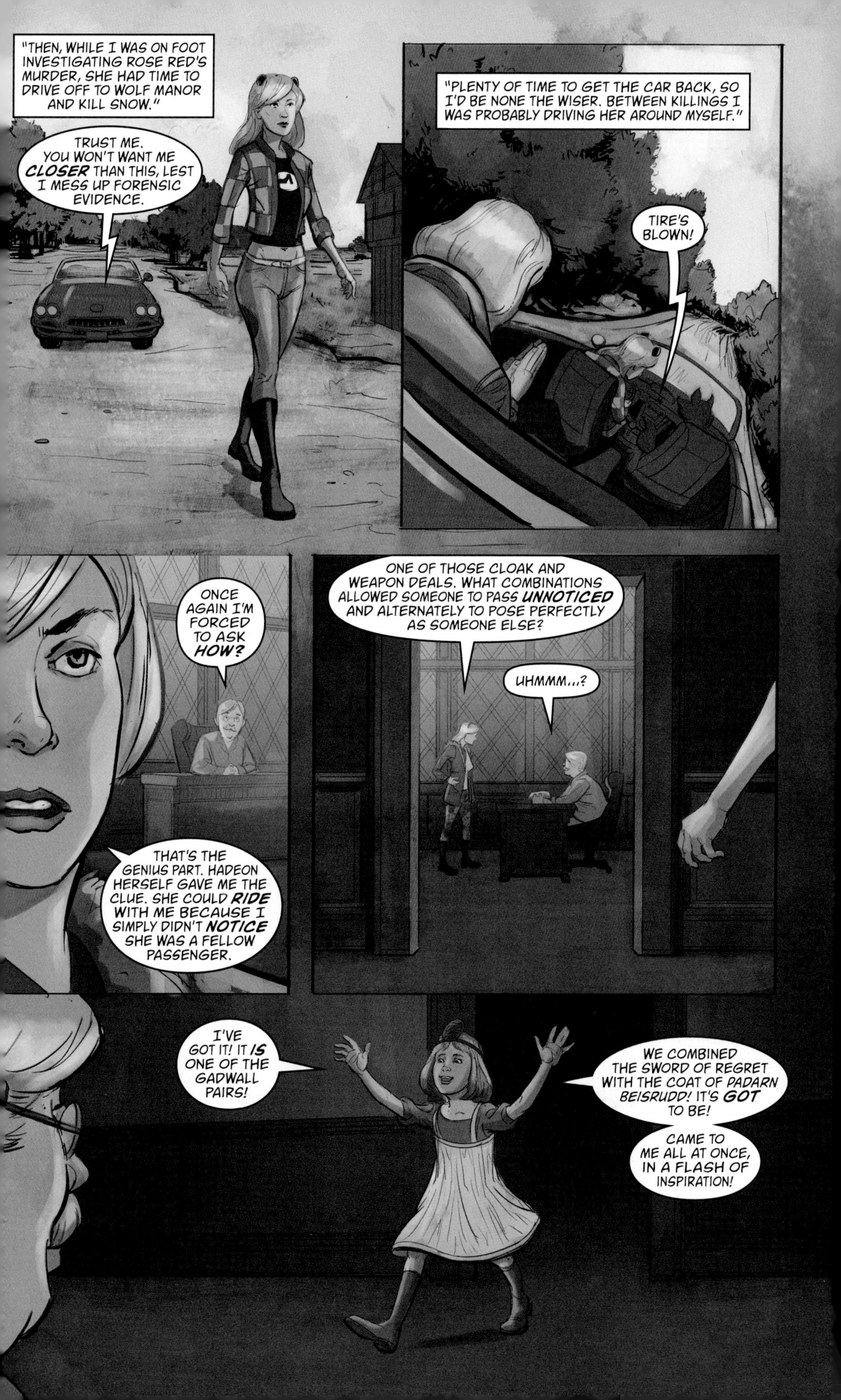
"THEN, WHILE I WAS ON FOOT INVESTIGATING ROSE RED'S MURDER, SHE HAD TIME TO DRIVE OFF TO WOLF MANOR AND KILL SNOW."
TRUST ME. YOU WON'T WANT ME CLOSER THAN THIS, LEST I MESS UP FORENSIC EVIDENCE.
"PLENTY OF TIME TO GET THE CAR BACK, SO I'D BE NONE THE WISER. BETWEEN KILLINGS I WAS PROBABLY DRIVING HER AROUND MYSELF."
TIRE'S BLOWN!
ONCE AGAIN I'M FORCED TO ASK HOW?
THAT'S THE GENIUS PART. HADEON HERSELF GAVE ME THE CLUE. SHE COULD RIDE WITH ME BECAUSE I SIMPLY DIDN'T NOTICE SHE WAS A FELLOW PASSENGER.
ONE OF THOSE CLOAK AND WEAPON DEALS. WHAT COMBINATIONS ALLOWED SOMEONE TO PASS UNNOTICED AND ALTERNATELY TO POSE PERFECTLY AS SOMEONE ELSE?
UHMMM...?
I'VE GOT IT! IT IS ONE OF THE GADWALL PAIRS!
WE COMBINED THE SWORD OF REGRET WITH THE COAT OF PADARN BEISRUDD! IT'S GOT TO BE!
CAME TO ME ALL AT ONCE, IN A FLASH OF INSPIRATION!

A FORESEEABLE RESULT OF SEQUESTERING SO MANY OF THE FAIREST IN ONE ROOM TOGETHER

Adam Hughes: artist

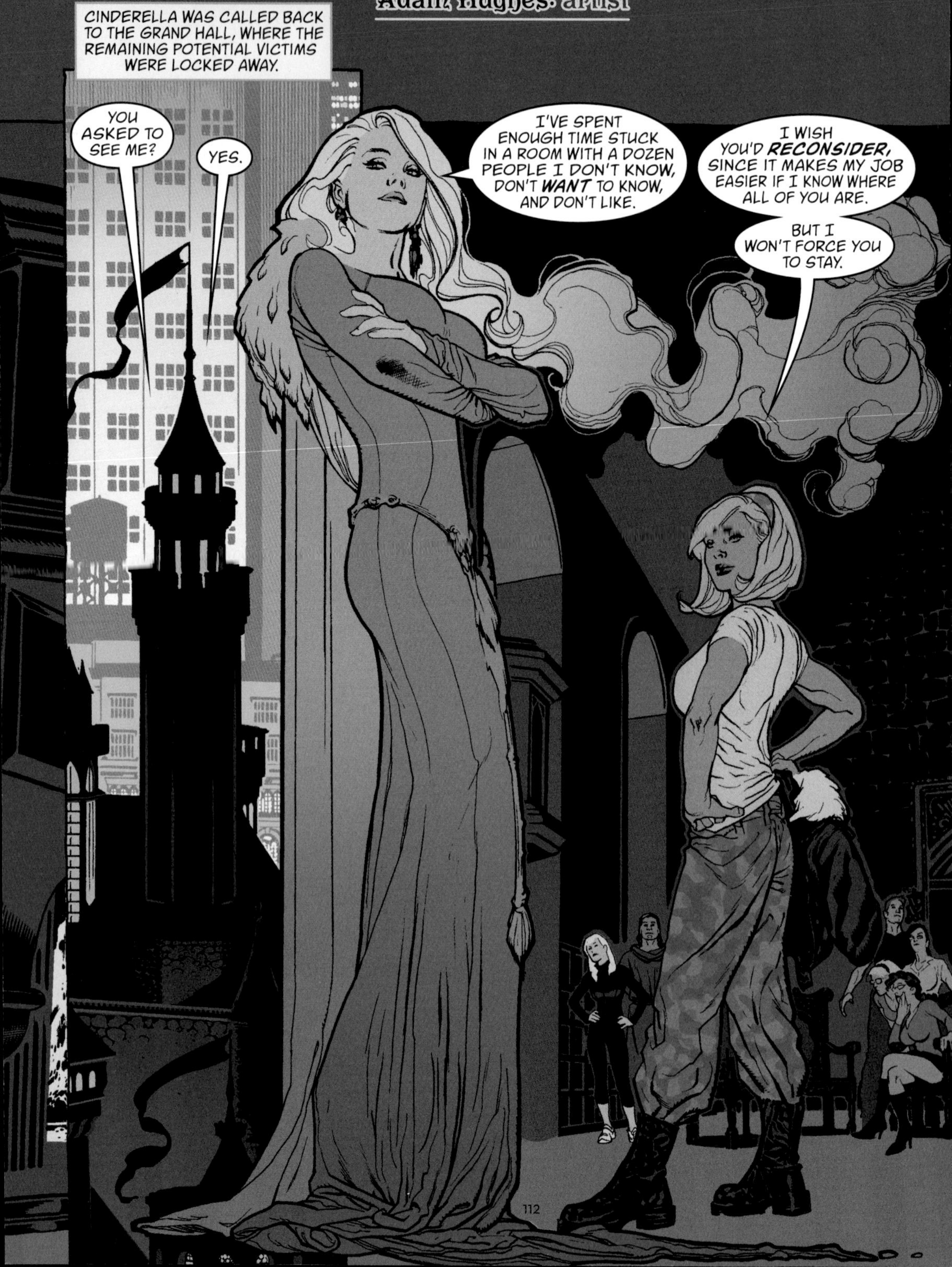
CINDERELLA WAS CALLED BACK TO THE GRAND HALL, WHERE THE REMAINING POTENTIAL VICTIMS WERE LOCKED AWAY.
YOU ASKED TO SEE ME?
YES.
I'VE SPENT ENOUGH TIME STUCK IN A ROOM WITH A DOZEN PEOPLE I DON'T KNOW, DON'T *WANT* TO KNOW, AND DON'T LIKE.
I WISH YOU'D **RECONSIDER,** SINCE IT MAKES MY JOB EASIER IF I KNOW WHERE ALL OF YOU ARE.
BUT I WON'T FORCE YOU TO STAY.

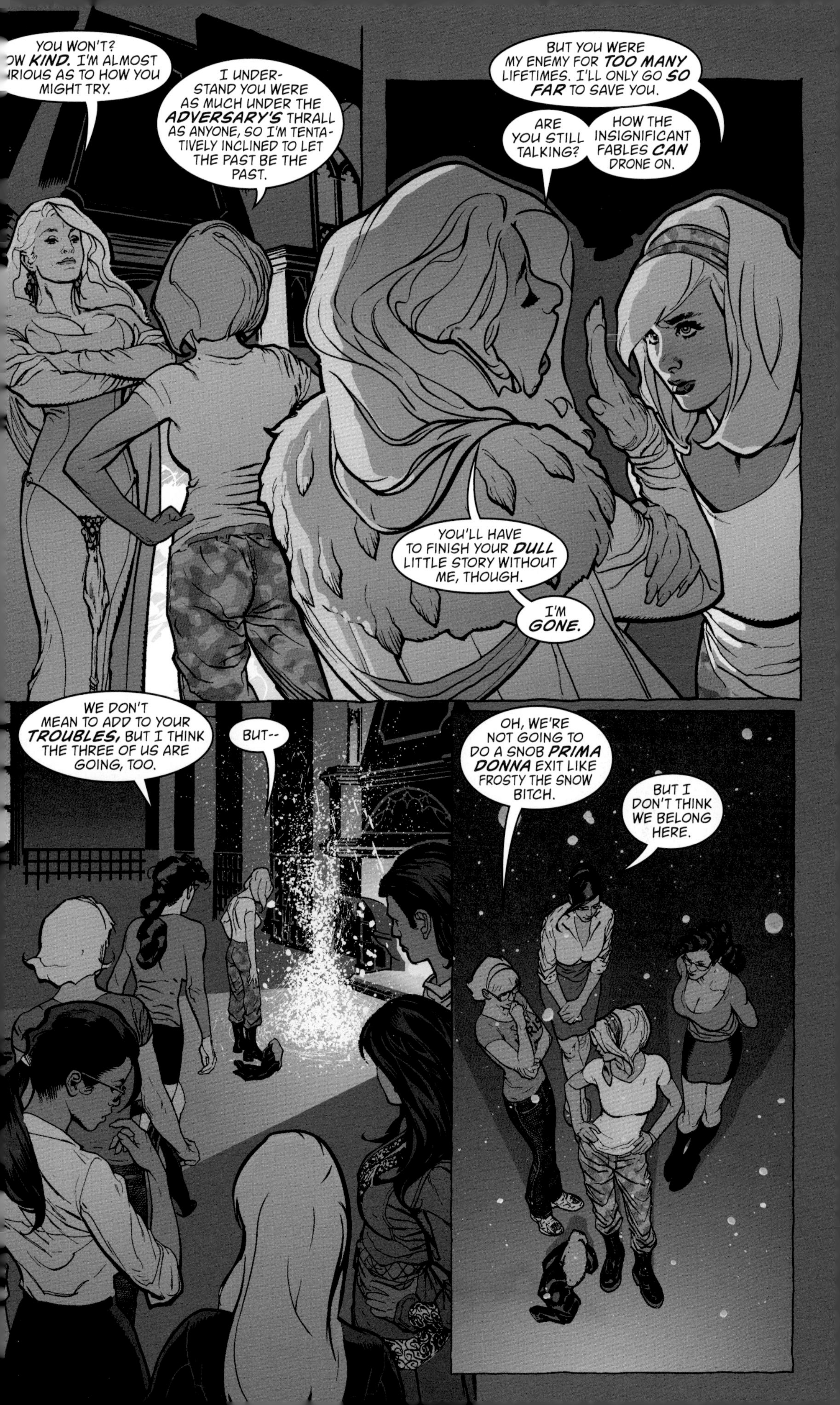

YOU WON'T? OW KIND. I'M ALMOST IRIOUS AS TO HOW YOU MIGHT TRY.
I UNDERSTAND YOU WERE AS MUCH UNDER THE ADVERSARY'S THRALL AS ANYONE, SO I'M TENTATIVELY INCLINED TO LET THE PAST BE THE PAST.
BUT YOU WERE MY ENEMY FOR TOO MANY LIFETIMES. I'LL ONLY GO SO FAR TO SAVE YOU.
ARE YOU STILL TALKING?
HOW THE INSIGNIFICANT FABLES CAN DRONE ON.
YOU'LL HAVE TO FINISH YOUR DULL LITTLE STORY WITHOUT ME, THOUGH.
I'M GONE.
WE DON'T MEAN TO ADD TO YOUR TROUBLES, BUT I THINK THE THREE OF US ARE GOING, TOO.
BUT--
OH, WE'RE NOT GOING TO DO A SNOB PRIMA DONNA EXIT LIKE FROSTY THE SNOW BITCH.
BUT I DON'T THINK WE BELONG HERE.

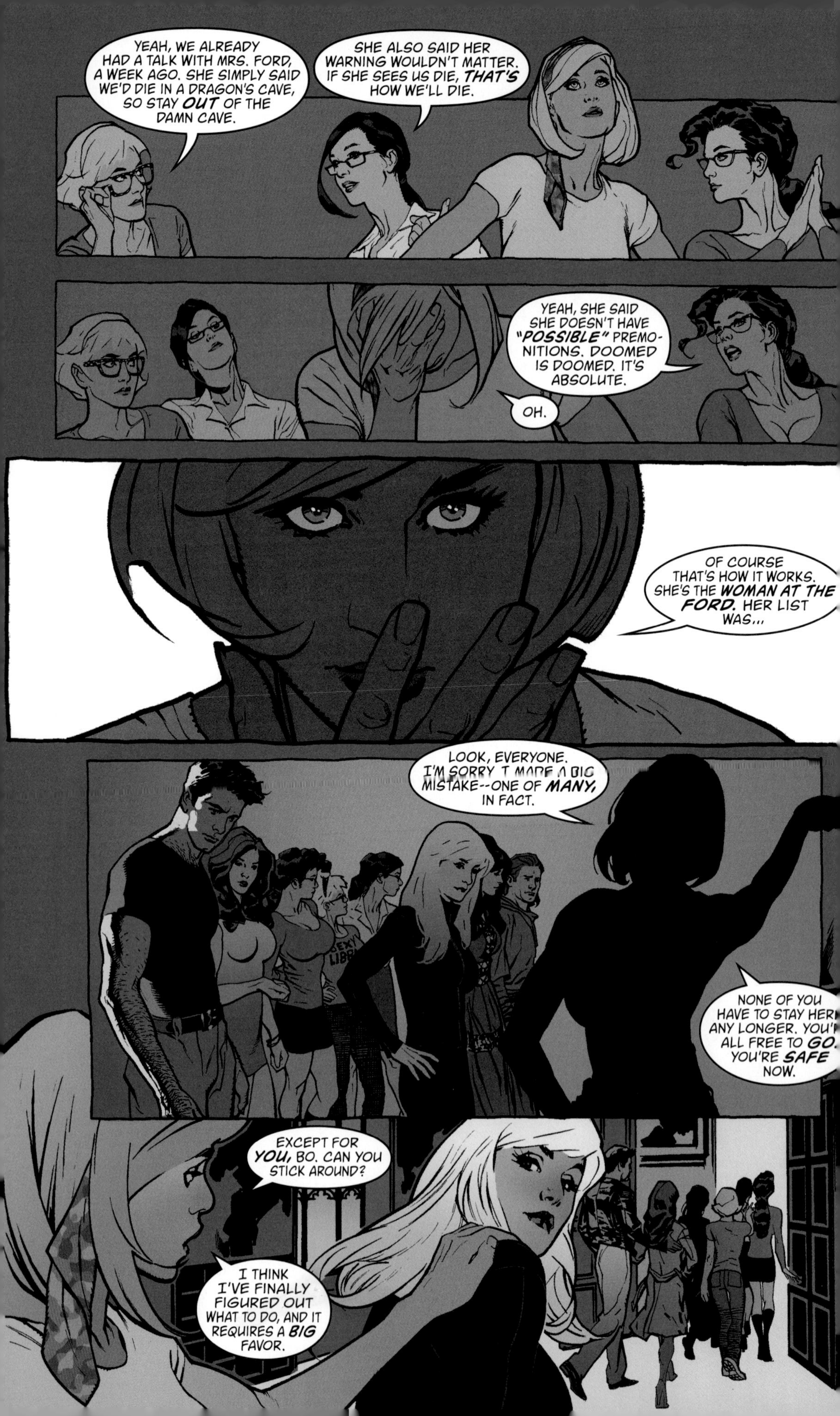
YEAH, WE ALREADY HAD A TALK WITH MRS. FORD, A WEEK AGO. SHE SIMPLY SAID WE'D DIE IN A DRAGON'S CAVE, SO STAY *OUT* OF THE DAMN CAVE.
SHE ALSO SAID HER WARNING WOULDN'T MATTER. IF SHE SEES US DIE, *THAT'S* HOW WE'LL DIE.
YEAH, SHE SAID SHE DOESN'T HAVE *"POSSIBLE"* PREMO-NITIONS. DOOMED IS DOOMED. IT'S ABSOLUTE.
OH.
OF COURSE THAT'S HOW IT WORKS. SHE'S THE *WOMAN AT THE FORD.* HER LIST WAS...
LOOK, EVERYONE. I'M SORRY. I MADE A BIG MISTAKE--ONE OF *MANY,* IN FACT.
NONE OF YOU HAVE TO STAY HER ANY LONGER. YOU' ALL FREE TO *GO.* YOU'RE *SAFE* NOW.
EXCEPT FOR *YOU,* BO. CAN YOU STICK AROUND?
I THINK I'VE FINALLY FIGURED OUT WHAT TO DO, AND IT REQUIRES A *BIG* FAVOR.

SATURDAY

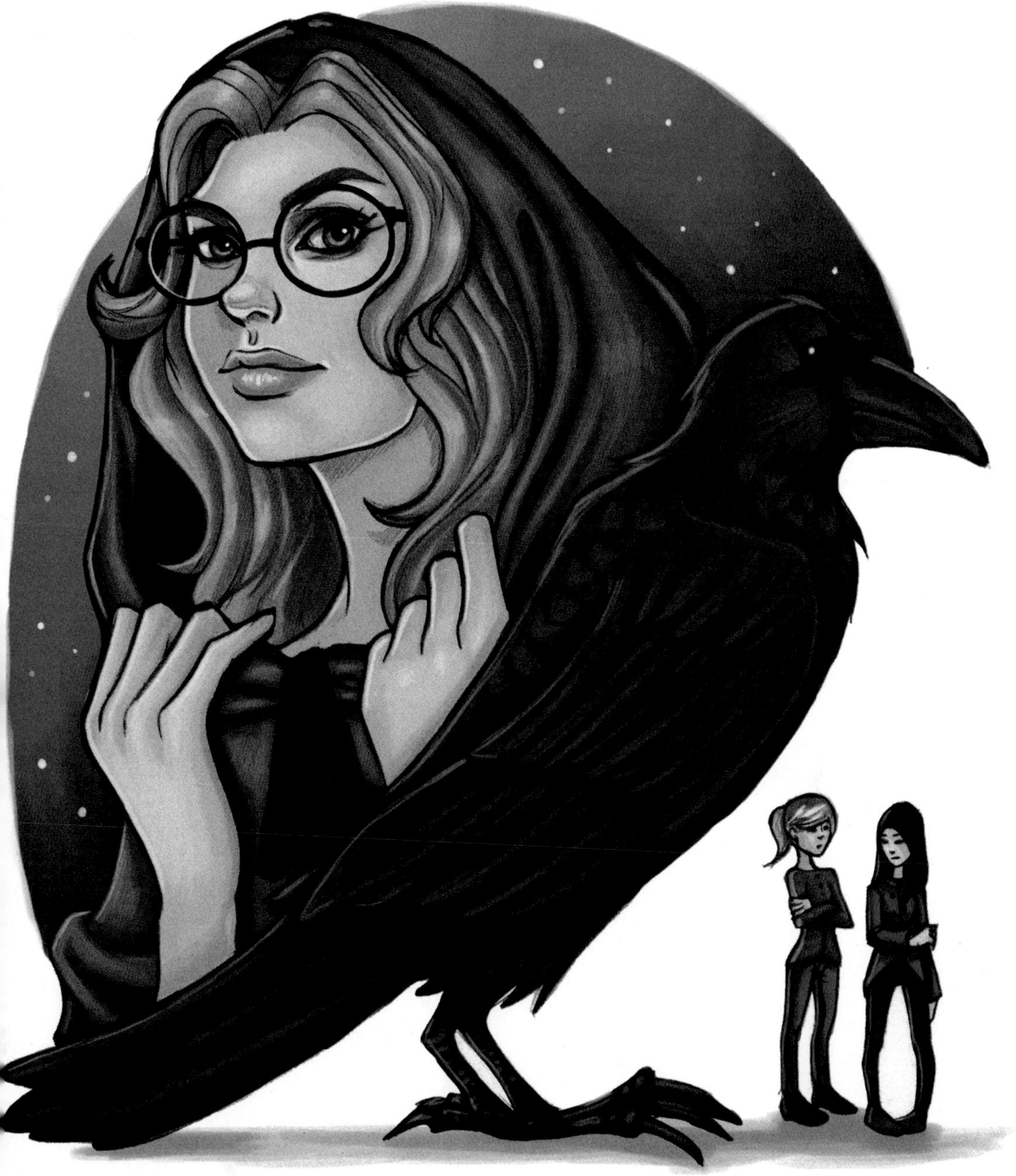

Did our attempted act of raw magic work? Or did Ozma come up with the connection on her own? I suppose it doesn't matter, as long as we got the result we were after. At long last it looks like Cinderella may be on the right track. Now, if only she can resolve this before the clock runs out. Less than two full days to go before the first of the victims pass beyond the point at which they can be recalled.

IN WHICH DIRTY DEEDS ARE HATCHED, FOR THE GREATER GOOD

Marley Zarcone: artist

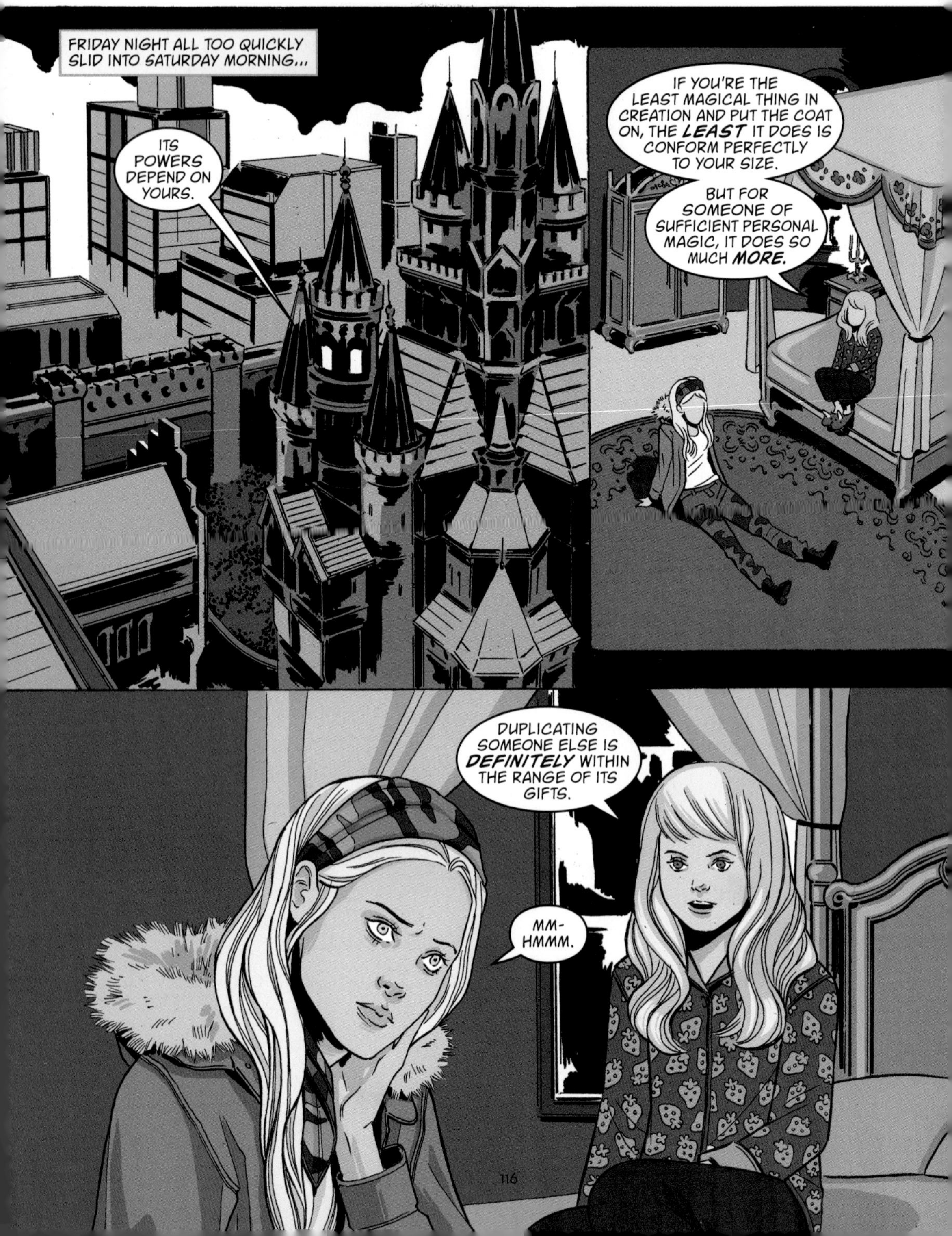
FRIDAY NIGHT ALL TOO QUICKLY SLID INTO SATURDAY MORNING...
ITS POWERS DEPEND ON YOURS.
IF YOU'RE THE LEAST MAGICAL THING IN CREATION AND PUT THE COAT ON, THE LEAST IT DOES IS CONFORM PERFECTLY TO YOUR SIZE.
BUT FOR SOMEONE OF SUFFICIENT PERSONAL MAGIC, IT DOES SO MUCH MORE.
DUPLICATING SOMEONE ELSE IS DEFINITELY WITHIN THE RANGE OF ITS GIFTS.
MM-HMMM.

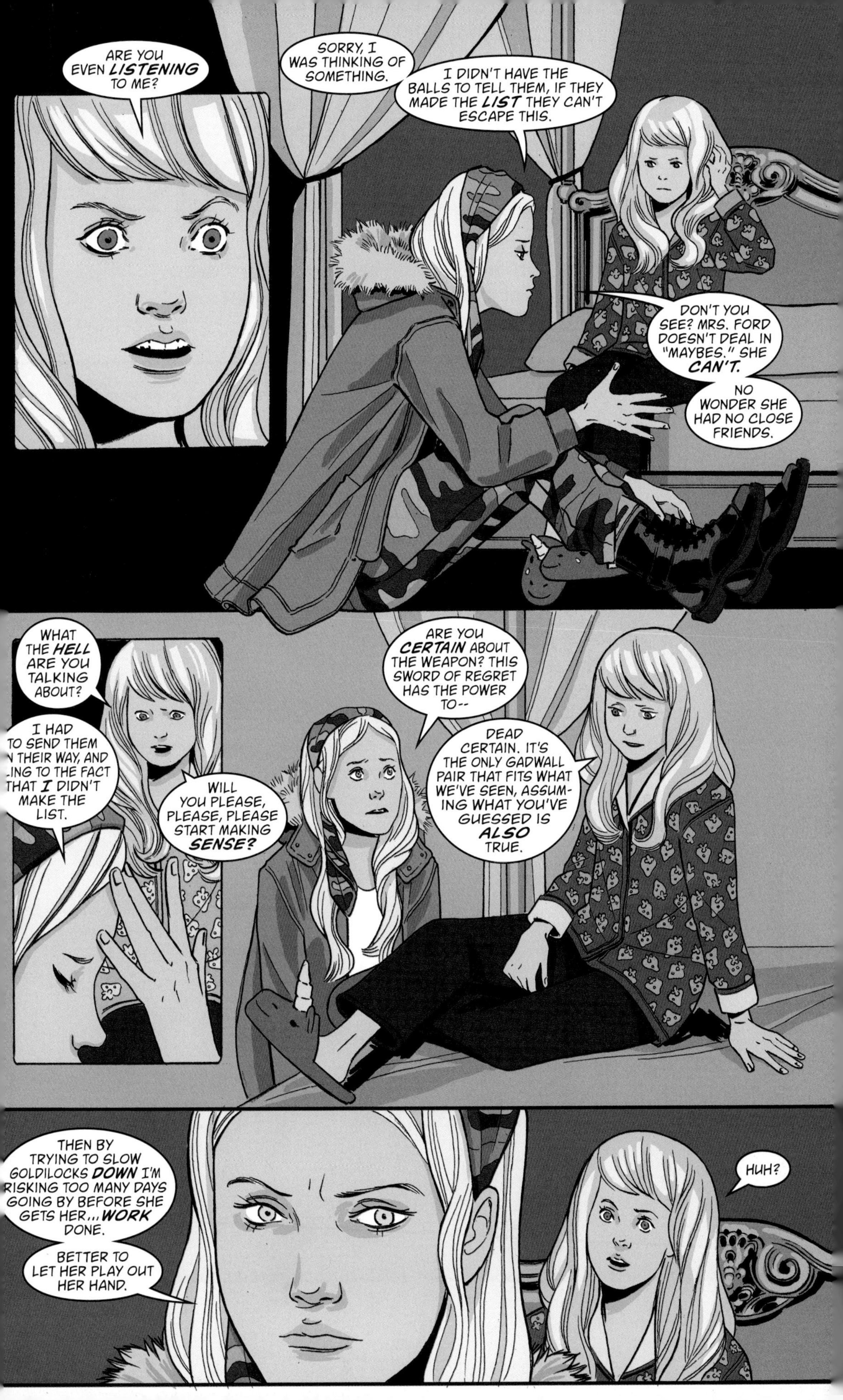
ARE YOU EVEN LISTENING TO ME?
SORRY, I WAS THINKING OF SOMETHING.
I DIDN'T HAVE THE BALLS TO TELL THEM, IF THEY MADE THE LIST THEY CAN'T ESCAPE THIS.
DON'T YOU SEE? MRS. FORD DOESN'T DEAL IN "MAYBES." SHE CAN'T.
NO WONDER SHE HAD NO CLOSE FRIENDS.
WHAT THE HELL ARE YOU TALKING ABOUT?
I HAD TO SEND THEM N THEIR WAY, AND ING TO THE FACT THAT I DIDN'T MAKE THE LIST.
WILL YOU PLEASE, PLEASE, PLEASE START MAKING SENSE?
ARE YOU CERTAIN ABOUT THE WEAPON? THIS SWORD OF REGRET HAS THE POWER TO--
DEAD CERTAIN. IT'S THE ONLY GADWALL PAIR THAT FITS WHAT WE'VE SEEN, ASSUMING WHAT YOU'VE GUESSED IS ALSO TRUE.
THEN BY TRYING TO SLOW GOLDILOCKS DOWN I'M RISKING TOO MANY DAYS GOING BY BEFORE SHE GETS HER... WORK DONE.
BETTER TO LET HER PLAY OUT HER HAND.
HUH?

GOLDILOCKS PLAYS OUT HER HAND

Al Davison: artist • Chris Chuckry: colorist
special thanks to Zander Cannon

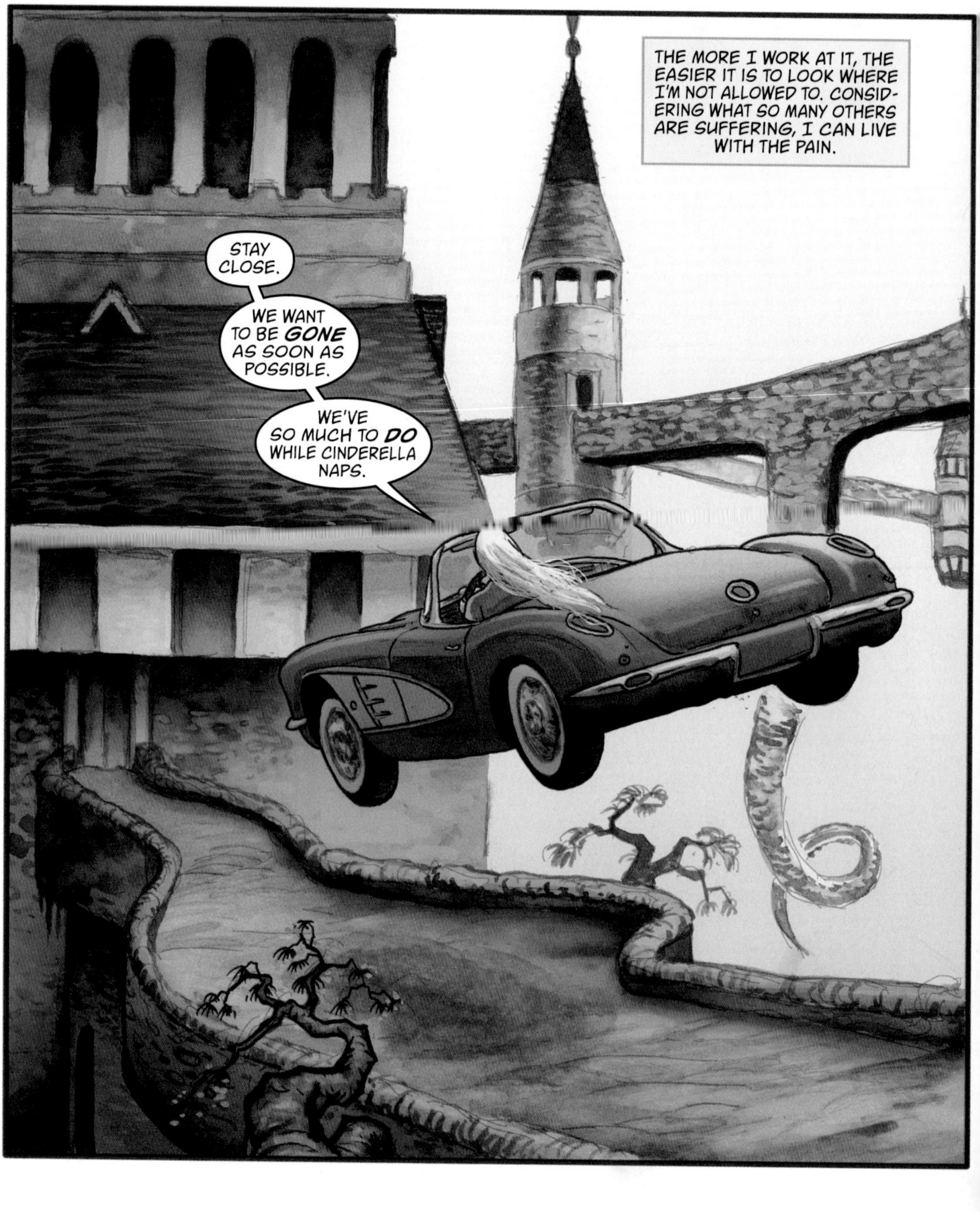
THE MORE I WORK AT IT, THE EASIER IT IS TO LOOK WHERE I'M NOT ALLOWED TO. CONSIDERING WHAT SO MANY OTHERS ARE SUFFERING, I CAN LIVE WITH THE PAIN.
STAY CLOSE.
WE WANT TO BE GONE AS SOON AS POSSIBLE.
WE'VE SO MUCH TO DO WHILE CINDERELLA NAPS.

WE WOULDN'T WANT HER TO WAKE AND FIND HER *CAR* MISSING.

DON'T DISMISS CINDER-ELLA SO BLITHELY. I FEAR SHE MAY BE *SMARTER* THAN SHE SEEMS.

SHE'S AN ARMED *THUG,* WORKING FOR THE STATE. INTELLIGENCE ISN'T A PREREQUISITE FOR HER JOB, JUST AN ABILITY TO KICK IN A DOOR IN THE MIDDLE OF THE NIGHT.

HUSH NOW. LET'S NOT RISK FLUSHING THE PREY TOO EARLY.

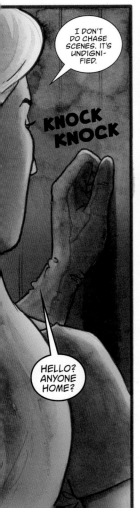

I DON'T DO CHASE SCENES. IT'S UNDIGNI-FIED.

KNOCK KNOCK

HELLO? ANYONE HOME?

IT'S ME, LAKE.

I DROPPED BY TO SEE IF YOU'RE STILL OKAY.

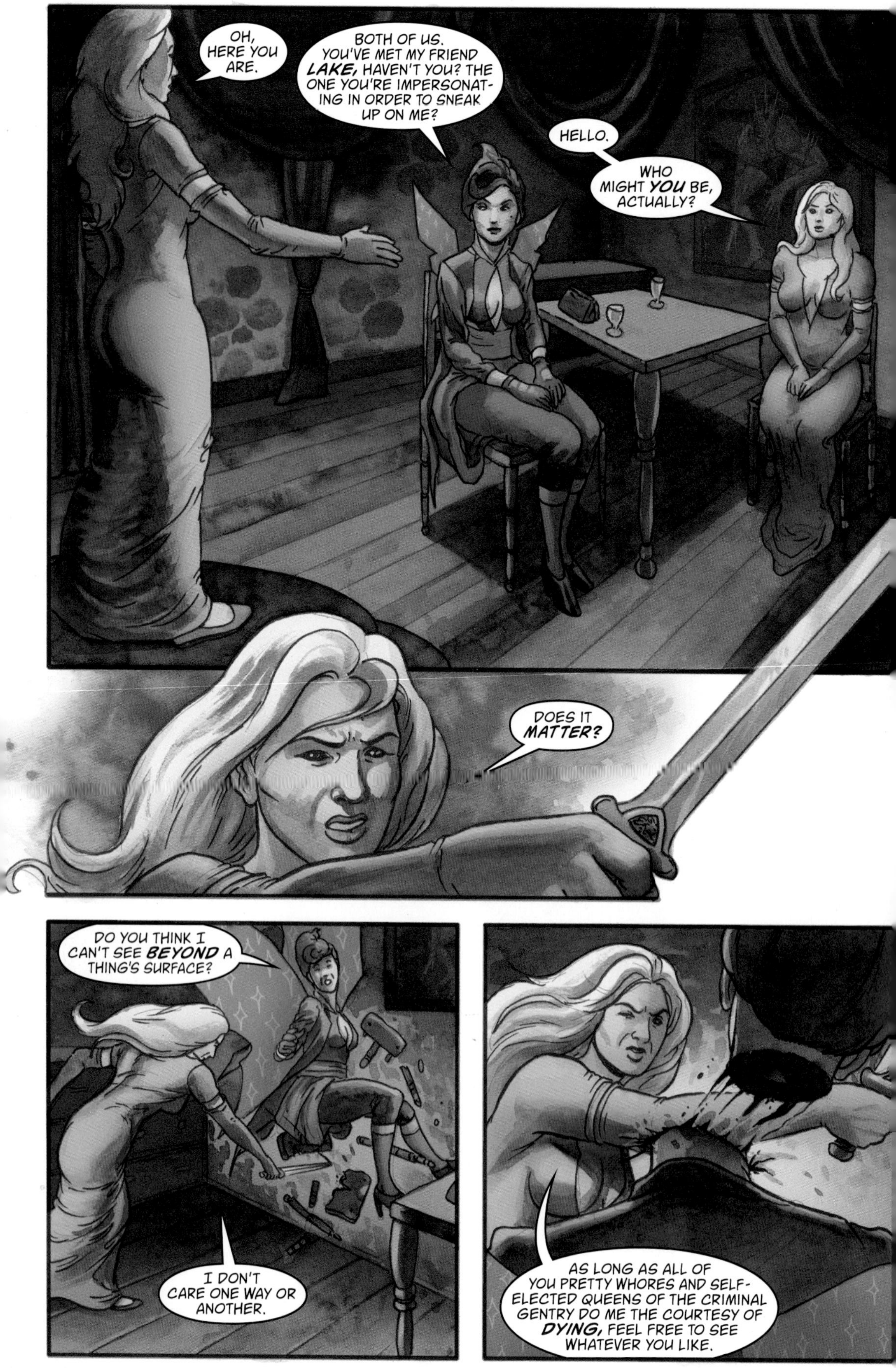
OH, HERE YOU ARE.
BOTH OF US. YOU'VE MET MY FRIEND LAKE, HAVEN'T YOU? THE ONE YOU'RE IMPERSONATING IN ORDER TO SNEAK UP ON ME?
HELLO.
WHO MIGHT YOU BE, ACTUALLY?
DOES IT MATTER?
DO YOU THINK I CAN'T SEE BEYOND A THING'S SURFACE?
I DON'T CARE ONE WAY OR ANOTHER.
AS LONG AS ALL OF YOU PRETTY WHORES AND SELF-ELECTED QUEENS OF THE CRIMINAL GENTRY DO ME THE COURTESY OF DYING, FEEL FREE TO SEE WHATEVER YOU LIKE.

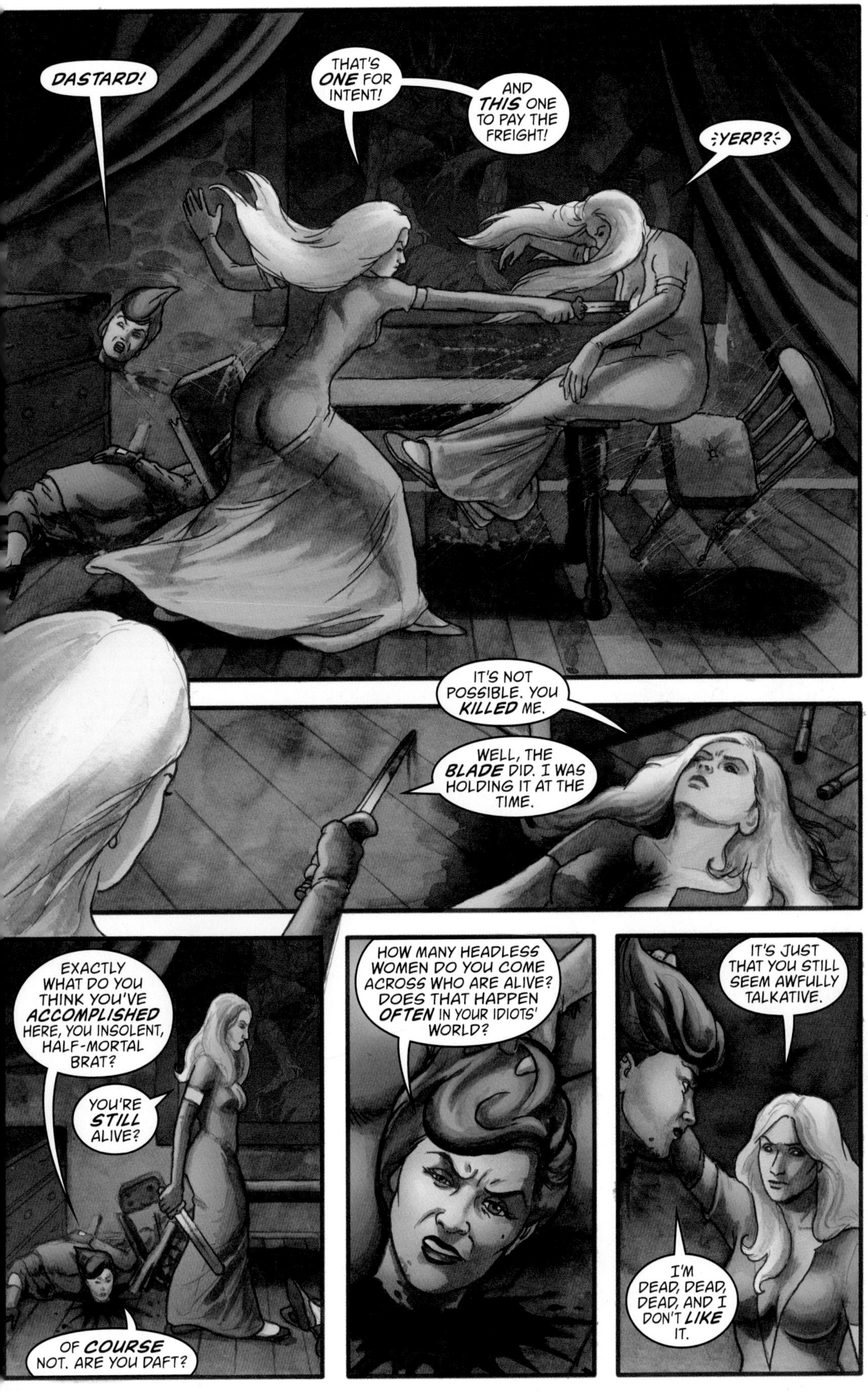
DASTARD!
THAT'S ONE FOR INTENT!
AND THIS ONE TO PAY THE FREIGHT!
YERP?
IT'S NOT POSSIBLE. YOU KILLED ME.
WELL, THE BLADE DID. I WAS HOLDING IT AT THE TIME.
EXACTLY WHAT DO YOU THINK YOU'VE ACCOMPLISHED HERE, YOU INSOLENT, HALF-MORTAL BRAT?
YOU'RE STILL ALIVE?
OF COURSE NOT. ARE YOU DAFT?
HOW MANY HEADLESS WOMEN DO YOU COME ACROSS WHO ARE ALIVE? DOES THAT HAPPEN OFTEN IN YOUR IDIOTS' WORLD?
IT'S JUST THAT YOU STILL SEEM AWFULLY TALKATIVE.
I'M DEAD, DEAD, DEAD, AND I DON'T LIKE IT.

NO, I **DON'T** LIKE IT, NOT ONE BIT!

YOU'VE UPSET **ALL** MY PLANS.

I WAS GOING TO BE MARRIED. BUT WHO WANTS TO MARRY A **DEAD** WOMAN? PEOPLE WILL **SNIGGER** BEHIND OUR BACKS. I **WON'T** BE EMBARRASSED SO.

I'LL HAVE TO CANCEL ANY NUMBER OF SOCIAL ENGAGEMENTS NOW. DO YOU SEE THE **BOTHER** YOU'VE CAUSED?

I SUPPOSE I CAN STILL ATTEND THE UNSEELIE MIDWINTER BALL. THEY'RE **BARBARIANS** ANYWAY, WITH **NO** STANDARDS.

WHAT **I** SEE IS A NEED TO BE ON MY WAY.

PUNT

OH!

OH, **THIS**...

...THIS IS A MOST **INELEGANT** TURN!

WHERE'S MY CAR?

Kurt Huggins: artist • Zelda Devon: colorist

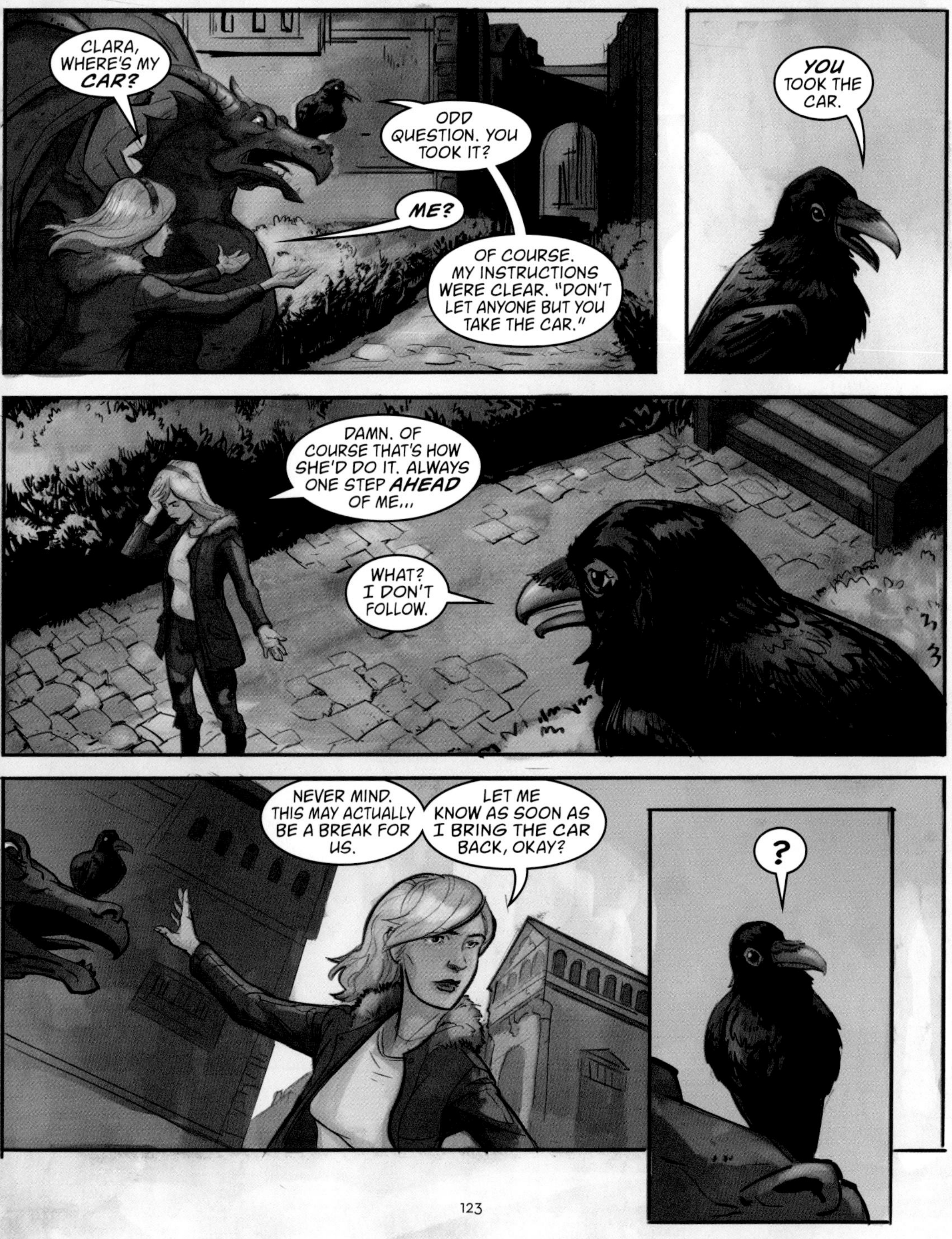

CLARA, WHERE'S MY *CAR?*
ODD QUESTION. YOU TOOK IT?
ME?
OF COURSE. MY INSTRUCTIONS WERE CLEAR. "DON'T LET ANYONE BUT YOU TAKE THE CAR."
YOU TOOK THE CAR.
DAMN. OF COURSE THAT'S HOW SHE'D DO IT. ALWAYS ONE STEP *AHEAD* OF ME...
WHAT? I DON'T FOLLOW.
NEVER MIND. THIS MAY ACTUALLY BE A BREAK FOR US.
LET ME KNOW AS SOON AS I BRING THE CAR BACK, OKAY?
?

THE BIG REVEAL

Shawn McManus: artist • Lee Loughridge: colorist

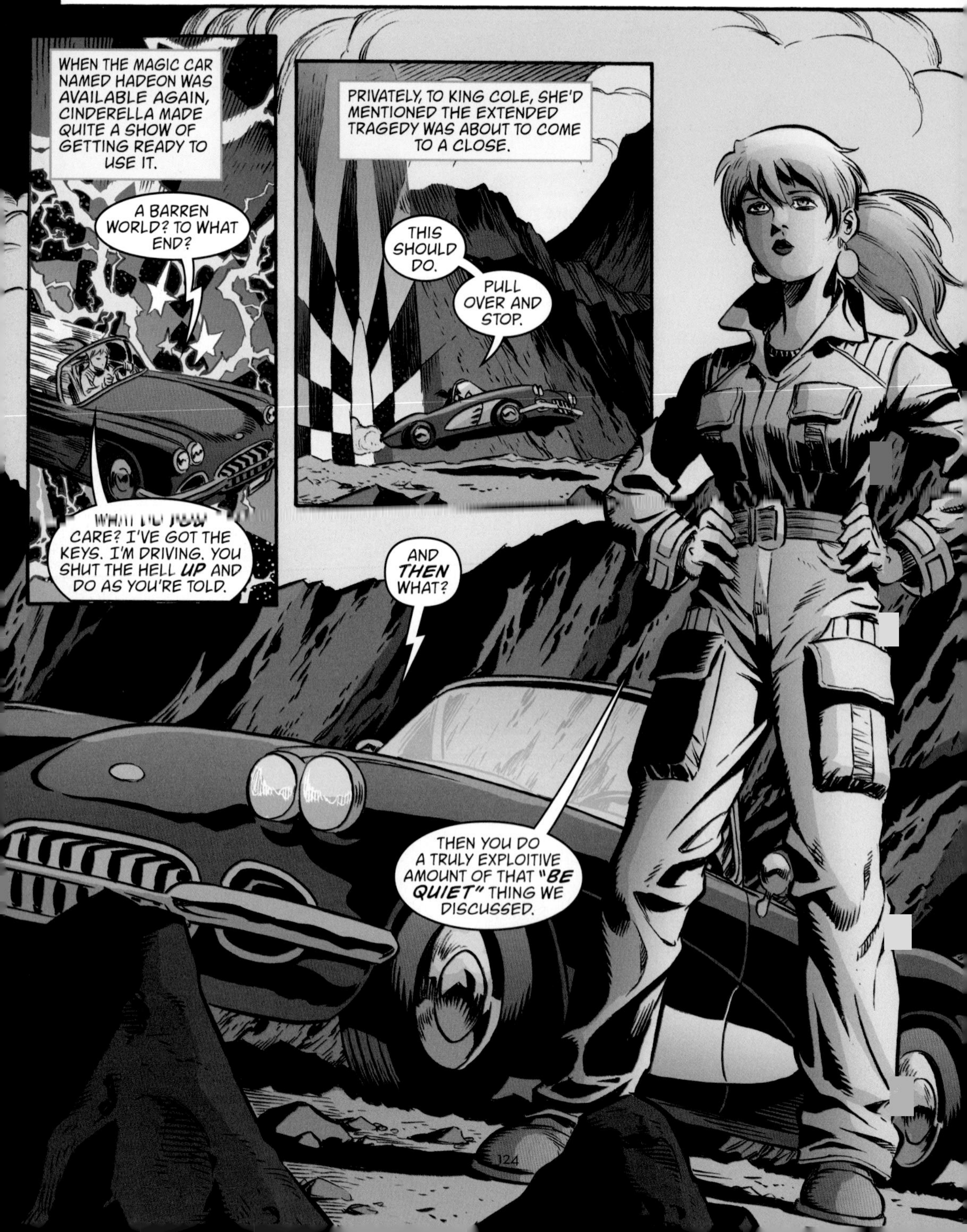
WHEN THE MAGIC CAR NAMED HADEON WAS AVAILABLE AGAIN, CINDERELLA MADE QUITE A SHOW OF GETTING READY TO USE IT.
A BARREN WORLD? TO WHAT END?
WHAT DO YOU CARE? I'VE GOT THE KEYS. I'M DRIVING. YOU SHUT THE HELL *UP* AND DO AS YOU'RE TOLD.
PRIVATELY, TO KING COLE, SHE'D MENTIONED THE EXTENDED TRAGEDY WAS ABOUT TO COME TO A CLOSE.
THIS SHOULD DO.
PULL OVER AND STOP.
AND *THEN* WHAT?
THEN YOU DO A TRULY EXPLOITIVE AMOUNT OF THAT ***"BE QUIET"*** THING WE DISCUSSED.

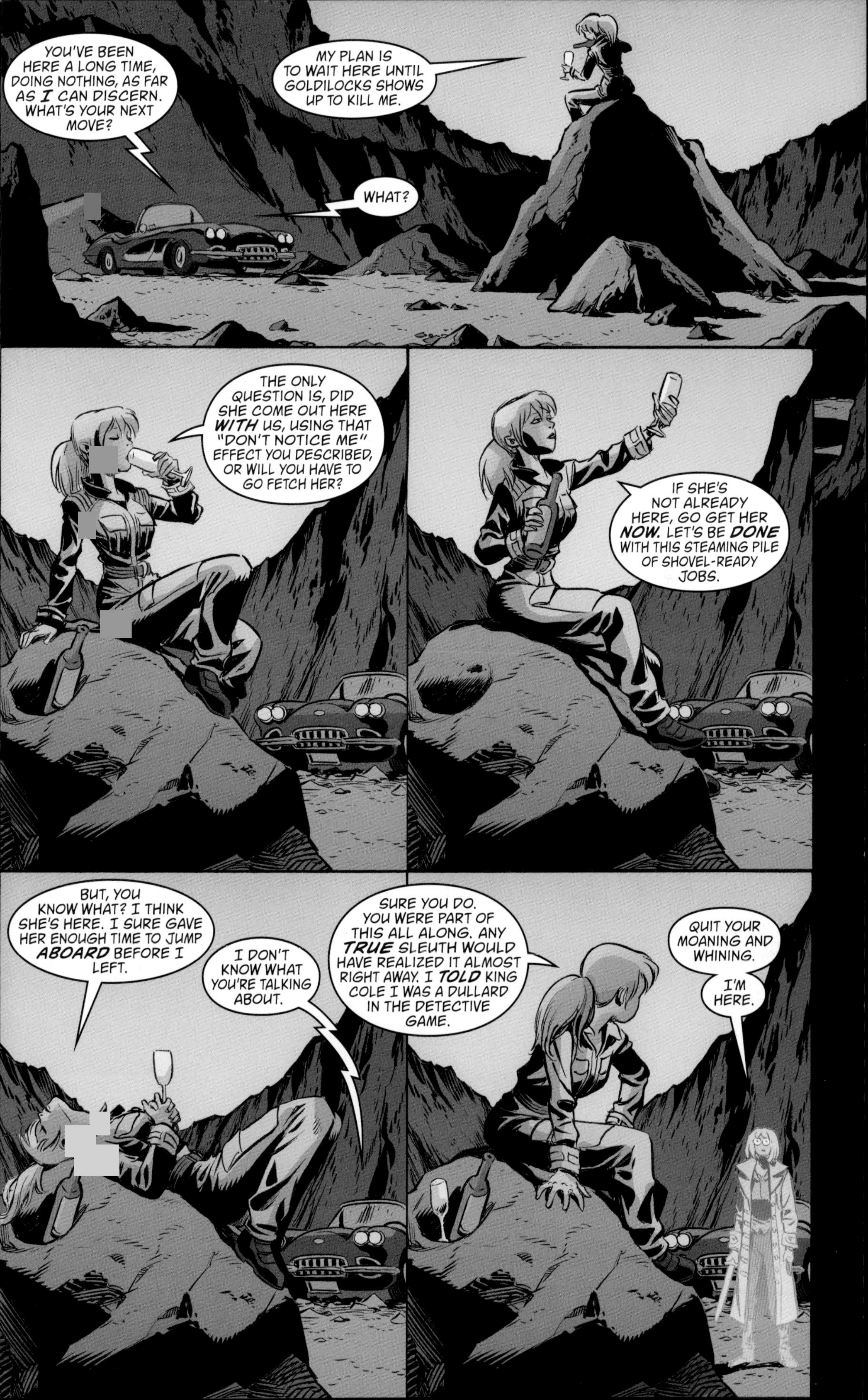

YOU'VE BEEN HERE A LONG TIME, DOING NOTHING, AS FAR AS *I* CAN DISCERN. WHAT'S YOUR NEXT MOVE?
MY PLAN IS TO WAIT HERE UNTIL GOLDILOCKS SHOWS UP TO KILL ME.
WHAT?
THE ONLY QUESTION IS, DID SHE COME OUT HERE *WITH* US, USING THAT "DON'T NOTICE ME" EFFECT YOU DESCRIBED, OR WILL YOU HAVE TO GO FETCH HER?
IF SHE'S NOT ALREADY HERE, GO GET HER *NOW.* LET'S BE *DONE* WITH THIS STEAMING PILE OF SHOVEL-READY JOBS.
BUT, YOU KNOW WHAT? I THINK SHE'S HERE. I SURE GAVE HER ENOUGH TIME TO JUMP *ABOARD* BEFORE I LEFT.
I DON'T KNOW WHAT YOU'RE TALKING ABOUT.
SURE YOU DO. YOU WERE PART OF THIS ALL ALONG. ANY *TRUE* SLEUTH WOULD HAVE REALIZED IT ALMOST RIGHT AWAY. I *TOLD* KING COLE I WAS A DULLARD IN THE DETECTIVE GAME.
QUIT YOUR MOANING AND WHINING.
I'M HERE.

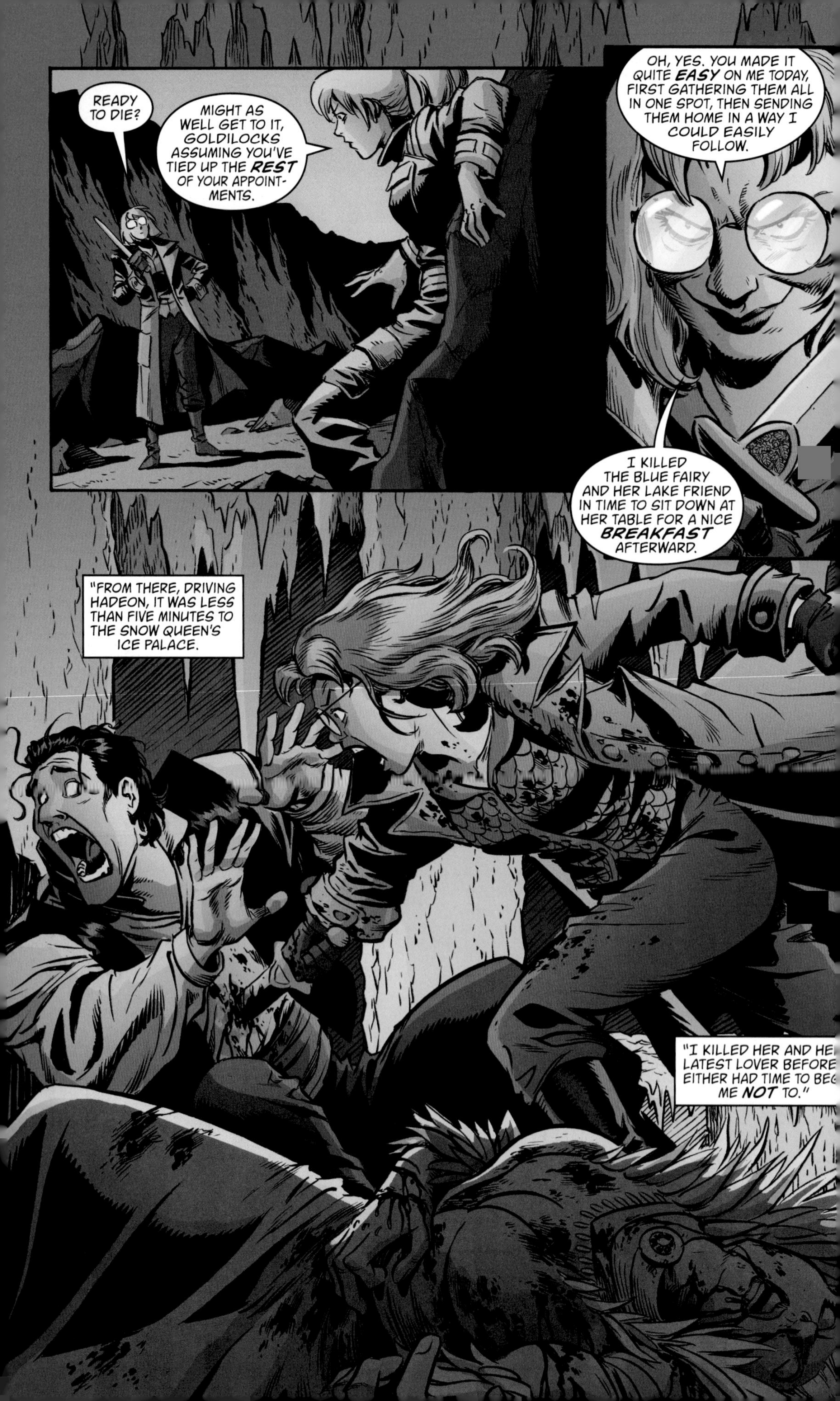
READY TO DIE?
MIGHT AS WELL GET TO IT, GOLDILOCKS ASSUMING YOU'VE TIED UP THE REST OF YOUR APPOINT-MENTS.
OH, YES. YOU MADE IT QUITE EASY ON ME TODAY, FIRST GATHERING THEM ALL IN ONE SPOT, THEN SENDING THEM HOME IN A WAY I COULD EASILY FOLLOW.
I KILLED THE BLUE FAIRY AND HER LAKE FRIEND IN TIME TO SIT DOWN AT HER TABLE FOR A NICE BREAKFAST AFTERWARD.
"FROM THERE, DRIVING HADEON, IT WAS LESS THAN FIVE MINUTES TO THE SNOW QUEEN'S ICE PALACE.
"I KILLED HER AND HE LATEST LOVER BEFORE EITHER HAD TIME TO BEG ME NOT TO."

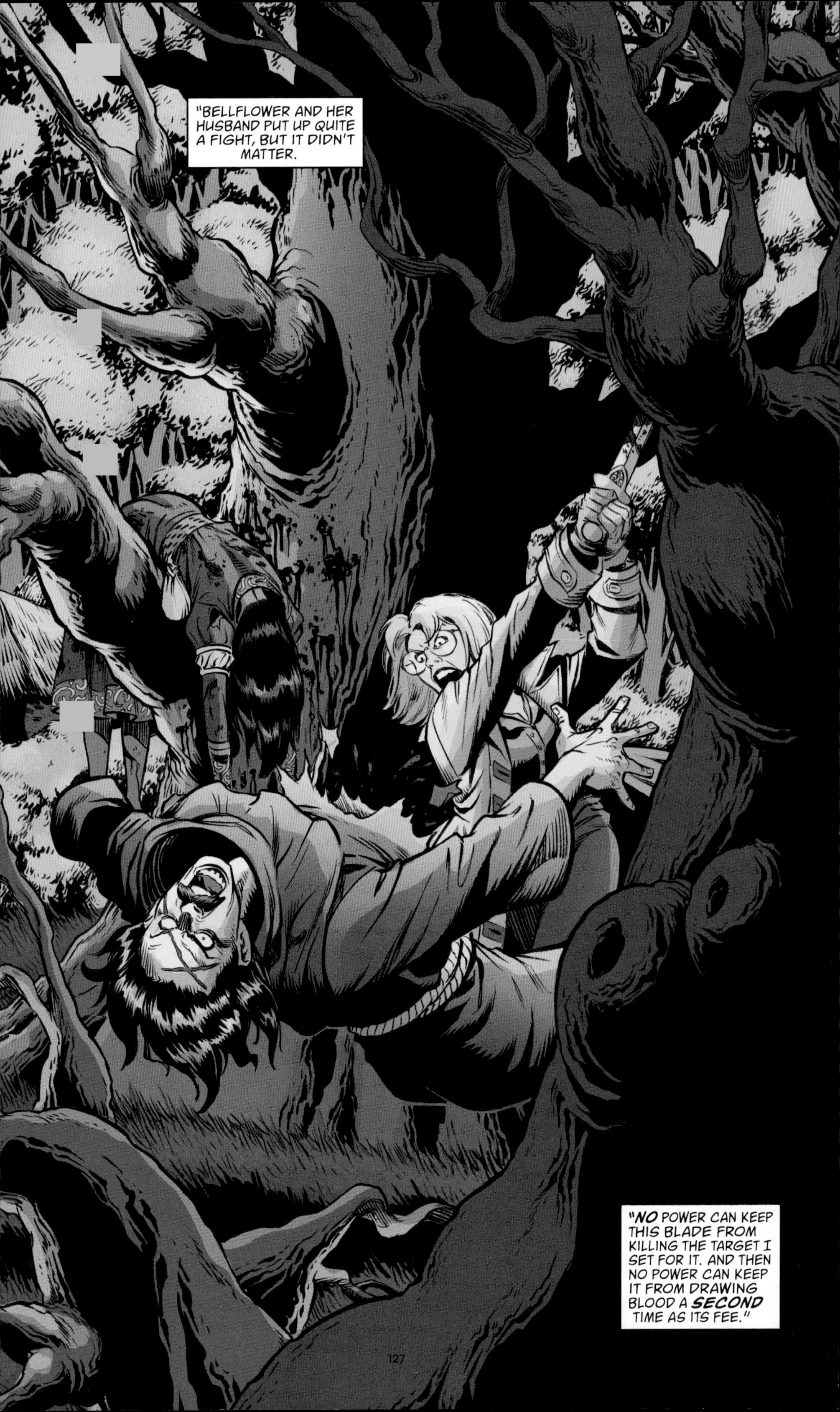
"BELLFLOWER AND HER HUSBAND PUT UP QUITE A FIGHT, BUT IT DIDN'T MATTER.
"NO POWER CAN KEEP THIS BLADE FROM KILLING THE TARGET I SET FOR IT. AND THEN NO POWER CAN KEEP IT FROM DRAWING BLOOD A SECOND TIME AS ITS FEE."

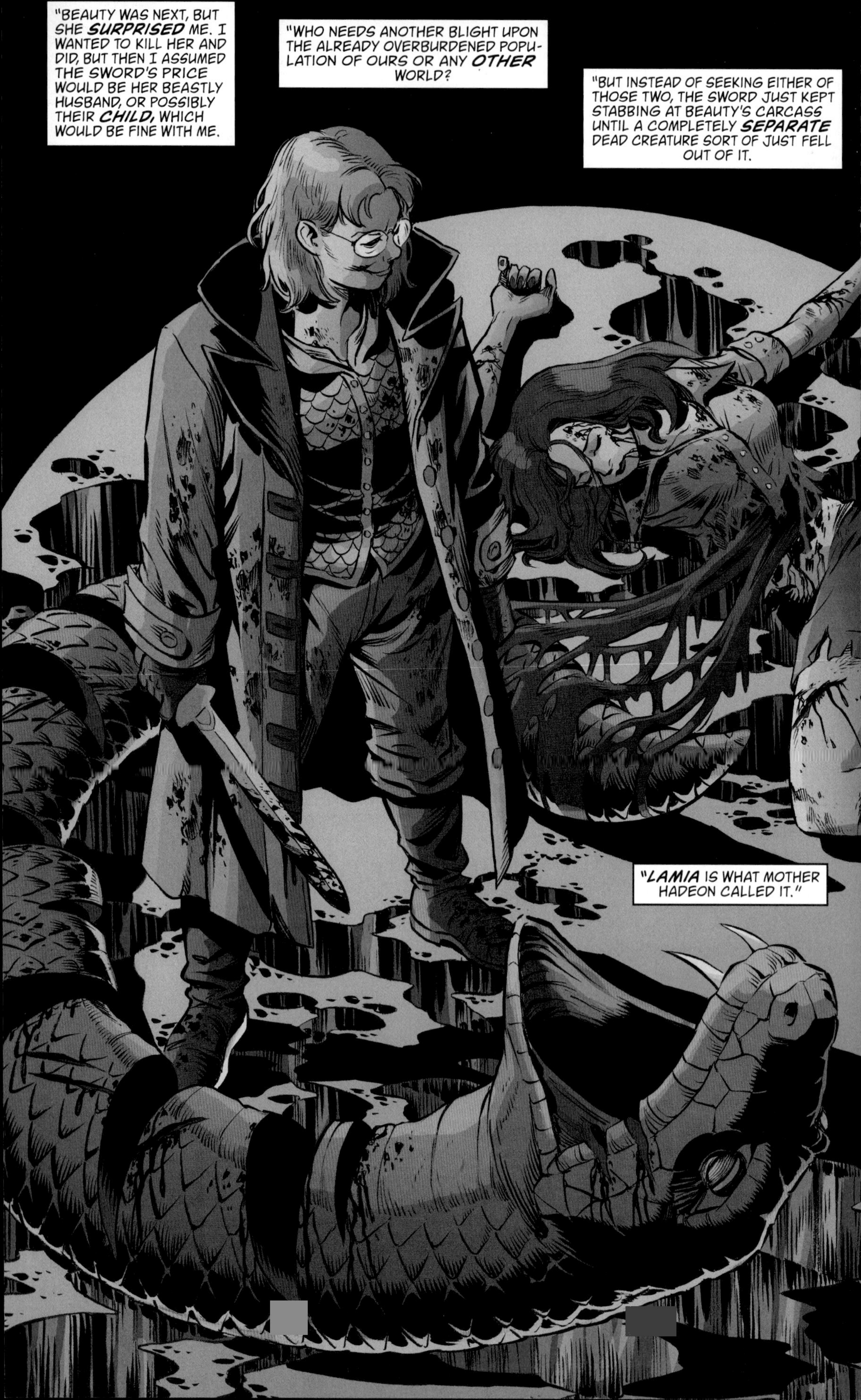
"BEAUTY WAS NEXT, BUT SHE SURPRISED ME. I WANTED TO KILL HER AND DID, BUT THEN I ASSUMED THE SWORD'S PRICE WOULD BE HER BEASTLY HUSBAND, OR POSSIBLY THEIR CHILD, WHICH WOULD BE FINE WITH ME.
"WHO NEEDS ANOTHER BLIGHT UPON THE ALREADY OVERBURDENED POPULATION OF OURS OR ANY OTHER WORLD?
"BUT INSTEAD OF SEEKING EITHER OF THOSE TWO, THE SWORD JUST KEPT STABBING AT BEAUTY'S CARCASS UNTIL A COMPLETELY SEPARATE DEAD CREATURE SORT OF JUST FELL OUT OF IT.
"LAMIA IS WHAT MOTHER HADEON CALLED IT."

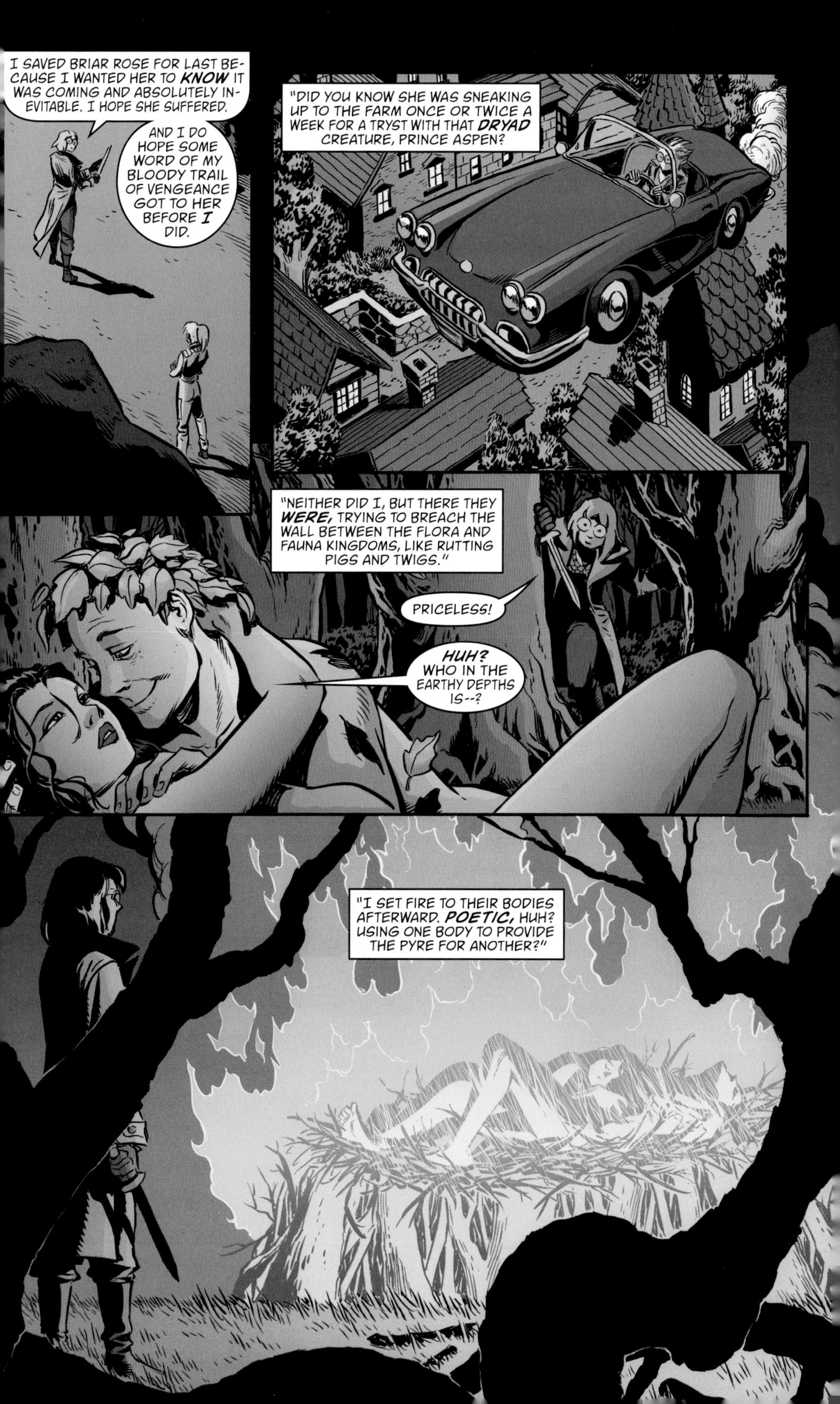

I SAVED BRIAR ROSE FOR LAST BECAUSE I WANTED HER TO **KNOW** IT WAS COMING AND ABSOLUTELY INEVITABLE. I HOPE SHE SUFFERED.
AND I DO HOPE SOME WORD OF MY BLOODY TRAIL OF VENGEANCE GOT TO HER BEFORE **I** DID.
"DID YOU KNOW SHE WAS SNEAKING UP TO THE FARM ONCE OR TWICE A WEEK FOR A TRYST WITH THAT **DRYAD** CREATURE, PRINCE ASPEN?
"NEITHER DID I, BUT THERE THEY **WERE,** TRYING TO BREACH THE WALL BETWEEN THE FLORA AND FAUNA KINGDOMS, LIKE RUTTING PIGS AND TWIGS."
PRICELESS!
HUH? WHO IN THE EARTHY DEPTHS IS--?
"I SET FIRE TO THEIR BODIES AFTERWARD. **POETIC,** HUH? USING ONE BODY TO PROVIDE THE PYRE FOR ANOTHER?"

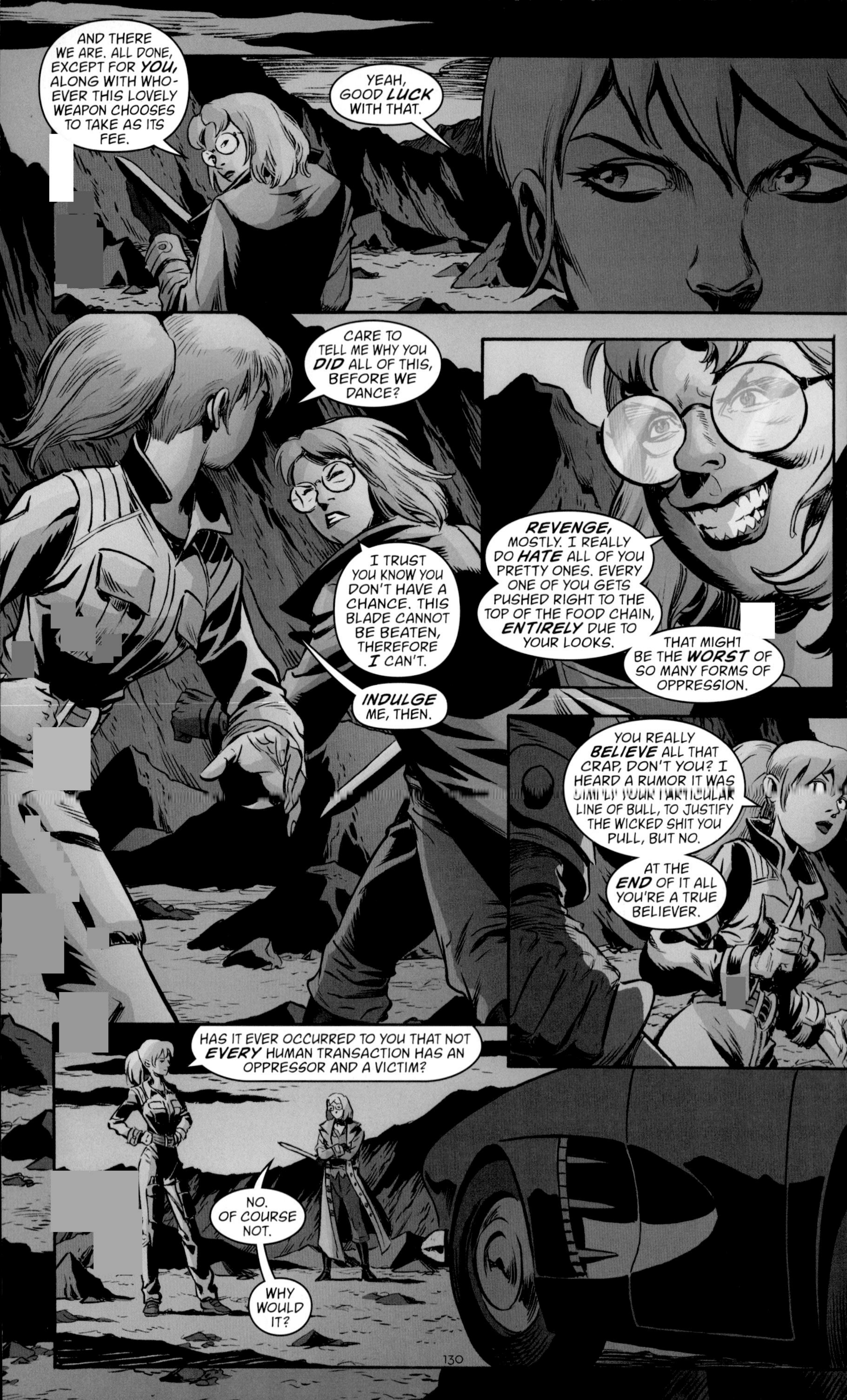
AND THERE WE ARE. ALL DONE, EXCEPT FOR YOU, ALONG WITH WHO-EVER THIS LOVELY WEAPON CHOOSES TO TAKE AS ITS FEE.
YEAH, GOOD LUCK WITH THAT.
CARE TO TELL ME WHY YOU DID ALL OF THIS, BEFORE WE DANCE?
I TRUST YOU KNOW YOU DON'T HAVE A CHANCE. THIS BLADE CANNOT BE BEATEN, THEREFORE I CAN'T.
INDULGE ME, THEN.
REVENGE, MOSTLY. I REALLY DO HATE ALL OF YOU PRETTY ONES. EVERY ONE OF YOU GETS PUSHED RIGHT TO THE TOP OF THE FOOD CHAIN, ENTIRELY DUE TO YOUR LOOKS.
THAT MIGHT BE THE WORST OF SO MANY FORMS OF OPPRESSION.
YOU REALLY BELIEVE ALL THAT CRAP, DON'T YOU? I HEARD A RUMOR IT WAS SIMPLY YOUR PARTICULAR LINE OF BULL, TO JUSTIFY THE WICKED SHIT YOU PULL, BUT NO.
AT THE END OF IT ALL YOU'RE A TRUE BELIEVER.
HAS IT EVER OCCURRED TO YOU THAT NOT EVERY HUMAN TRANSACTION HAS AN OPPRESSOR AND A VICTIM?
NO. OF COURSE NOT.
WHY WOULD IT?

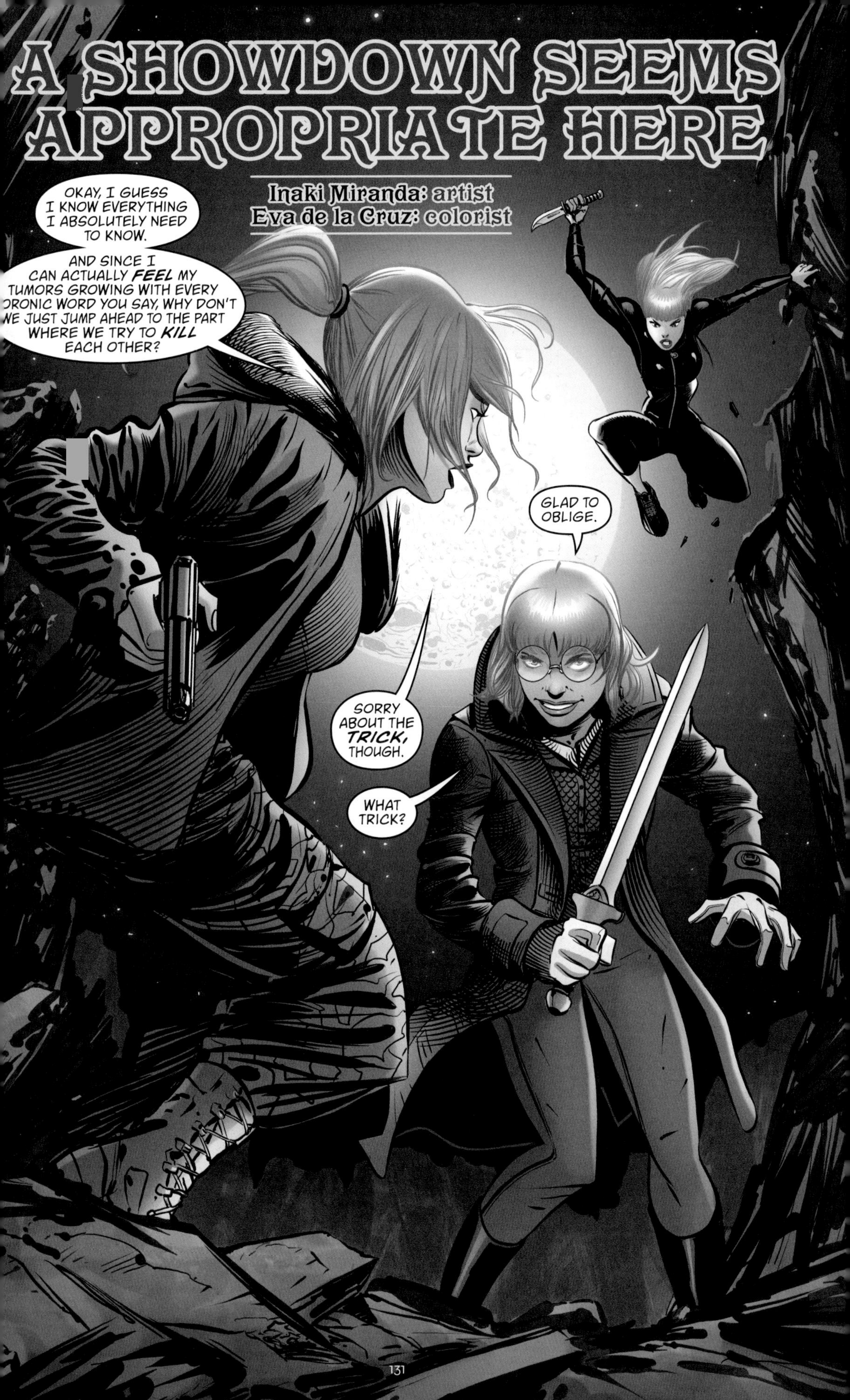

A SHOWDOWN SEEMS APPROPRIATE HERE
Inaki Miranda: artist
Eva de la Cruz: colorist
OKAY, I GUESS I KNOW EVERYTHING I ABSOLUTELY NEED TO KNOW.
AND SINCE I CAN ACTUALLY FEEL MY TUMORS GROWING WITH EVERY RONIC WORD YOU SAY, WHY DON'T E JUST JUMP AHEAD TO THE PART WHERE WE TRY TO KILL EACH OTHER?
GLAD TO OBLIGE.
SORRY ABOUT THE TRICK, THOUGH.
WHAT TRICK?

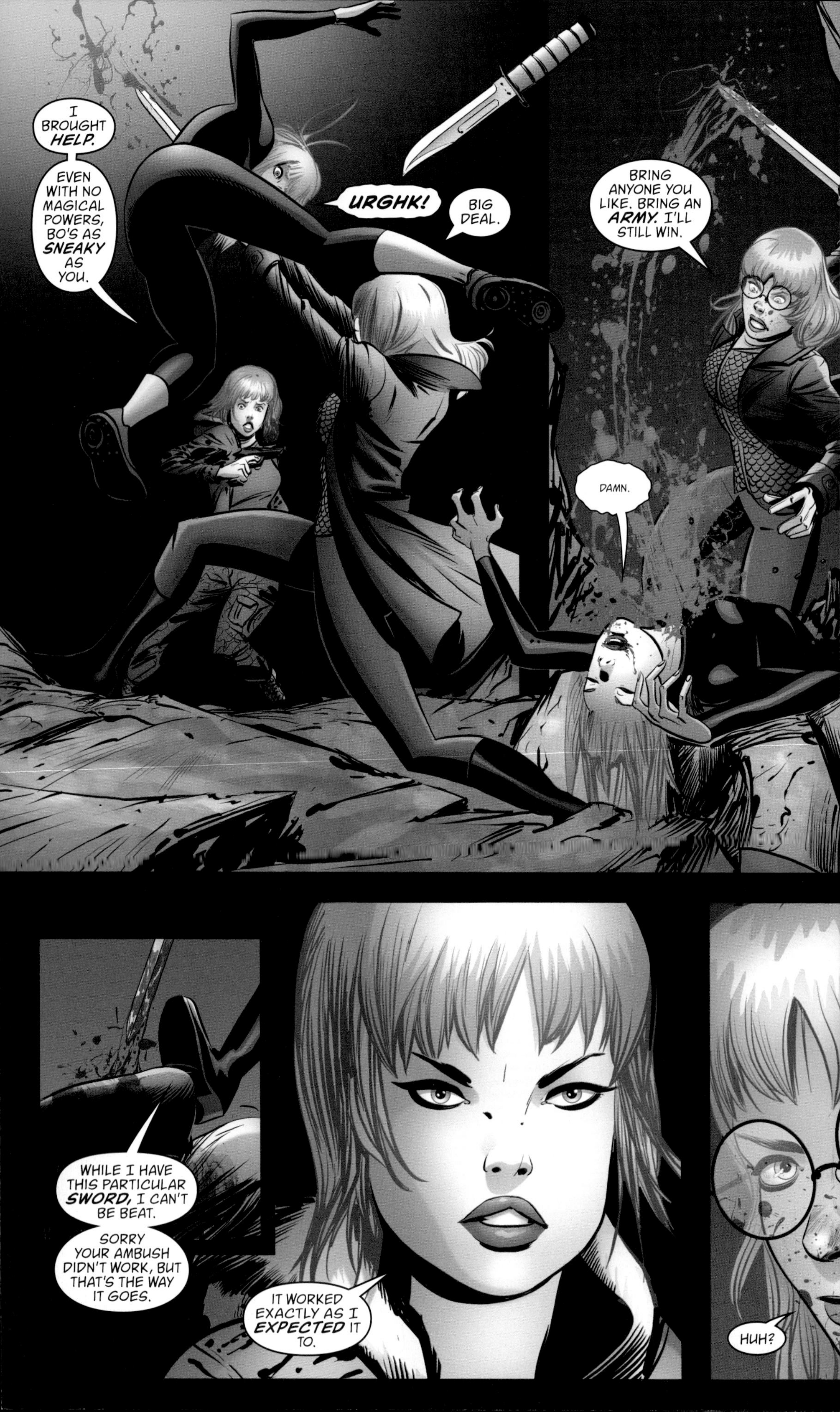

I BROUGHT HELP.
EVEN WITH NO MAGICAL POWERS, BO'S AS SNEAKY AS YOU.
URGHK!
BIG DEAL.
BRING ANYONE YOU LIKE. BRING AN ARMY. I'LL STILL WIN.
DAMN.
WHILE I HAVE THIS PARTICULAR SWORD, I CAN'T BE BEAT.
SORRY YOUR AMBUSH DIDN'T WORK, BUT THAT'S THE WAY IT GOES.
IT WORKED EXACTLY AS I EXPECTED IT TO.
HUH?

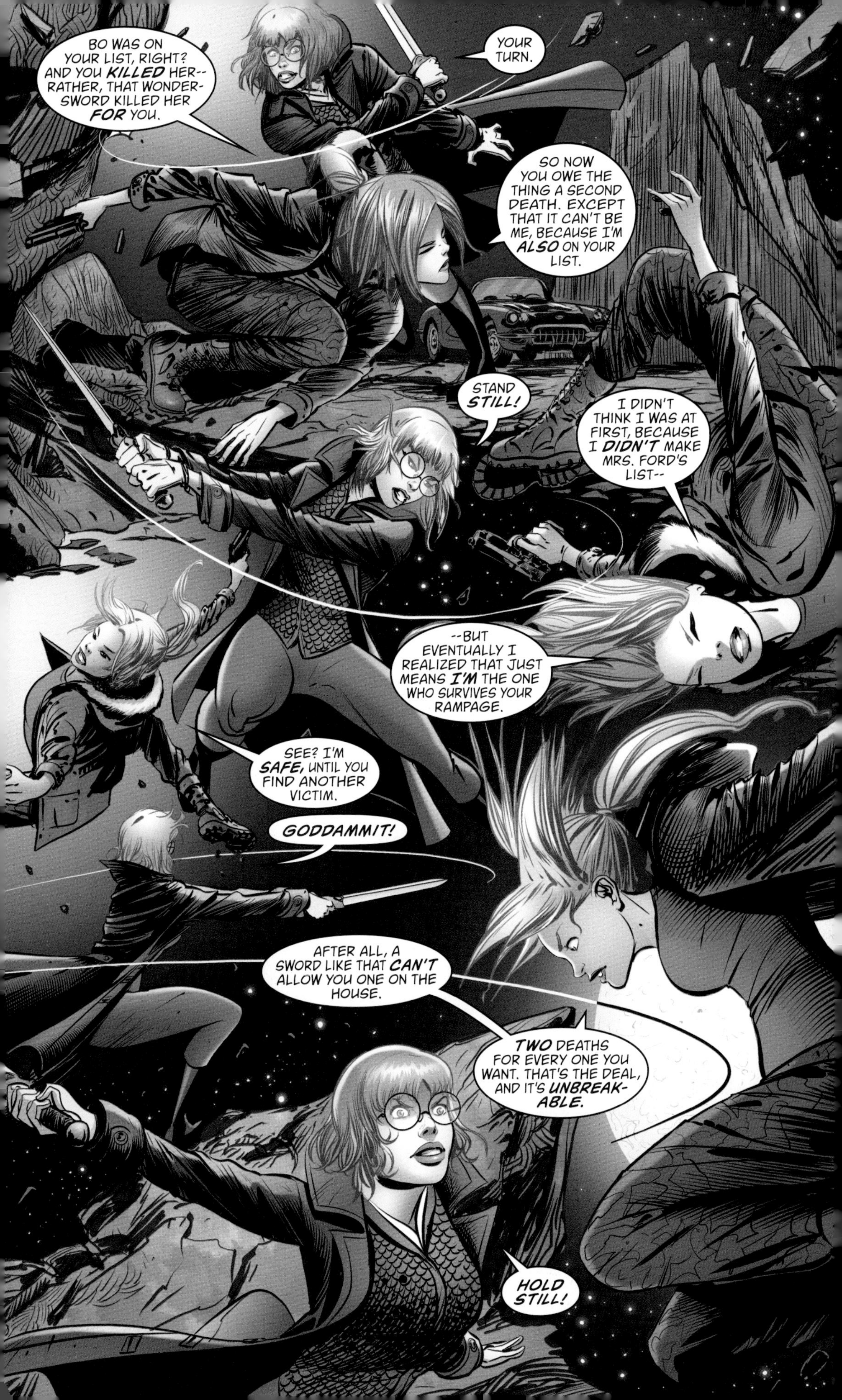
BO WAS ON YOUR LIST, RIGHT? AND YOU KILLED HER-- RATHER, THAT WONDER-SWORD KILLED HER FOR YOU.
YOUR TURN.
SO NOW YOU OWE THE THING A SECOND DEATH. EXCEPT THAT IT CAN'T BE ME, BECAUSE I'M ALSO ON YOUR LIST.
STAND STILL!
I DIDN'T THINK I WAS AT FIRST, BECAUSE I DIDN'T MAKE MRS. FORD'S LIST--
--BUT EVENTUALLY I REALIZED THAT JUST MEANS I'M THE ONE WHO SURVIVES YOUR RAMPAGE.
SEE? I'M SAFE, UNTIL YOU FIND ANOTHER VICTIM.
GODDAMMIT!
AFTER ALL, A SWORD LIKE THAT CAN'T ALLOW YOU ONE ON THE HOUSE.
TWO DEATHS FOR EVERY ONE YOU WANT. THAT'S THE DEAL, AND IT'S UNBREAK-ABLE.
HOLD STILL!

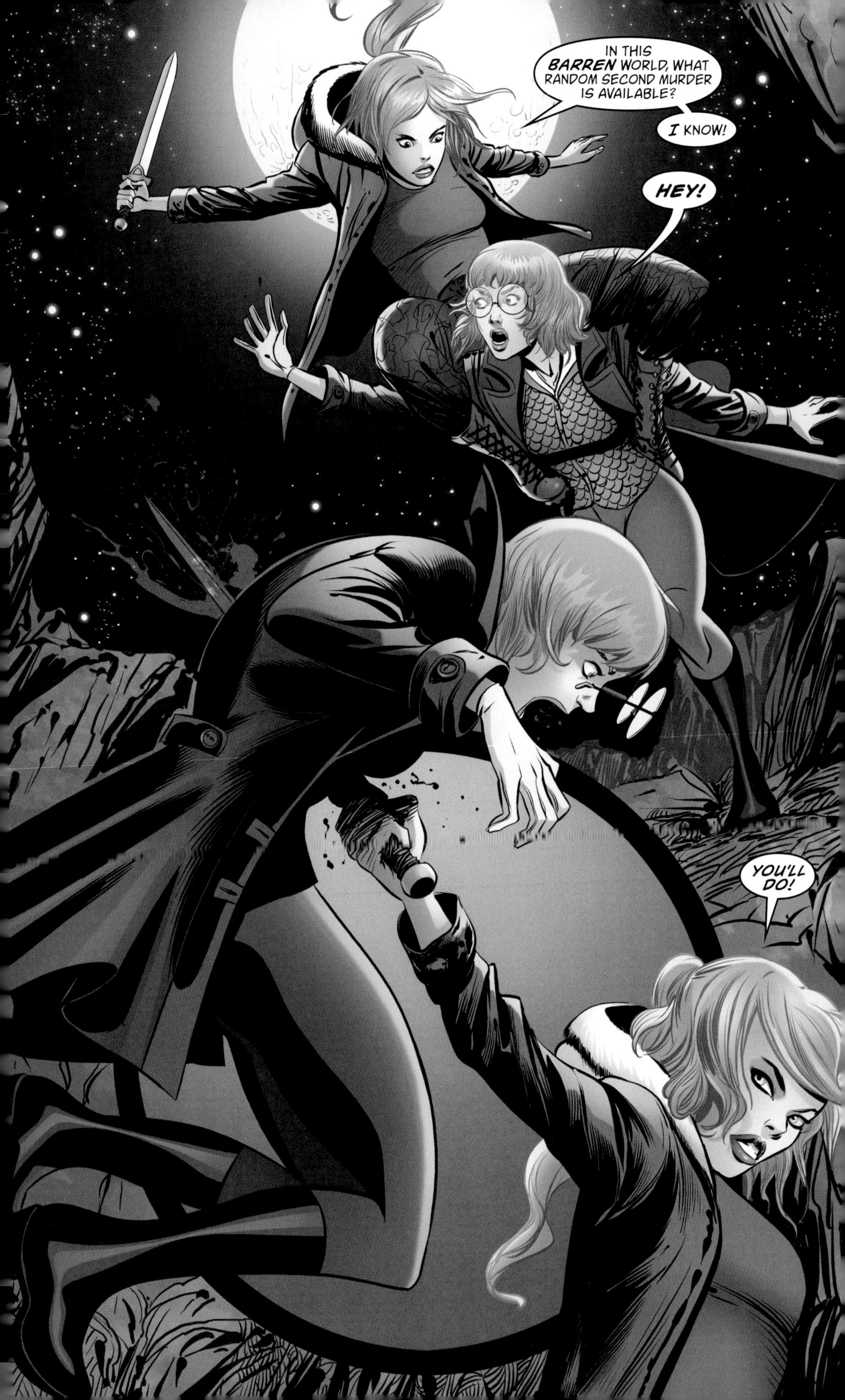
IN THIS BARREN WORLD, WHAT RANDOM SECOND MURDER IS AVAILABLE?
I KNOW!
HEY!
YOU'LL DO!

SUNDAY

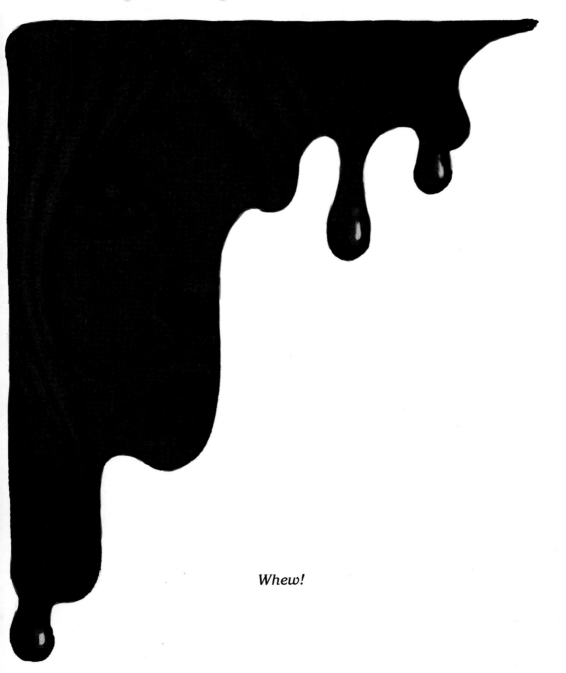

Whew!

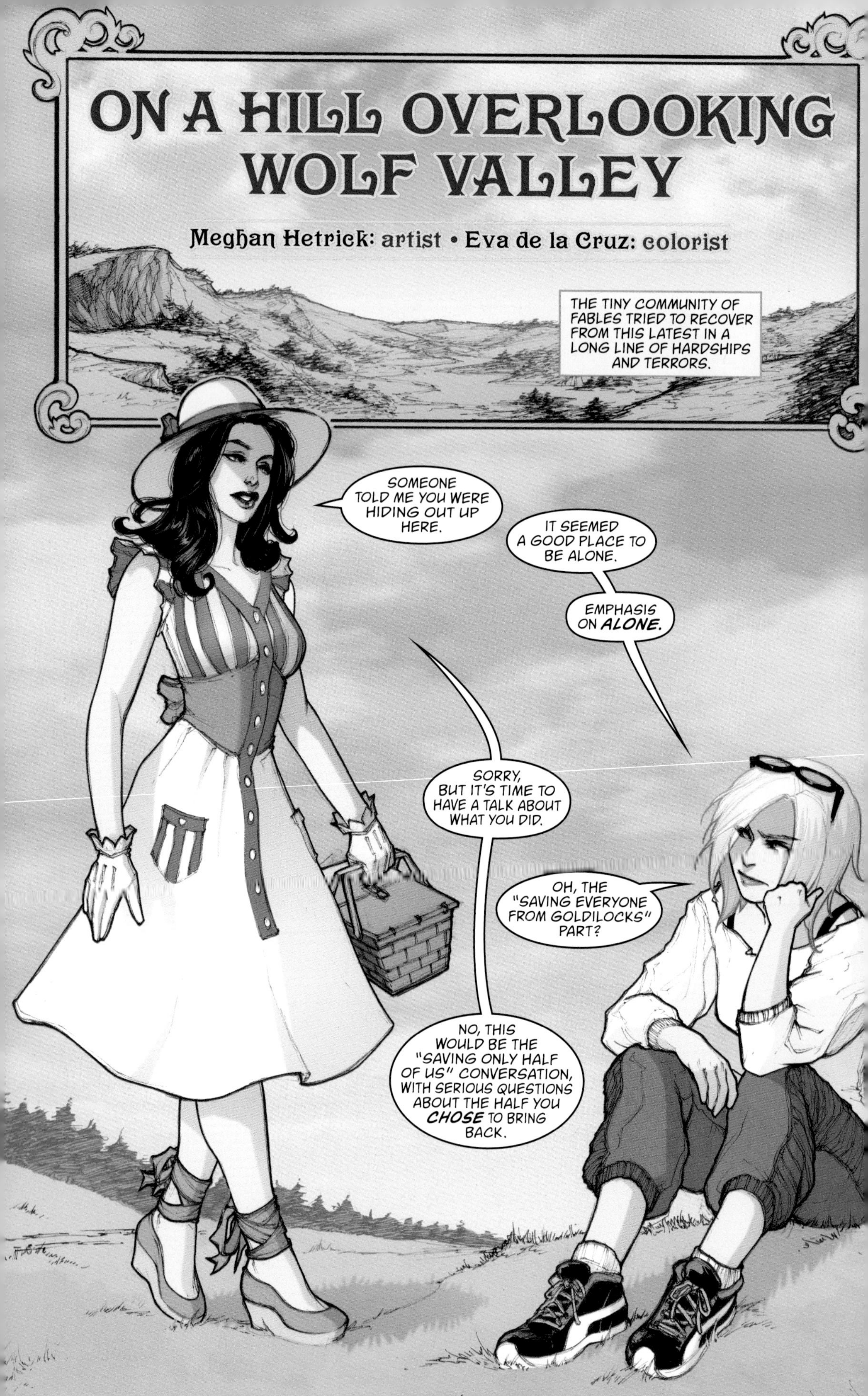
ON A HILL OVERLOOKING WOLF VALLEY
Meghan Hetrick: artist • Eva de la Cruz: colorist
THE TINY COMMUNITY OF FABLES TRIED TO RECOVER FROM THIS LATEST IN A LONG LINE OF HARDSHIPS AND TERRORS.
SOMEONE TOLD ME YOU WERE HIDING OUT UP HERE.
IT SEEMED A GOOD PLACE TO BE ALONE.
EMPHASIS ON ALONE.
SORRY, BUT IT'S TIME TO HAVE A TALK ABOUT WHAT YOU DID.
OH, THE "SAVING EVERYONE FROM GOLDILOCKS" PART?
NO, THIS WOULD BE THE "SAVING ONLY HALF OF US" CONVERSATION, WITH SERIOUS QUESTIONS ABOUT THE HALF YOU CHOSE TO BRING BACK.

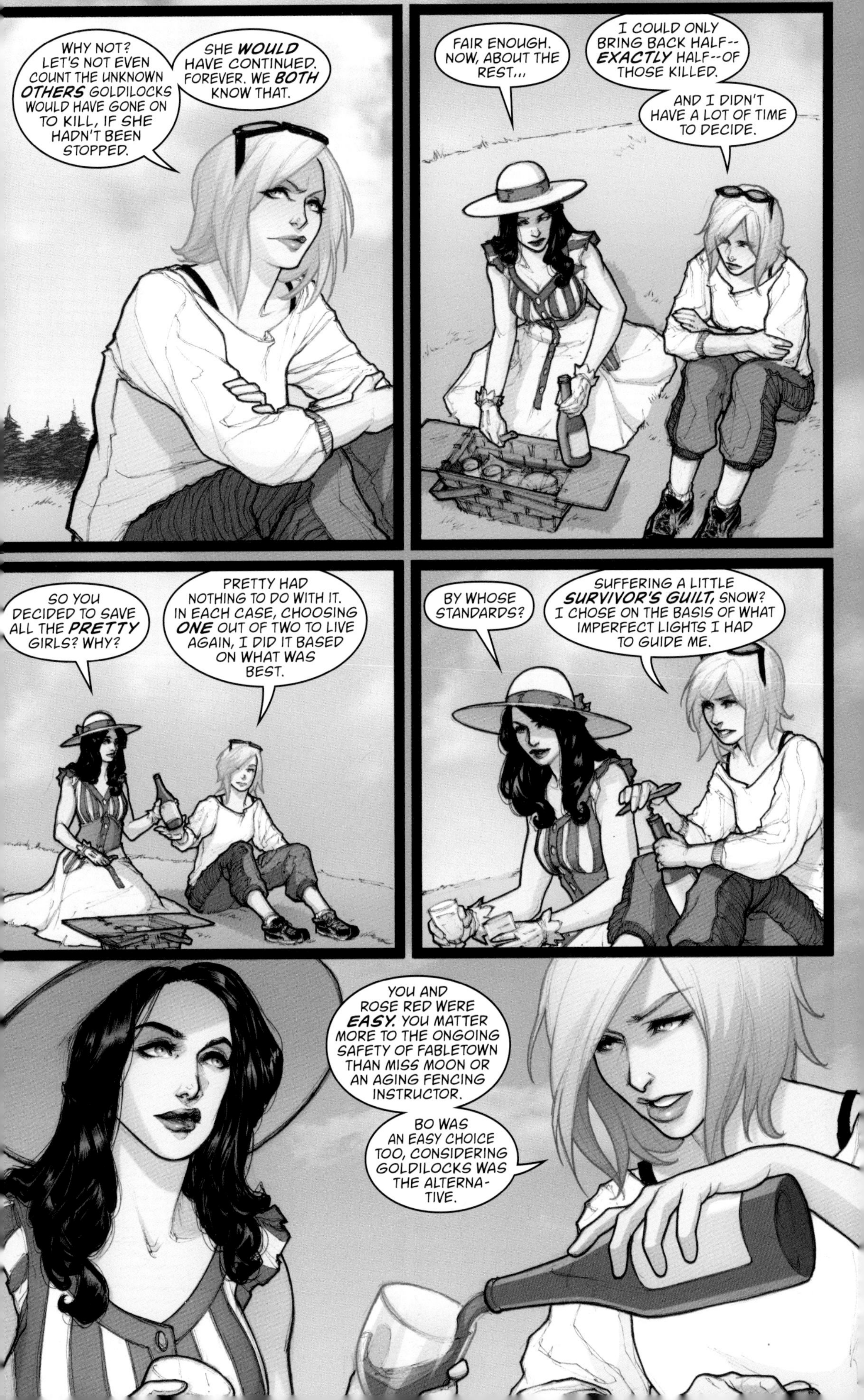
WHY NOT? LET'S NOT EVEN COUNT THE UNKNOWN OTHERS GOLDILOCKS WOULD HAVE GONE ON TO KILL, IF SHE HADN'T BEEN STOPPED.
SHE WOULD HAVE CONTINUED. FOREVER. WE BOTH KNOW THAT.
FAIR ENOUGH. NOW, ABOUT THE REST...
I COULD ONLY BRING BACK HALF-- EXACTLY HALF--OF THOSE KILLED.
AND I DIDN'T HAVE A LOT OF TIME TO DECIDE.
SO YOU DECIDED TO SAVE ALL THE PRETTY GIRLS? WHY?
PRETTY HAD NOTHING TO DO WITH IT. IN EACH CASE, CHOOSING ONE OUT OF TWO TO LIVE AGAIN, I DID IT BASED ON WHAT WAS BEST.
BY WHOSE STANDARDS?
SUFFERING A LITTLE SURVIVOR'S GUILT, SNOW? I CHOSE ON THE BASIS OF WHAT IMPERFECT LIGHTS I HAD TO GUIDE ME.
YOU AND ROSE RED WERE EASY. YOU MATTER MORE TO THE ONGOING SAFETY OF FABLETOWN THAN MISS MOON OR AN AGING FENCING INSTRUCTOR.
BO WAS AN EASY CHOICE TOO, CONSIDERING GOLDILOCKS WAS THE ALTERNA-TIVE.

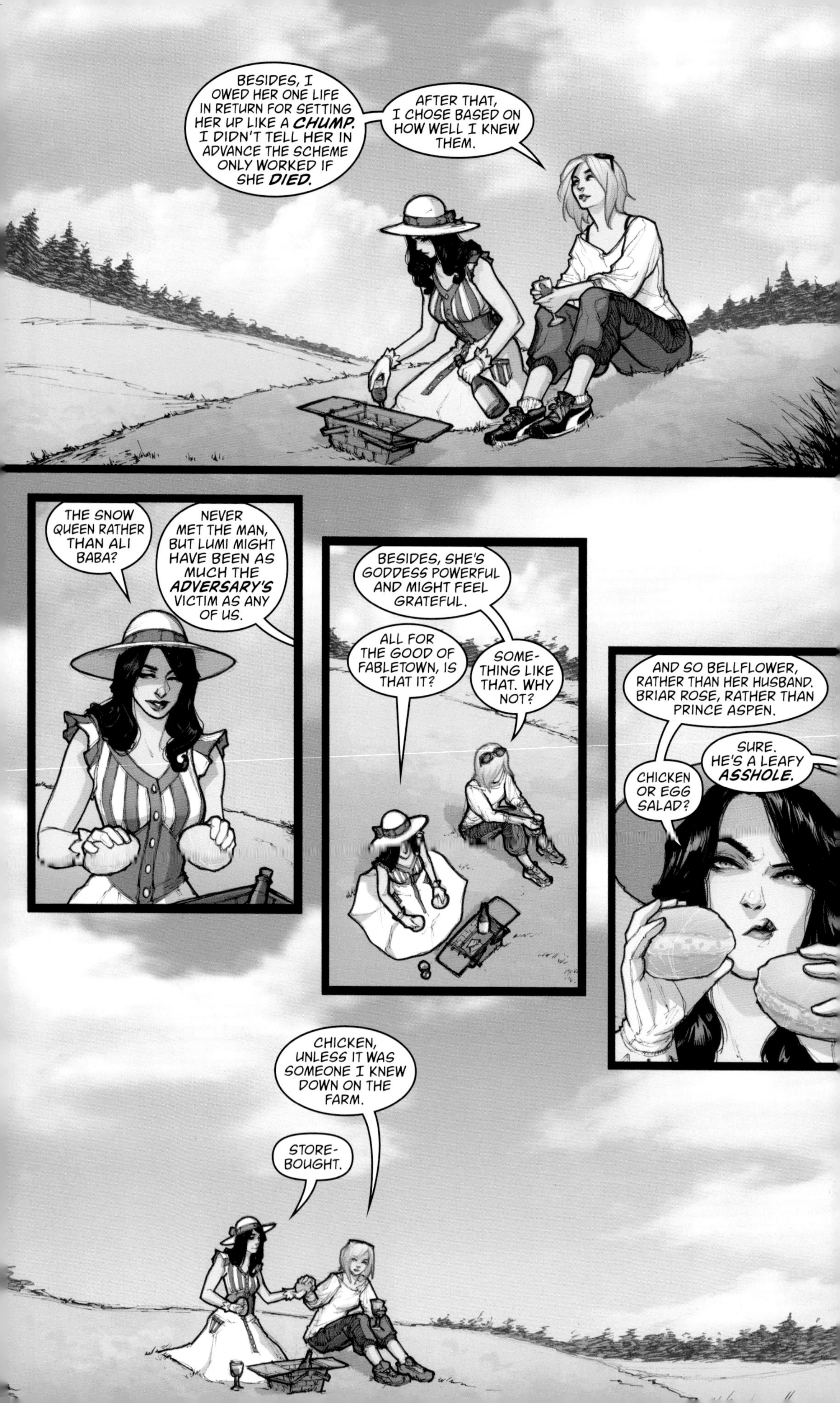
BESIDES, I OWED HER ONE LIFE IN RETURN FOR SETTING HER UP LIKE A CHUMP. I DIDN'T TELL HER IN ADVANCE THE SCHEME ONLY WORKED IF SHE DIED.
AFTER THAT, I CHOSE BASED ON HOW WELL I KNEW THEM.
THE SNOW QUEEN RATHER THAN ALI BABA?
NEVER MET THE MAN, BUT LUMI MIGHT HAVE BEEN AS MUCH THE ADVERSARY'S VICTIM AS ANY OF US.
BESIDES, SHE'S GODDESS POWERFUL AND MIGHT FEEL GRATEFUL.
ALL FOR THE GOOD OF FABLETOWN, IS THAT IT?
SOME-THING LIKE THAT. WHY NOT?
AND SO BELLFLOWER, RATHER THAN HER HUSBAND. BRIAR ROSE, RATHER THAN PRINCE ASPEN.
SURE. HE'S A LEAFY ASSHOLE.
CHICKEN OR EGG SALAD?
CHICKEN, UNLESS IT WAS SOMEONE I KNEW DOWN ON THE FARM.
STORE-BOUGHT.

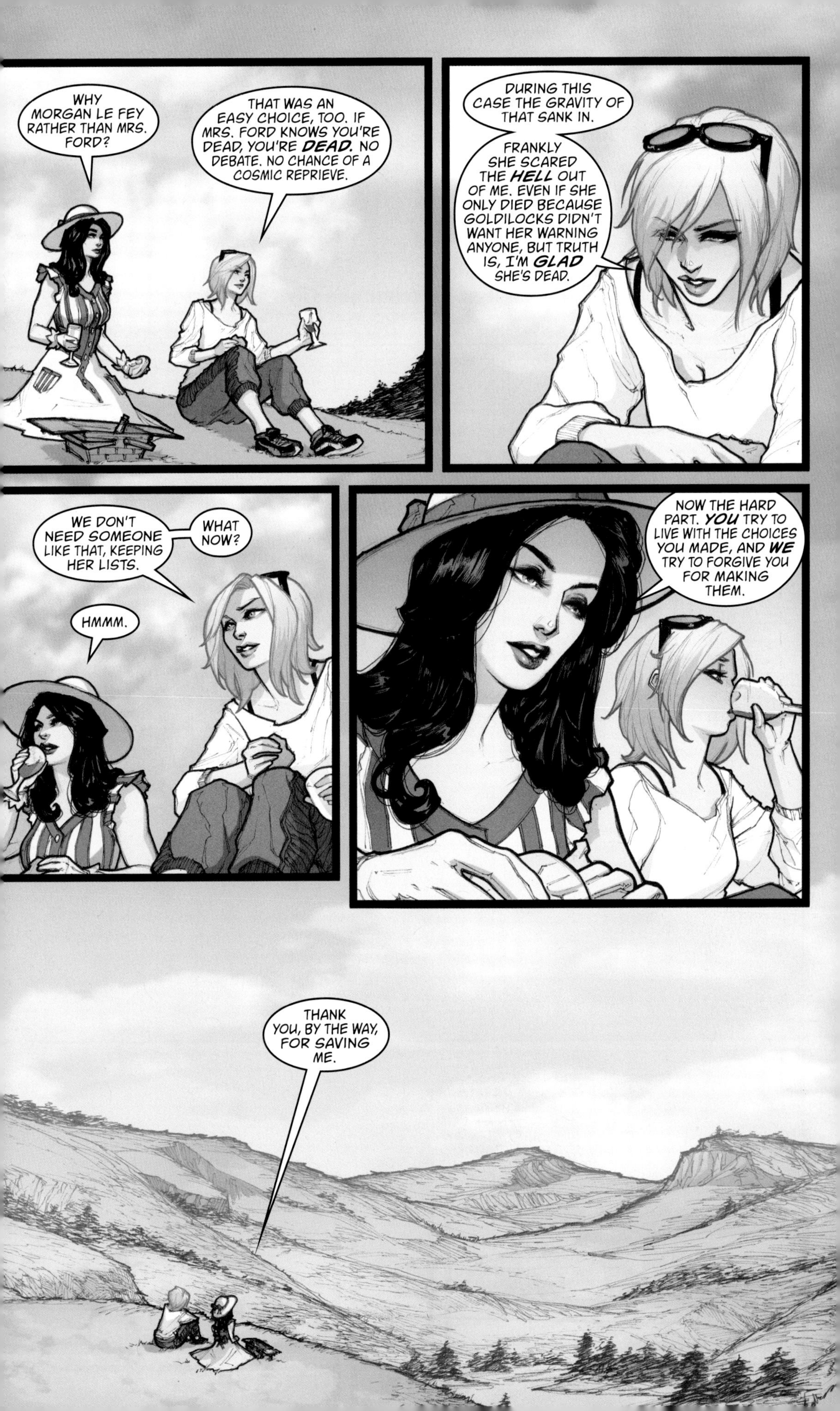

WHY MORGAN LE FEY RATHER THAN MRS. FORD?
THAT WAS AN EASY CHOICE, TOO. IF MRS. FORD KNOWS YOU'RE DEAD, YOU'RE DEAD. NO DEBATE. NO CHANCE OF A COSMIC REPRIEVE.
DURING THIS CASE THE GRAVITY OF THAT SANK IN.
FRANKLY SHE SCARED THE HELL OUT OF ME. EVEN IF SHE ONLY DIED BECAUSE GOLDILOCKS DIDN'T WANT HER WARNING ANYONE, BUT TRUTH IS, I'M GLAD SHE'S DEAD.
WE DON'T NEED SOMEONE LIKE THAT, KEEPING HER LISTS.
WHAT NOW?
HMMM.
NOW THE HARD PART. YOU TRY TO LIVE WITH THE CHOICES YOU MADE, AND WE TRY TO FORGIVE YOU FOR MAKING THEM.
THANK YOU, BY THE WAY, FOR SAVING ME.

MY MOTHER THE CAR

Kevin Maquire: artist • Rosemary Cheetham: colorist

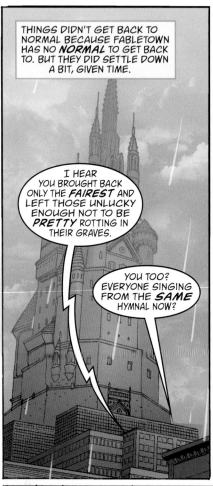

THINGS DIDN'T GET BACK TO NORMAL BECAUSE FABLETOWN HAS NO **NORMAL** TO GET BACK TO. BUT THEY DID SETTLE DOWN A BIT, GIVEN TIME.

I HEAR YOU BROUGHT BACK ONLY THE **FAIREST** AND LEFT THOSE UNLUCKY ENOUGH NOT TO BE **PRETTY** ROTTING IN THEIR GRAVES.

YOU TOO? EVERYONE SINGING FROM THE **SAME** HYMNAL NOW?

I'M JUST POINTING OUT THAT GOLDILOCKS HAD THE **TRUTH** OF IT ALL ALONG. THIS WRETCHED PLACE IS A **TYRANNY** OF THE BEAUTIFUL PEOPLE.

CRY ME A RIVER.

YOU AND I ARE GOING FOR A RIDE. DEPENDING ON HOW WELL AND **ENTHUSIASTICALLY** YOU ANSWER QUESTIONS, YOU **MAY** BE ALLOWED TO RETURN FROM IT.

OH, I'M HARDLY WORRIED ABOUT THAT. I'M NOT SURE YOU COULD **DO** ME PERMANENT HARM.

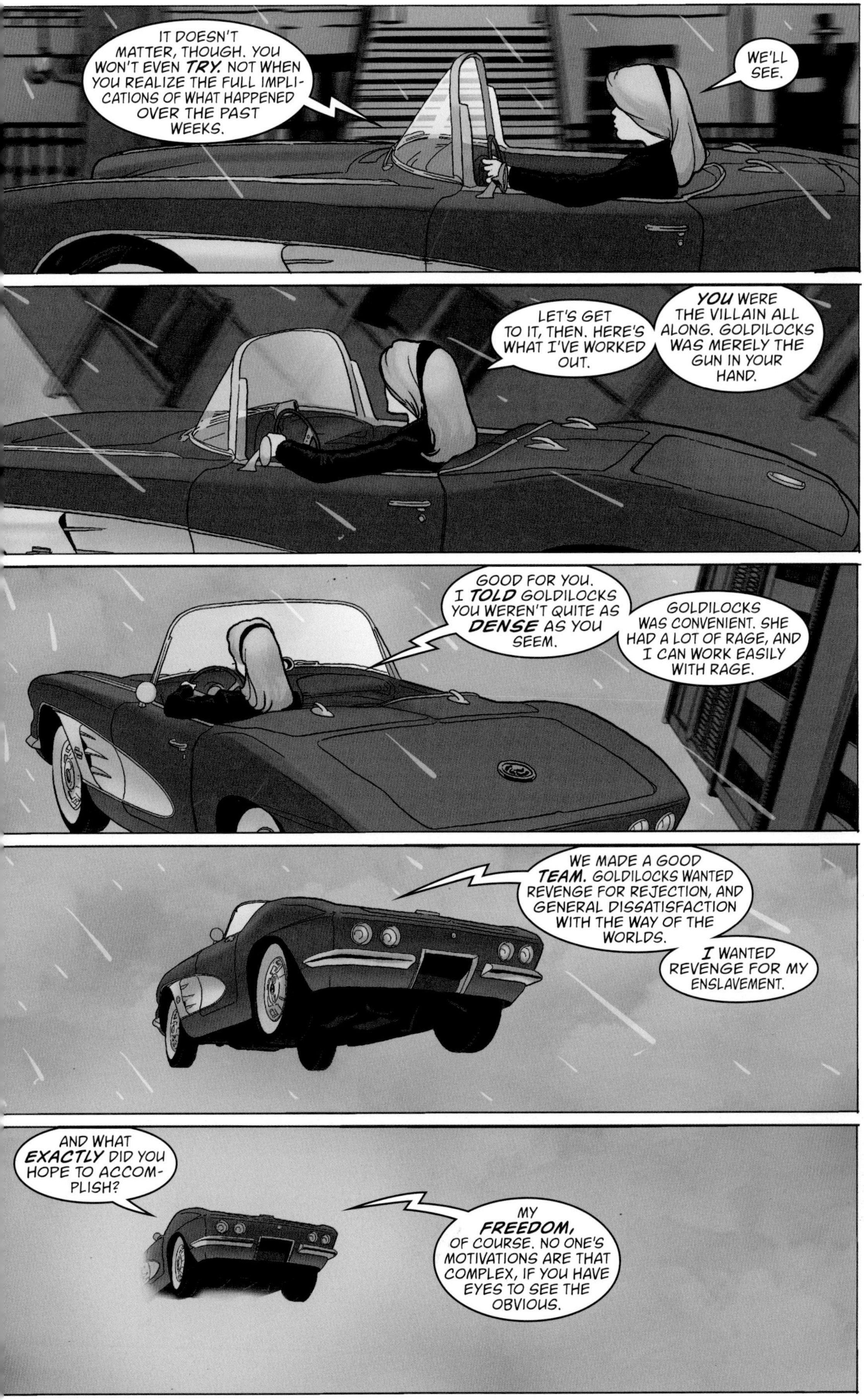
IT DOESN'T MATTER, THOUGH. YOU WON'T EVEN TRY. NOT WHEN YOU REALIZE THE FULL IMPLICATIONS OF WHAT HAPPENED OVER THE PAST WEEKS.
WE'LL SEE.
LET'S GET TO IT, THEN. HERE'S WHAT I'VE WORKED OUT.
YOU WERE THE VILLAIN ALL ALONG. GOLDILOCKS WAS MERELY THE GUN IN YOUR HAND.
GOOD FOR YOU. I TOLD GOLDILOCKS YOU WEREN'T QUITE AS DENSE AS YOU SEEM.
GOLDILOCKS WAS CONVENIENT. SHE HAD A LOT OF RAGE, AND I CAN WORK EASILY WITH RAGE.
WE MADE A GOOD TEAM. GOLDILOCKS WANTED REVENGE FOR REJECTION, AND GENERAL DISSATISFACTION WITH THE WAY OF THE WORLDS.
I WANTED REVENGE FOR MY ENSLAVEMENT.
AND WHAT EXACTLY DID YOU HOPE TO ACCOMPLISH?
MY FREEDOM, OF COURSE. NO ONE'S MOTIVATIONS ARE THAT COMPLEX, IF YOU HAVE EYES TO SEE THE OBVIOUS.

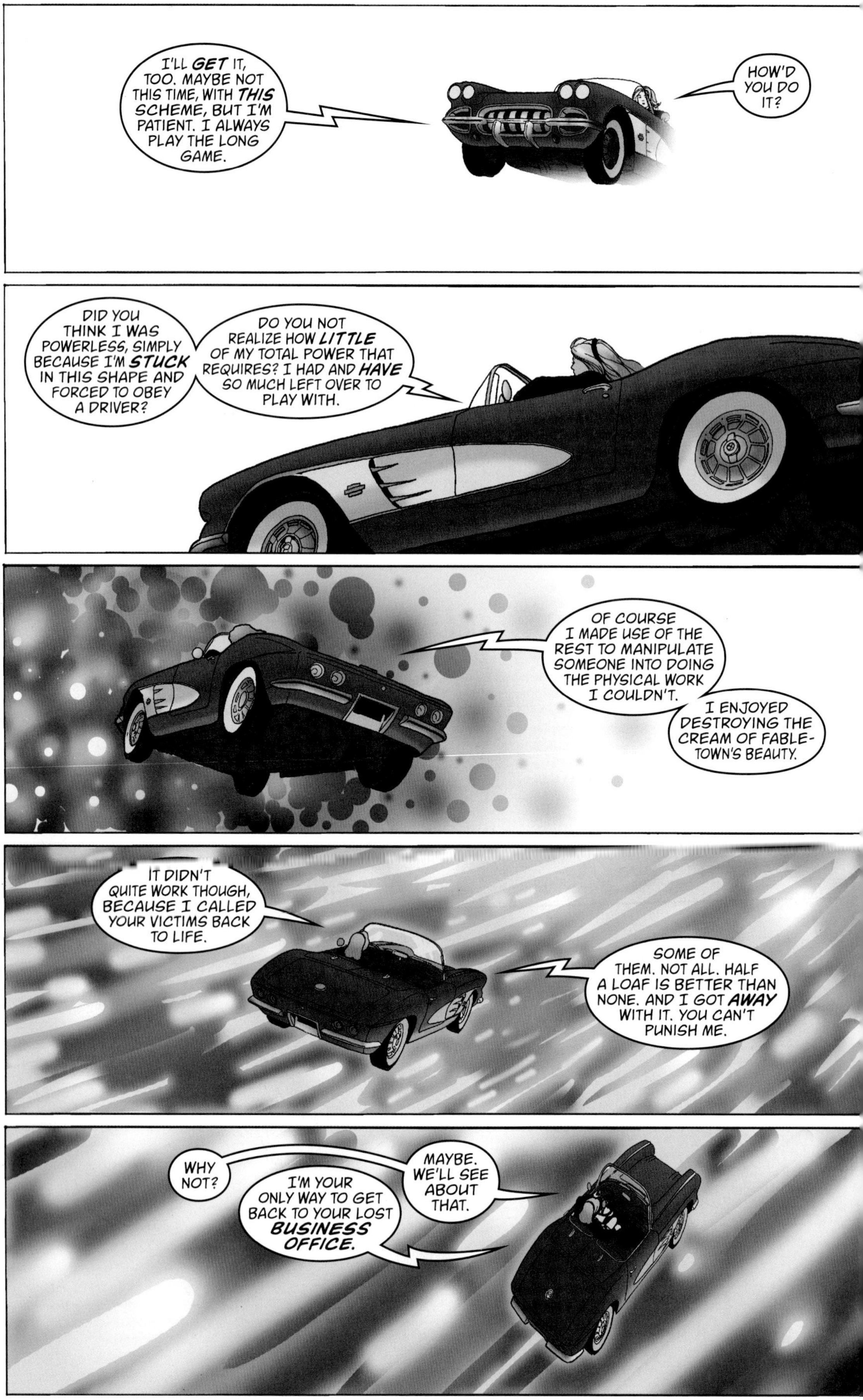
I'LL GET IT, TOO. MAYBE NOT THIS TIME, WITH THIS SCHEME, BUT I'M PATIENT. I ALWAYS PLAY THE LONG GAME.
HOW'D YOU DO IT?
DID YOU THINK I WAS POWERLESS, SIMPLY BECAUSE I'M STUCK IN THIS SHAPE AND FORCED TO OBEY A DRIVER?
DO YOU NOT REALIZE HOW LITTLE OF MY TOTAL POWER THAT REQUIRES? I HAD AND HAVE SO MUCH LEFT OVER TO PLAY WITH.
OF COURSE I MADE USE OF THE REST TO MANIPULATE SOMEONE INTO DOING THE PHYSICAL WORK I COULDN'T.
I ENJOYED DESTROYING THE CREAM OF FABLE-TOWN'S BEAUTY.
IT DIDN'T QUITE WORK THOUGH, BECAUSE I CALLED YOUR VICTIMS BACK TO LIFE.
SOME OF THEM. NOT ALL. HALF A LOAF IS BETTER THAN NONE. AND I GOT AWAY WITH IT. YOU CAN'T PUNISH ME.
MAYBE. WE'LL SEE ABOUT THAT.
WHY NOT?
I'M YOUR ONLY WAY TO GET BACK TO YOUR LOST BUSINESS OFFICE.

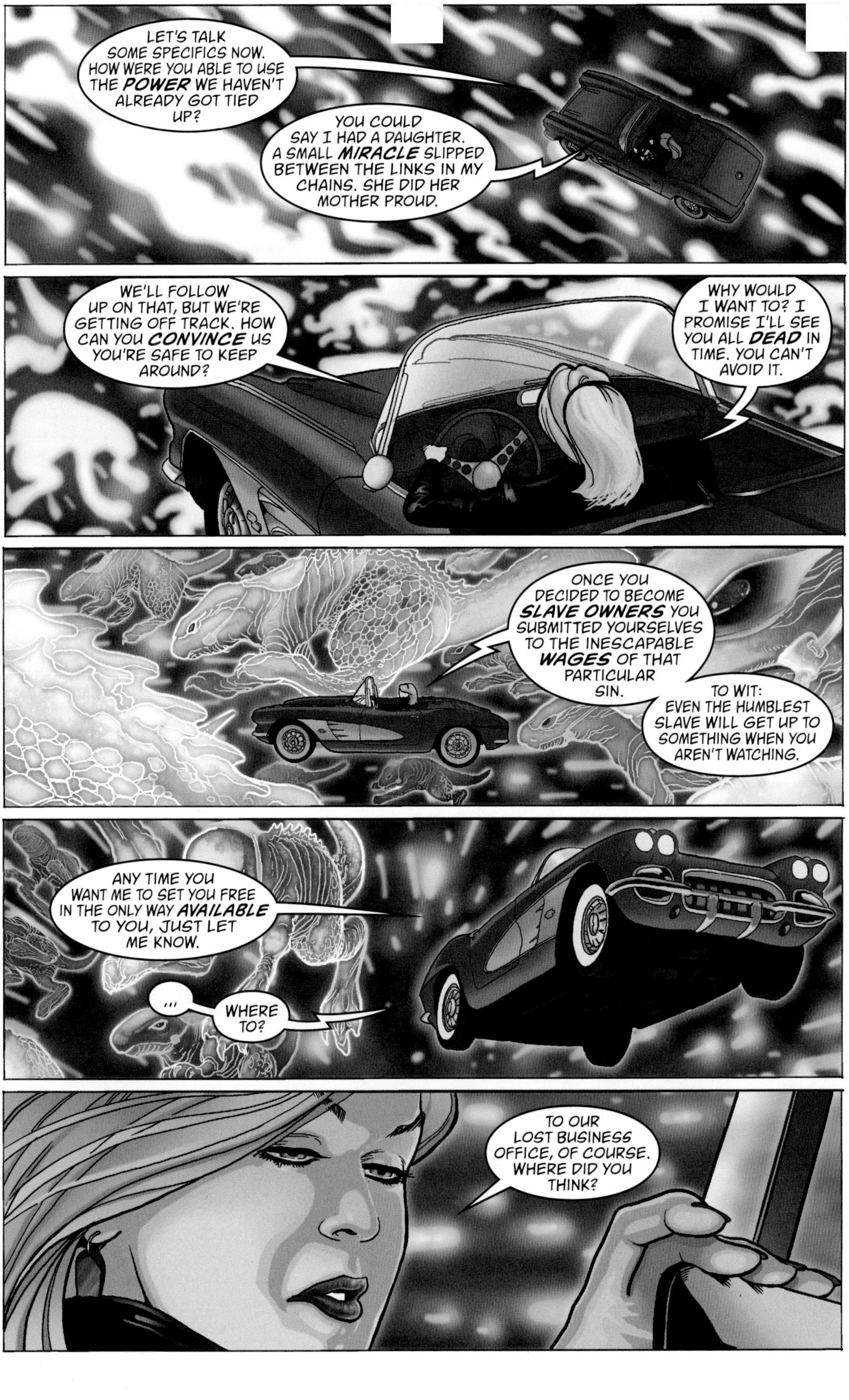
LET'S TALK SOME SPECIFICS NOW. HOW WERE YOU ABLE TO USE THE POWER WE HAVEN'T ALREADY GOT TIED UP?
YOU COULD SAY I HAD A DAUGHTER. A SMALL MIRACLE SLIPPED BETWEEN THE LINKS IN MY CHAINS. SHE DID HER MOTHER PROUD.
WE'LL FOLLOW UP ON THAT, BUT WE'RE GETTING OFF TRACK. HOW CAN YOU CONVINCE US YOU'RE SAFE TO KEEP AROUND?
WHY WOULD I WANT TO? I PROMISE I'LL SEE YOU ALL DEAD IN TIME. YOU CAN'T AVOID IT.
ONCE YOU DECIDED TO BECOME SLAVE OWNERS YOU SUBMITTED YOURSELVES TO THE INESCAPABLE WAGES OF THAT PARTICULAR SIN.
TO WIT: EVEN THE HUMBLEST SLAVE WILL GET UP TO SOMETHING WHEN YOU AREN'T WATCHING.
ANY TIME YOU WANT ME TO SET YOU FREE IN THE ONLY WAY AVAILABLE TO YOU, JUST LET ME KNOW.
...
WHERE TO?
TO OUR LOST BUSINESS OFFICE, OF COURSE. WHERE DID YOU THINK?

RESTORATION

Hectic days followed.

Cinderella arrived late Sunday night, driving the demonic fairy car that had caused all the trouble. They shot into existence just above Snow White's old desk and landed at speed. Taking a wide turn around the main floor, they came to a stop directly over the previous tire tracks, not much more than a purposeful stride or two beyond the bleachers of heads.

"Welcome back," I said, before she could even climb out of the car. "Or maybe even welcome *home* is in order. We've missed you."

"I'll be damned," Cinderella said.

She took a long moment to look the place over.

"What a collection of underachievers we've been," she said. "The moment Briar Rose arrived with her go-anywhere car, we should have seen its potential to reunite us with the Business Office."

"I missed it too," I said. And I'm supposed to be the one who knows everything.

"We could have found you months ago."

"From what I could see, the whole bunch of you were kept pretty busy at the time," I said. "No one can blame you for being tardy on epiphanies."

I reintroduced Cindy to Frankie and the Woodenheads, which caused her to remark on how much that sounded like a great name for a doo-wop band. Bad choice of words on her part, for of course they inspired Frankie and the Woodenheads to immediately break into a selection of *a cappella* choral numbers. Poor Cindy was obligated by the rules of historically important reunions to politely listen to each song, until I finally stepped in to save her.

"Life sans mobility can be tedious," Bartholomew Woodenhead said, "without things like choir practice to help keep our wits about us. Besides, disbanded military units of defunct old empires are practically ordained by the gods of martial nostalgia to sing old campaign songs. Not just our own war ballads, either. Frankie leads us in a rendition of *Men of Harlech* that'll tear your heart out."

"Nothing to apologize for," Cindy said. "You guys are actually good. I

hope you'll consider performing again when the real big wigs show up."

"Others will be along?" Frankie said. "All of my old office pals?"

"Some," Cindy said. "We'll talk about that later. But, yes, others will absolutely follow after me. Now that we finally have a way to reach you, you can bet your absent asses we aren't about to lose touch again."

Afterwards I introduced the Barleycorn Women.

"I didn't realize there were any of you outside of Smalltown," Cindy said.

"There weren't," Crowtop said. "Bufkin hatched us and grew us long after you lost connection to the Business Office, when he needed an army to help him conquer various witches and geniis, along with a few assorted demons, ghouls and grumpins."

"I can see we have lots to catch up on," Cindy said.

And eventually, we did.

* * * * * * * *

The next group arrived in a bus. It was still Hadeon, but this time transformed into a vehicle more suited to larger traffic. This more official envoy included a team of witches from the 13th Floor group (which I see is back to residing on an actual 13th floor — traditions often being their own justification). Barely off the bus, they went immediately to work on installing a new office door where the old one had long faded.

"Now that we can accurately place you in time and space, we can rebuild a direct link to Fabletown," Morgan le Fey said.

Ozma wasn't among the sorcerers' group, or I'd have been sorely tempted to grill her on her flash of deduction (or was it true inspiration?) identifying the particular coat and sword being used against them. Did our efforts in fact influence her, or did she come up with it entirely on her own? She might have done. She knew all about the weapons packages, way back when. She could have remembered them without outside intervention. There's no way of knowing, one way or another, but I prefer to believe we helped.

"We should have everything up and running within the month," le Fey said. "The spells are being rebuilt even as we speak. By this time next month one will once again be able to take a step from here directly into one of the corridors of Fabletown Castle, or vice versa."

"At least those with more mobility than the majority of us here," I said.

* * * * * * * *

One day King Flycatcher arrived to talk to the Woodenheads.

"You have some choices to make," he said, concerning both your immediate and long-range futures. You can stay here. You can relocate to Fabletown, or you can come live in Haven. Once there, should you choose, you can be replanted among your brothers and sisters in the new Sacred Grove."

"What about making us new bodies?" Günter Woodenhead asked.

"No," Flycatcher said. "That's the one option no longer possible. I won't be doing any carving."

Even those six who chose to stay here were moved away from my vicinity, so that Cindy and I could have a private chat.

"We're using up an awful lot of Hadeon's one-thousand trips, coming and going from here," she said. "So far we're keeping a good eye on her, never leaving her alone again – especially never leaving her alone with only one person on whom she can work her seductive wiles. But sooner, rather than later, we need to decide what we're going to do with her. What we're going to do *to* her."

"And you want my advice?" I said.

"You do have a perspective everyone else in the universe lacks," she said.

"In most cases," I said, "when my free and uncoerced advice is sought, the only answer I find worth giving is, 'figure out what you want to do and do it.' But I understand this is a special case, wherein I'm also looking after my own welfare, as well as for those in my community. So I'll do my part, by advising you as best I can. Make of it what you will."

"Fair enough."

"I think we should do exactly what Briar Rose planned all along. Make Hadeon serve out the remainder of her sentence as Fabletown's miracle private and public transportation. Then, as her last task comes due, find a way to kill her. I suspect there are many deadly things stored here in the Business Office that can do the job nicely."

"Except that leaves her alive for now, active and dangerous. We need to consider all of the extra power she has that isn't spent in performing her duties. What's to stop her from getting up to new shenanigans with it?"

"That's the genius part," I said. "Now that we know about it, we'll want to put that to work too. For the past weeks I've been watching the 13th Floor group complain about how much power their project to restore Bigby is burning up. Why not tap all that extra power from Hadeon and put it to

use as their Special Projects Reserve Gas supply? Why waste their own powers, when they can take hers? Considering how much extra magic Hadeon claims to have, it might even cut Bigby's restoration time in half — or at least whittle it down a good bit."

I let Cinderella sit and mull that a bit, before moving on to the next item of business.

"You know I can see, hear and pretty much know everything, right?"

"Sure," she said. "I guess so. Why do you — ?"

"No one who's my friend has an easy time of it," I said. "There's no privacy to be had from me. I can easily do what every police state has only ever dreamed of doing."

"Fine," Cindy said. "What's your point?"

"Only that I've seen what you've been dealing with. I think it's high time some nosy bastard in your very small circle of friends tells you this: You did fine. Of the sixteen killed, you gave us back Snow, Rose Red, Lumi, Bo Peep, Morgan le Fey, Lake, Bellflower and Beauty. Those were objectively good choices."

"I left just as many dead," she said.

"So?" I said. "In the entire history of everything ever, when has anyone been able to accomplish all worth doing? This is what it's about. I've had a good look, and I can tell you with authority that all of life boils down to the struggle for 'good enough' at best, and most often for 'it's better than nothing.' Period. End of sentence. That's all any victory will ever get you. You scored a perfect 50% — or even higher than that, when you consider Goldilocks and Lamia are among those in the stay-dead group. Statistically that places you squarely in the category of wildly successful. So, why don't you quit your moping and — uh — what's that mundy phrase I love?"

"Tough it out?"

"No."

"Stiff upper lip?"

"No."

"Carry on?"

"Nope. Not quite."

"Get over yourself?"

"That's it! Why don't you do that?"

* * * * * * * *

They were ready to make the big reconnection. The new door between here and Fabletown was about to be opened for the first time. People gathered around the door, far across the hall, anxious for the event. No one's attention was directed my way, and that afforded me the chance to do something I hadn't often been able to do since the rediscovery. I had a private chat with one — and only one — of the Barleycorn Women.

"Goose, can you step over here for a minute?" I said. "Come close, so there's no chance of our being overheard."

"But I want to go see the Grand Opening," she said.

"You'll have plenty of time to get over there before anything important happens. They're still in the long countdown, checking and rechecking a thousand things."

"What did you want?" she said.

"Goldilocks is dead and not coming back this time," I said. "Hadeon is close to powerless now, and her death will come, after we've wrung the last mile of debt out of her. Now it's time to settle matters with the last member of their conspiracy. You didn't actually dye your hair, did you? There's no evidence you ever gathered the materials to do it. I checked — rather I had some of the other Barleycorn Women check for me."

There was a sudden flash of rage across her features, almost too quick to notice, before the shy and awkward Goose of old reasserted herself.

"What can you mean?" she said. Her look of confusion was expertly manufactured.

"Hadeon mentioned she'd had a daughter, in order to carry out her schemes. Everyone assumed she spoke metaphorically and referred to Goldilocks. Everyone was wrong. Goldilocks was never more than a useful tool in Hadeon's hands. It was clear Hadeon had no love for her. A daughter,

even one not directly related, is a more intimate and important relationship. Hadeon needed an agent here, in our lost Business Office, in order to work her plans. She turned her power on you."

"That's ridiculous!" Goose said. "She was never here, before that day. I never met her!"

"I've no doubt of that," I said. "She worked from a distance. She didn't know who she was seducing, only that her victim would be the most alone and emotionally vulnerable of the group. The outcast. And once you'd accepted her, you started the transformation into a miniature version of her. Your hair turned dark, your skin deathly pale, and if I'm not mistaken, the buds of fairy wings have even started to show, despite the way you cover

them with a loose blouse."

"I think you've gone insane!" she said, no longer able to keep the venom out of her voice. "We're reunited with Fabletown, and you've lost all your power over us. Now the paranoia sets in."

"You intentionally shoved Christoph into me, shattering my glass," I said. "Just in time to blind me for Hadeon to show up. Timing that perfect doesn't happen by accident. And you were the one who spoke the spell binding me. You were the one who listed all of the places I wasn't allowed to watch."

"You're just making things up!"

"The spell would have worked better if you'd done it while my glass was intact. But then I would have known who was pulling my strings. You very much needed me not to know who Hadeon's ally was, or even that she had one in our camp."

"You can't actually do anything to me," she said. "You can't do anything but talk, and no one's close enough to hear you right now. You can't stop me from breaking you again — or better yet, I'll pronounce the spell again while you're whole, and this time it will work more fully. This time you'll have to obey me, without resistance."

"Good plan," I said. "You should have carried it out before I exposed you."

That's when Cinderella slapped the shoebox down over Goose, and quickly slipped a metal cookie sheet underneath, trapping Goose inside. My job was to fully attract Goose's attention, while Cindy snuck up from behind. Getting the confession was gravy.

Cindy picked the box up, carefully keeping it closed tight. Each time Goose tried to speak from within — trying to start the spell that would bind me — Cindy would give the box a few vigorous shakes and Goose would settle right down again.

"Ozma and her crew have a better box ready," Cinderella said.

"I hope they can clean Hadeon out of her, leaving the original Goose intact," I said. "It wasn't really her fault. She was the outcast of the group and

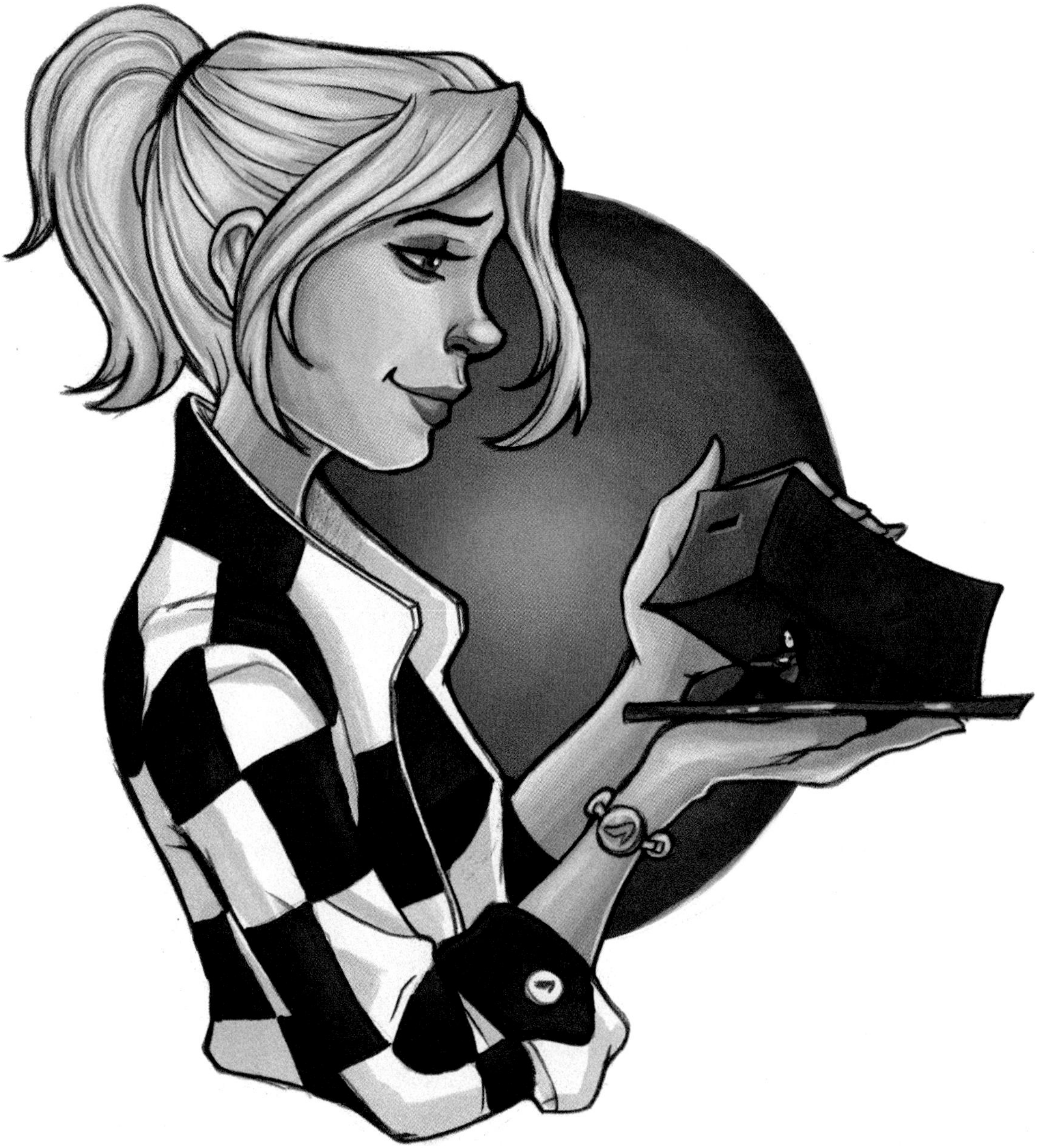

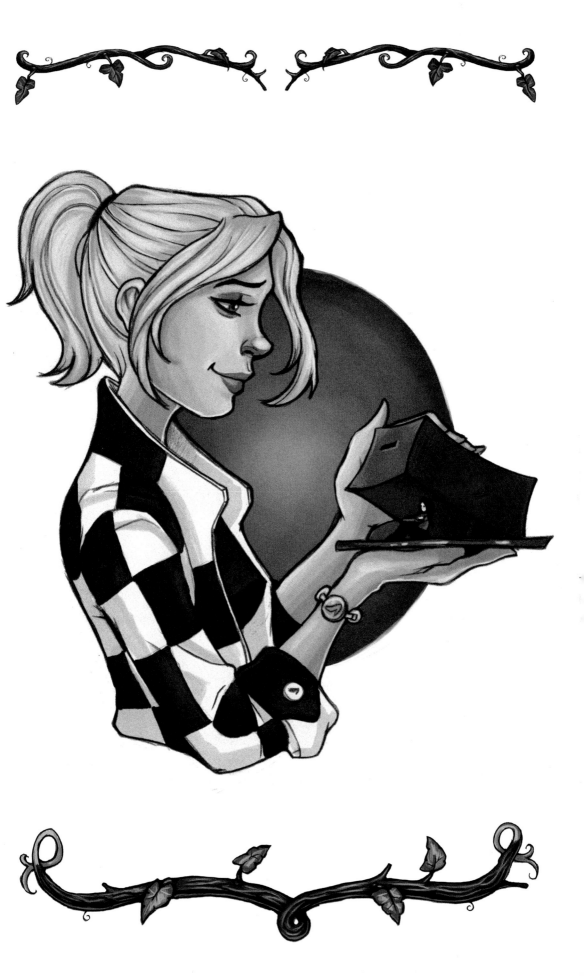

therefore most vulnerable to Hadeon's transforming charms. No daughter's in a position to ask to be born."

"We'll see," Cindy said. "So, what have you decided? Going to stay here, or move into Fabletown?"

"They're about to become substantially the same place again," I said. "Besides, this is my home."

And that, more or less, is how the Business Office was reunited with Fabletown, only they didn't call it the Business Office from then on. They called it Mirror's House, and thereafter came and went as my guests.

THE END

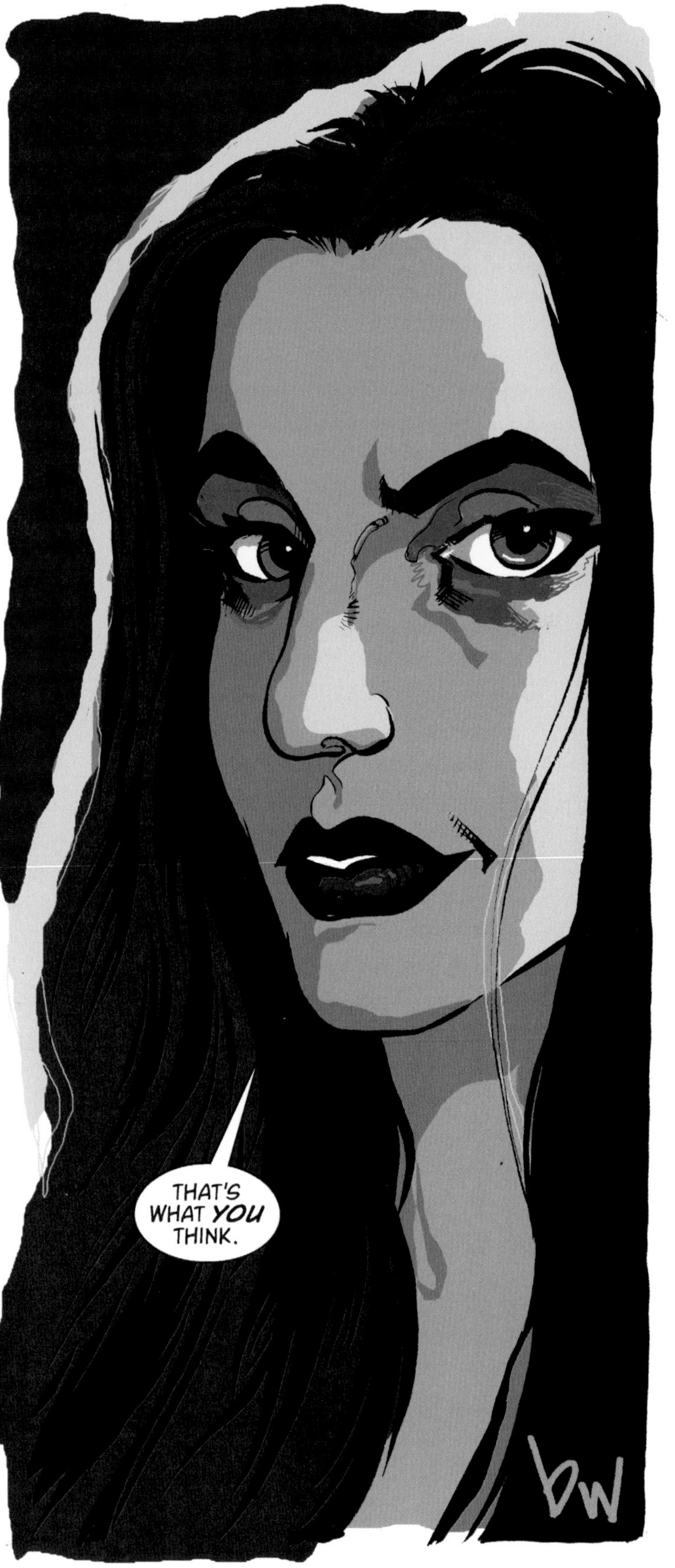
THAT'S WHAT *YOU* THINK.
bw

With increasingly few exceptions, **Bill Willingham** does not work or play well with others, which is as it should be when pushing 60.

When not drawing for the Fairest, **Tony Akins** enjoys life in Seattle and waltzing with bears.

Jordie Bellaire currently colors TOM STRONG for Vertigo alongside her favorite frequent collaborator Chris Sprouse!

Russ Braun, twenty-year comics veteran drawer of stuff, raised by wolves.

Mark Buckingham, regular artist, irregular showman, the polite English gentleman permanently residing in the worlds of all things FABLES.

Rosemary Cheetham colors comics. She's an English astronomy geek—living in Toronto—where there are no stars.

Illustrator and colorist **Chris Chuckry** lives in Winnipeg and can be seen monthly in THE UNWRITTEN making Peter Gross look great.

Andrew Dalhouse, colorist, has a way with light and shadow.

Al Davison, Image conjurer: Bigby's feet, Merlyn's beard... Bruce Lee's hands: Confused he is.

Eva de la Cruz, colorist, is very happy to have contributed to the FABLES universe.

Renae De Liz and **Ray Dillon** are hidden in the woods of Maine creating fantastic fairy tales.

Zelda Devon, illustrator, loves the way bats move, as if in a stop-motion film. Also, a big fan of sharpened pencils and sharpened minds.

Ming Doyle lives in Massachusetts with her partner Neil, their Siamese cat Maui, and an ever-expanding collection of vintage Halloween masks.

Meghan Hetrick, artist, is quite handy with an extensive array of sharp, pointy things.

Kurt Huggins is an artist, writer and future king of a faraway land that's completely made up.

Gene Ha. Artist of SHADE, FABLES, JUSTICE LEAGUE and *Adv Cyclps+Phnx*. 1+3 Eisners for Top10 books. Pro NWAL, RL in Berwyn IL w PYT wife Lisa + pup Fina.

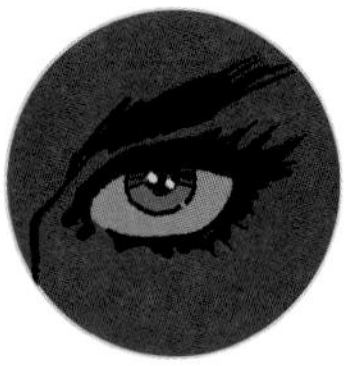

Adam Hughes: Harvey, Eisner, and Inkpot award-winning artist and *New York Times* best-selling author. Take THAT, high school guidance counselor!

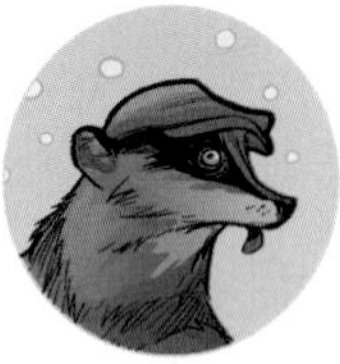

Karl Kerschl is hidden in the woods with the *Abominable Charles Christopher*.

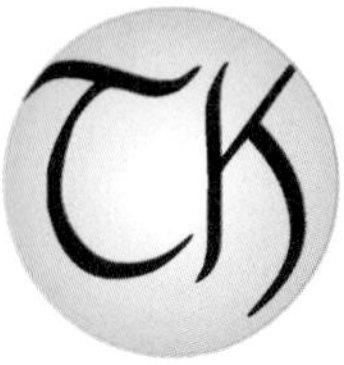
TK

Todd Klein, letterer, alphabetically bedecks comics, designed eagerly for geniuses herein, inscribing jolly Klein lettering meaningfully.

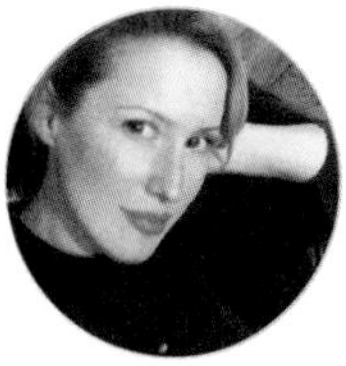

Tula Lotay is an artist hailing from the mythical land of Yorkshire. She shot first, is best in life, and mostly comes out at night. Mostly.

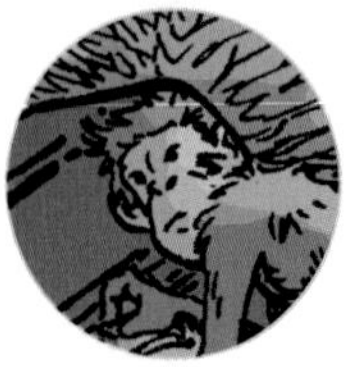

Colorist extraordinaire **Lee Loughridge** would rather be surfing.

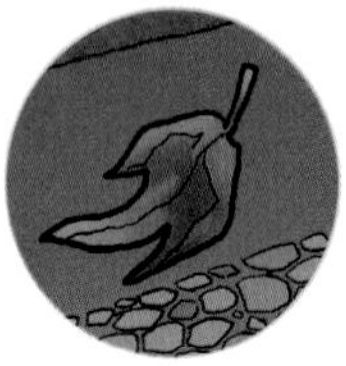

Kevin Maguire has illustrated numerous beautiful women in the DCU, but this graphic novel marks his Vertigo debut.

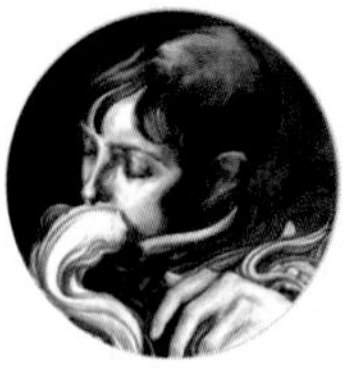

Nimit Malavia, illustrator and cover artist, believes himself to be Prince Charming, when in reality he's probably closer to a dwarf.

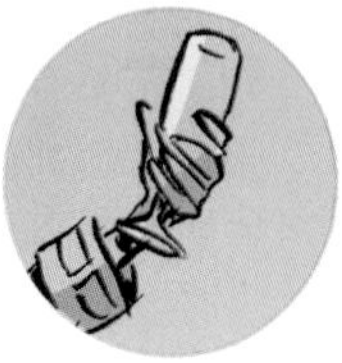

Shawn McManus is in a non-disclosed location allegedly working with FABLES super-spy CINDERELLA.

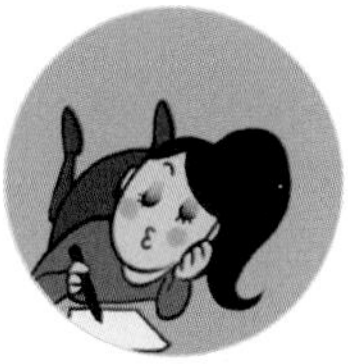

Fiona Meng is an illustrator, graphic novel artist, dog lover. She's really good at TV watching and is in serious need of some exercise.

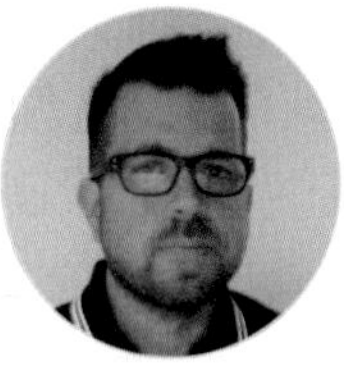

When **Phil Noto** isn't drawing gorgeous women in the pages of FAIREST, he's drawing gorgeous women in the pages of... everything!

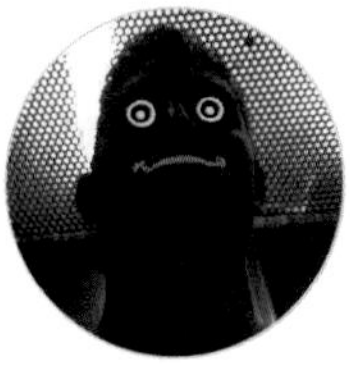

Inaki Miranda is moving to his new studio in Madrid, and is inviting everybody for mojitos and margaritas.

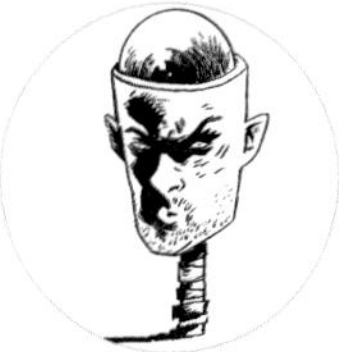

Dean Ormston, illustrator and part-time pig wrestler, decided to take up art after his efforts to "huff and puff and blow houses down" failed miserably.

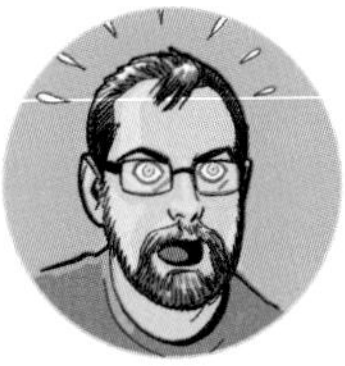

Chris Sprouse is probably drawing comics pages and listening to music while you're reading this... that's pretty much all he does.

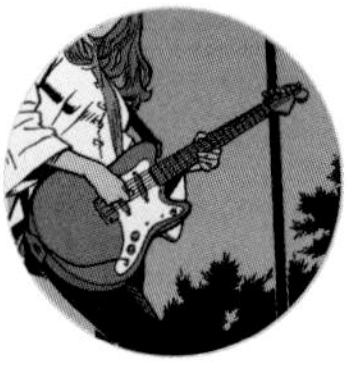

Karl Story extraordinarily inks Chris Sprouse with as much natural grace as alphabetical order.

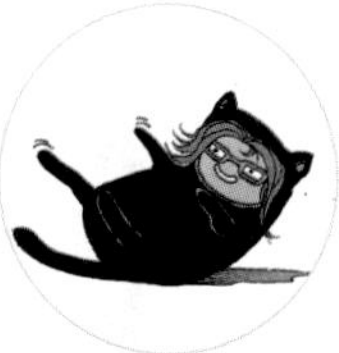

Marley Zarcone hasn't spoken to the Magic Mirror since he told her drawing lots of cats wouldn't turn her into one. One day she will be a cat.

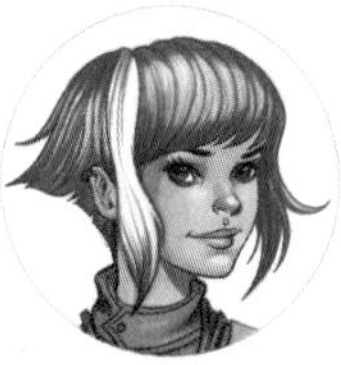

Chrissie Zullo, illustrator, desperately longs to be Snow White, with a bit of Rose Red in there, too.

FROM THE PAGES OF THE
EISNER AWARD-WINNING *FABLES*

BILL WILLINGHAM

with PHIL JIMENEZ

FAIREST VOL. 2:
THE HIDDEN KINGDOM

with LAUREN BEUKES,
INAKI MIRANDA and
BARRY KITSON

CINDERELLA: FROM
FABLETOWN
WITH LOVE

with CHRIS ROBERSON and
SHAWN McMANUS

CINDERELLA: FABLES
ARE FOREVER

with CHRIS ROBERSON and
SHAWN McMANUS

"Entertaining... It's briskly paced and full of all the action and intrigue that one would hope for." —IGN

From the pages of F A B L E S

FAIREST
Wide Awake

BILL WILLINGHAM · PHIL JIMENEZ
ANDY LANNING · MATTHEW STURGES · SHAWN McMANUS

VERTIGO

VERTIGO

"Fables is an excellent series in the tradition of Sandman, one that rewards careful attention and loyalty."
—PUBLISHERS WEEKLY

"[A] wonderfully twisted concept..." "features fairy tale characters banished to the noirish world of present-day New York." —WASHINGTON POST

"Great fun." —BOOKLIST

BILL WILLINGHAM
FABLES VOL. 1: LEGENDS IN EXILE

THE #1 NEW YORK TIMES BEST-SELLING SERIES

FABLES

Legends in Exile

"A top-notch fantasy comic that is on a par with SANDMAN." — *Variety*

BULLFINCH STREET

DIRECTOR

Bill Willingham
Lan Medina
Steve Leialoha
Craig Hamilton

VERTIGO